JN086586

2030年までに知っておきたい

最重要

Essential Vocabulary
for Surviving 2030

ボキャブラリー
1000

アンドリュー・ロビンス［著］

岡本 茂紀［編・訳］

山久瀬 洋二［解説］

IBCパブリッシング

カバーデザイン＝菊池　祐

はじめに

　言葉は時と共に変化します。それは英語でも同様です。

　いま、コンピューターサイエンスやAI技術が目覚ましく進歩し、それと並行するように社会の常識も変わろうとしています。しかし、もっと大切なことは、こうした社会の変化によって、人々の意識も変わろうとしていることです。

　20世紀が終わり、21世紀もすでに中盤に差し掛かろうとしている中で、この20年間で人々の生活や社会との関わり方、さらにはコミュニケーションのあり方についての考え方、感覚が大きく変化しているのです。その影響が言葉遣いそのものにも現れようとしているのです。

　この現象がもっとも鮮明に現れている言語が英語かもしれません。というのも、ITやAIの進化の核となったのがアメリカを中心とした英語圏だったからです。さらに、こうした地域ではジェンダーや人種などの分野で、社会規範そのものもどんどん進化し、例えばジェンダーでいうならば、男女という二極化によって表現を規定せず、多様な価値観や趣向に対して寛容に、さらには平等に対応しようという社会変革も進められました。それが新たな用語を創造し、日常生活の中でも使用されるようになってきているのです。

　この変化は単にジェンダーへの認識の変化だけではなく、社会を構成するありとあらゆる場面でそれぞれ新たな言葉や表現を生み出しました。その頻度がもっとも顕著な言語が英語だと言っても差し支えないはずです。

　そして、この現象に押されるように、2030年ごろには今新たに生み出された言葉がごく普通の日常用語になっている可能性も多々あるのです。おそらくそれらの単語や表現方法の一部は、外来語となって日本語の中にも取り入れられてくるかもしれません。

　そんなごく近未来を見据えたとき、今すでに使用されている言葉も含め、これだけは知っておかなければ会話にも支障をきたすのではと思われる1000語をここに集めてみました。これらは近未来の常識を象徴するような言葉であると共に、さらにその先の時代に向けて変化を続ける表現であるはずです。

我々はまだこうした発想で英語に接していないかもしれません。近未来の会話の中で必須となるような言葉を学ぶ機会は思いの外少ないのです。それだけに、ここで取り上げた1000語には、特に注意を払っておきたいのです。

　また、どうしてこうした単語が重要になってきているのかという社会的背景も理解すれば、英語を学ぶと同時に、よりグローバルな感性も磨くことができるはずです。世界のあちこちで、政治、経済、国際情勢に加え、社会、そして技術革新が人々の生活に変化をもたらしているからこそ、これらの英単語や熟語、さらには英語表現が生み出されているのだということを理解してほしいのです。

　本書を単なる単語帳と思わずに、未来学への一つのアプローチとして活用してもらえればと祈念しています。

山久瀬　洋二

Preface

When I was a kid, my family had a clunky, old TV from the 70s. We controlled it with a clicker—people called it that because it clicked. Pressing any of the four oversized buttons would cause an aluminum bar to vibrate at a specific frequency, shooting sound waves out through the air. A circuit in the TV would receive the signal and change the channel or adjust the volume accordingly. Sometimes, if you sneezed forcefully enough, you could hit that same ultrasonic range, and the TV would abruptly switch off. Pollen season was a mess.

Our first VCR had a remote tethered to the unit by a long wire. That remote had five buttons: play, stop, pause, fast forward, and rewind. You always had to rewind a video after you finished watching it. That took a while. Some video rental stores charged customers a small fee when they forgot. Stickers with reminders were often affixed to videotape cases. "BE KIND. REWIND." That was Blockbuster's slogan. For a time, Blockbuster was the largest video rental store chain in the US. Then, it succumbed to poor management and competing business models. Streaming services put the final nail in the coffin.

This sliver of late 20th-century nostalgia persists in memory, media, and, in some cases, museums. With enough time, I could paint you a vivid picture of the period: the technology and the fashion, the politics and the culture, even the atmosphere—both figuratively and literally. And, of course, the language. Some things might surprise you. You might even say, "Well, how do you like that?" Or at least, that's what my late grandfather Irving would have said. Nobody says that anymore. Or "clicker." Or "BE KIND. REWIND." Or "Blockbuster," I suppose. The times have changed. As society evolves, language evolves along with it. What sorts of things will we be talking about in the year 2030? Remote surgery? Already happening. Mass adoption of autonomous vehicles? Picking up speed every day. Instantaneous matter transporters? No, certainly not, which is why I didn't include it in this dictionary.

What I have included are technologies, concepts, and other terms I found likely enough to be pervasive. My commentary in the first half of the book will give you insight into why some terms will achieve widespread adoption as well as what effects the widespread adoption of other terms will have. Maybe I got a few wrong here and there—no one knows the future, after all—but I guarantee most of them are right. I tried to strike a balance between bleakness and hope. The latest climate change news might cause you to choke with ecoanxiety, but the progressive nature of Generation Z might also inspire some woke introspection. It is my hope that this dictionary ignites conversations, sparks curiosity, and invites you to explore the vast possibilities that lie ahead. The words we use not only reflect reality but also have the power to shape the future. Perhaps this reference will help lead to a better tomorrow.

Lastly, I would like to express my appreciation to some of the people who helped make this project possible. My co-author, Okamoto-san, and my editor, Kyoko, for their enduring patience and invaluable feedback. My mentors, Hiroshi and Nyangotani, for helping me navigate my winding career path. And, of course, my family for their unyielding support. Ami, Noah, Kyle, Sarah, Dad, Mom, Alex, Missy, Dave, Jonas, Ryan, Mikey, Nico, and Annie, I love you and thank you from the bottom of my heart.

Andrew Robbins

もくじ

近未来をのぞき見する楽しみを
本書の構成とお勧めアプローチ

　英語の語彙集は、ちまたにあふれています。その中において、本書に異彩を放つ点があるとすれば、集められた語彙が「今」ではなく「近未来」を向いていることでしょう。本書に収載された1,000のボキャブラリーは、(A)比較的最近生まれた新語の部類に属するものと、(B)長く使われてきて社会的に熟成されたもの、に大別できます。そして、いずれのグループにも共通するのが、本書の刊行時点から見た近未来である2030年およびそれ以降において、依然として古びることなく、むしろ、いっそう時代を映すキーワードとして重要度を増すだろう、と予想される点です。つまり、皆さんは今、ここにある1,000の語彙を通じて、来たるべき近未来をのぞき見する楽しみを手に入れたのだ、と言い換えることもできるでしょう。なお、本書で取り扱う1,000の語句については、単語・フレーズ・略語・頭字語などが混在していることから、以降、「ターム(term)」と呼ぶことにします。

さて、本書の構成には、次の3つの特徴があります。

1. 1,000の語彙が500ずつ、Part 1と2に分割されている
2. 中心となるターム＝「キーターム」1つと、その関連ターム4つからなるグループの単位で提示されている
3. 各タームに例文は付されず、代わりに「定義（語義）」が英語と日本語で示されている

これらの構成上の特徴は、本書を効果的に利用するための鍵となるものです。以下に詳しく見ていきましょう。

1 Part 1は、より身近な近未来キーワード集

Part 1では、キータームのアルファベット順に、分野横断的にタームのグループを並べてあります。この点で、タームが分野・カテゴリー別に分類されているPart 2とは対照的です。これは、Part 1には、特定の分野への興味や専門性、関わりの強い人に限らず、誰もが日常的に見聞きすることになるだろうと予想される「身近な近未来キーワード」を集めてあるからです。各タームグループの冒頭

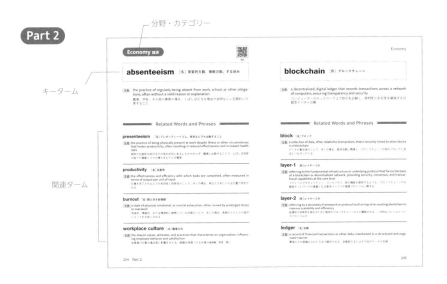

ix

に分野・カテゴリーを表示してありますが、ここではそれにとらわれず、2030年以降の世界を俯瞰するつもりで各タームを眺めてください。

　各キータームの直下に、その言葉にまつわる世の中の情勢・実情に関する、現在から近未来への予想を含めた「解説」が書かれています。また、Part 1の全タームに、［2030］のラベル付きで、当該のタームやその周辺の物事の背景に関する予測が記されています。これを基に、各タームがどんな文脈＝コンテクストで用いられることになりそうか、言葉の未来に思いを馳せてみてください。

　一方、Part 2では、分野・カテゴリー別にタームを分類した上で、キータームのアルファベット順に語彙を整理してあります。Part 2のタームは、各分野・カテゴリーとより強く結び付く形で使われるだろうと予想されるものです。したがって、自分の興味・関心が強いカテゴリーを優先してタームをチェックするのがいいでしょう。

② キータームと関連タームで文脈を予測する

　Part 1・2ともに、キーターム1つと、その関連ターム4つからなるグループの単位でページが展開します。この構成は、「キーターム1＋関連ターム4＝5ターム」で1つの文脈＝コンテクストが形作られる、という考えに基づいています。つまり、実際の場面では、キータームを核に、周辺に残りの4タームが散りばめられるような形で会話や文章が展開することを想定しているのです。

　単語やフレーズが、何の脈絡もなく単独で現れることはありません。必ず話者や書き手の意図、あるいは会話の流れに応じて、文脈に沿う形で用いられます。そこで、本書では「キーターム1＋関連ターム4＝5ターム」を一塊の文脈に見立て、そこから実際の場面での使われ方をイメージしつつ語句を捉えられるように工夫しました。これによって、一見すると何の変哲もない、使い古されたように見えるタームでも、近未来の文脈の中で新たな輝きをまとって使われる可能性が見えてくるはずです。

③ 例文よりも「定義」で言葉のイメージを膨らませる

　一般の語彙集には普通、語句の使い方を把握するための例文・用例が掲載されています。しかし、本書ではあえて例文を外しました。これは、ごく短い例文の

中に埋め込まれることで、むしろ各タームの近未来におけるイメージや存在意義が誤認される可能性があると判断したからです。例えば、job market（労働市場）というタームの例文としてAfter the invention of the automobile, the job market rapidly expanded.（自動車が発明されると、求人市場が急速に拡大した）という英文があるとします。これだけ見ると、とても2030年代の話とは思えません。しかし、もしこの文が「歴史的には、自動車の発明などで求人市場が急速に拡大したが、今やAIや自動化の影響で、2030年までに約23パーセントの雇用が失われてしまい、この先、求人市場の10パーセント程度が過去に存在しなかった職で占められるだろう」といった大きな文脈の中で語られたものであれば、近未来の会話の中で当該のタームがどう使われるかを示す例として十分に機能するでしょう。とはいえ、残念ながら、本書の限られた紙幅の中でそこまでの文脈をカバーした長い文例を掲載するのは困難でした。そこで、本書ではあえて例文を載せずに、①や②で示した要素・構成と、英日で記した「定義」でタームの役割やイメージを伝える方法を選びました。

　各タームに添えられた「定義」は、通常の英英辞典に掲載されている定義文よりも長めで、かつ予想される2030年以降での中心的な語義を説明しています。ぜひ「定義」を読み込みつつ、各タームの近未来での使われ方のイメージを膨らませてください。なお、出版社のウェブサイト上では、各タームの短い例文を確認することが可能です（次ページ参照）。

　言葉は生き物だ、とよく言われます。語句の意味や使われ方は、世の中の推移や人間の発展に応じて、日々刻々と変化しています。事実上の国際共通語である英語の語句も、その例外でないばかりか、むしろ世界の他のどの言語よりもダイナミックな進化を遂げてきたと言えるでしょう。ここに挙がった1,000の英語ボキャブラリーを通じて、2030年代という、すぐに手が届きそうな近未来を少しだけ先取りし、私たちの世界で何がどう変わるのか、あるいは変わらないのかを、楽しみながら予想してみてください。

編者・訳者　岡本 茂紀

■分野・カテゴリーについて

分野・カテゴリーは以下の13種類です。本文中の見出しおよび索引の表記は、一部省略されている場合があります。

- Economy　経済
- Politics　政治
- Society　社会
- Diversity, Equity, and Inclusion　多様性、公平性、包括性
- Education　教育
- Culture, Fashion, Art and Sports　文化、ファッション、アート、スポーツ
- Healthcare　医療・健康管理
- Technology　テクノロジー
- Computing　コンピューティング
- Environment and Sustainability　環境、持続可能性
- Climate Change　気候変動
- Miscellaneous　その他
- Slang and Casual Conversation　俗語、日常の会話

■音声ダウンロードについて

本書に掲載の英文の音声（MP3形式）を下記URLとQRコードから無料でPCなどに一括ダウンロードすることができます。

https://ibcpub.co.jp/audio_dl/0770/

※ダウンロードしたファイルはZIP形式で圧縮されていますので、解凍ソフトが必要です。

※MP3ファイルを再生するには、iTunesやWindows Media Playerなどのアプリケーションが必要です。

※PCや端末、アプリケーションの操作方法については、編集部ではお答えできません。付属のマニュアルやインターネットの検索を利用するか、開発元にお問い合わせください。

■例文について

本書でとりあげた各タームを使用した例文は、小社ウェブサイトに掲載しています。トップページの検索スペースに本書名（一部でも可）を入力し、書籍ページを表示してご確認ください。

https://ibcpub.co.jp

近未来へのガイドブック

　AIにしろ、バイオテクノロジーにしろ、技術の進化は我々の言語環境にも大きな変化をもたらします。現在は専門用語として一部の人の間でしか使われていない言葉でも、10年もするとごく一般的に使われる言葉となるかもしれません。

　Part 1では、「近未来の日常を乗り切る」ために必要な語彙500が集められています。中にはごく日常の常識として、すでに使用されている言葉も含まれています。例えばAIというキータームがあります。誰でも知っている言葉だなと思われるでしょう。しかし、その関連語として紹介されているstrong AI、weak AIという言葉を重ねて読むと、今後のAIの行方と現在のコンピューターテクノロジーの位置付けがわかってきます。キータームからその延長にある用語を知ることで、今後世の中がどのように変わっていくかが見えてくるようです。

　さらにページをめくると、chatbotという語句が出てきます。これは、ChatGPTなど、我々が今まさに出会い、これから共存していこうとする技術に他なりません。一見、専門的に見える語句も、その解説を読むと、確かに、それが今の社会で問題になっていたり、話題になっている現象であることがわかると思います。そうしたことをヒントに、2030年、さらにはその後の我々の世界を予見してみてはどうでしょう。

　本書には単なる語句の意味を知るだけではない、その背景を知りながら味わう面白さがあります。言葉の繋がりから見える近未来を楽しみ、現在から近未来に至る社会を眺めてもらいたいのです。つまり、本書は、近未来へのガイドブックの役割を担っていることになるわけです。

　Part 1「近未来の日常を乗り切る」を読んで、キータームのうち半分の語句に見覚えがなかった人は、現在の社会をさらに注意深く観察する必要があるかもしれません。つまりPart 1ではすでに現在の我々の社会にも深く根ざした語句が集められているからです。

Part 1を読み終えたら、Part 2「多様な分野の近未来に精通する」で、興味のあるカテゴリーを読むのも良いでしょう。自分の専門や興味のあるカテゴリーで扱われている語彙で、知っている語が半分に満たないと、2030年には英語での会話や世界の人々との交流に取り残されかねないほどの、大事な表現が集められています。

　社会は刻一刻と変化をし、技術が進化すれば、人の常識も変化します。そして常識が変化すれば価値観も変わってきます。それが人類にとってプラスの方向にいこうとしているのか、それとも逆なのかは、簡単には結論づけられません。未来は常に不安定なのです。それを実感しながらより良い社会へと調整してきたのが人類の歴史の有りようだったのでしょう。

　であれば、本書に紹介する語彙、表現を味わいながら知ることは、今我々はどこに向かおうとしているのか、そしてどこへ向かうべきかを考えるヒントになるのではと思っています。

　ここに収載したほとんどは、明らかに100年前には存在しなかった単語や表現です。ではこれから100年後にはどんな言葉が生まれてくるのでしょうか。それをこの単語や表現のコレクションから占うのも楽しいものです。

山久瀬洋二

この**500**
タームで

近未来の日常を
乗り切る

001

agroecology

［名］農業生態学

解説

As the global population expands and environmental challenges become more pressing, **agroecology** has emerged as a promising approach to sustainable agriculture. The adoption of techniques such as permaculture exemplifies the shift toward more resource-efficient farming practices. **Agroecology** has gained support from organizations like the United Nations, which has recognized its potential to address global food security and climate change.

世界人口の増加と環境問題の深刻化に伴い、農業生態学は持続可能な農業への有望な手法として浮上してきた。持続型農業のような技術の採用は、より資源効率の高い農法への移行を象徴している。農業生態学は、国連などの機関からの支持を受けており、世界の食糧安全保障と気候変動に対処できる潜在的可能性が認められている。

定義 the study of ecological processes applied to agricultural production systems, aiming to create diversified, resilient, and sustainable systems
農業生産システムに適用される生態学的過程の研究で、多様で弾力的かつ持続可能なシステムの構築を目指すもの

 The food production industry will change to meet the needs of the growing global population.
世界人口の増加に伴い、食糧生産業は変容するでしょう。

agrovoltaics [名]営農型太陽光発電

 定義 the co-utilization of land for both solar photovoltaic power and agriculture
太陽光発電と農業の両方の目的で土地を共同活用すること

2030 It will eventually become rare to find large-scale farms that do not harvest solar photovoltaic power in addition to their crops or livestock.
いずれは、農作物や家畜だけで太陽光発電を取り入れないような大規模農場は珍しくなるでしょう。

permaculture [名]持続型農業

 定義 an agricultural design system that adopts arrangements observed in flourishing natural ecosystems
豊かな自然生態系に見られるような秩序を採用した農業設計方式

2030 Large permaculture communities will sprout up all over the world.
大規模な持続型農業に従事するコミュニティーが、世界中に誕生するでしょう。

bioenergy [名]生物燃料エネルギー

 定義 renewable energy produced from materials derived from biological sources, such as plant materials and animal waste
植物原料や動物の排泄物など、生物由来の材料から生産される再生可能エネルギー

2030 Small-scale bioreactors will help address the energy concerns of local communities.
小規模な生物反応器が、地域社会のエネルギーに関する懸念の払しょくに貢献するでしょう。

precision agriculture [名]精密農業

 定義 an agricultural approach that utilizes advanced technologies, such as remote sensing, GPS, and data analytics, to optimize crop production, enhance resource efficiency, and minimize environmental impact
遠隔測定や GPS、データ解析などの先端技術を活用する農業手法で、作物生産の最適化や資源効率の向上、環境負荷の最小化を図る

2030 Both water and pesticide use will decrease as technology yields smarter agricultural practices.
テクノロジーによってより高精度の農業が実現されるにつれて、水と農薬の使用量が減少していくでしょう。

002

AI

［名］人工知能、AI

解説

AI is practically unmatched in its ability to disrupt society—for the better and for the worse. Many industries were transformed seemingly overnight as ChatGPT and similar LLMs were made available for use. We may not be able to predict how AI will progress, but we can be sure that every major industry will make use of it.

人工知能は事実上、社会を破壊する能力において比類なきものである——良くも悪しくもだ。ChatGPTや類似の大規模言語モデルが利用できるようになったことで、多くの産業が一夜にして変貌を遂げたかのようだ。AIがどのように進化するかは予測できないかもしれないが、あらゆる主要産業がAIを活用することは間違いないだろう。

定義 short for "artificial intelligence," a branch of technology that involves the creation and development of computer systems and software capable of imitating and simulating human cognitive abilities

「人工知能」の頭字語で、コンピューターシステムやソフトウェアの制作と開発に関わるテクノロジーの一分野。人間の認知能力を模倣し、シミュレートすることができる

 AI will play an essential role in every major industry, from education to healthcare.

AI は、教育から医療まで、あらゆる主要産業で不可欠な役割を果たすでしょう。

black box ［名］ブラックボックス

 定義 a system, device, or process whose internal workings are not easily understood or explained
内部の仕組みが容易に理解・説明できないシステムや装置、工程のこと

2030 Developers will produce new tools that provide insight into AI output.
開発者は、AI の出力に洞察を与える新しいツールを制作するでしょう。

intelligent agent ［名］知的エージェント

 定義 a software entity or system designed to autonomously perceive and interpret its environment, make decisions, and take actions to achieve specific goals or tasks
特定の目標や課題を達成するために、自律的に環境を認識・解釈し、意思決定を行い、行動を起こすように設計されたソフトウェアの実体またはシステム

2030 Intelligent agents will play a significant role in daily life, managing everything from personal schedules to home automation systems.
知的エージェントが、個人のスケジュールからホームオートメーションシステムまで、あらゆるものを管理し、日常生活で重要な役割を果たすようになるでしょう。

strong AI ［名］強い人工知能

 定義 AI systems that possess cognitive abilities similar to human intelligence, enabling them to perform a wide range of intellectual tasks
人間の知能に近い認知能力を持った AI システムで、さまざまな知的課題をこなせるもの

2030 Everyday AI will become more versatile, but it will not be considered strong AI.
日常的な AI はより多機能になりますが、強い人工知能とは言えないでしょう。

weak AI ［名］弱い人工知能

 定義 AI systems designed to perform specific tasks, without possessing broader cognitive abilities like human intelligence
特定の課題をこなすために設計された AI システムで、人間の知能のような広範な認知能力を持たない

2030 Weak AI tutors will assist students in all subjects.
弱い人工知能のチューターが全教科で生徒をサポートするでしょう。

air quality

003

［名］大気質、大気環境

解説

After several wildfires broke out in Canada in June 2023, a red haze of smoke filled the sky all the way to New York. New York City reported that it was the worst **air quality** on record. As climate change makes wildfires occur more frequently worldwide, the visible signs of deteriorating **air quality** become more apparent.

2023年6月にカナダで複数の山火事が発生した後、赤い霧のような煙がニューヨークに至る空一面に広がった。ニューヨーク市は、記録上最悪の大気環境だったと報告した。気候変動によって世界中で山火事が頻発するようになると、大気質悪化の目に見える兆候がより鮮明になる。

定義 the condition of the air based on the presence of pollutants, such as particulate matter and harmful gases, which can affect human health and the environment
汚染物質の存在に基づいた待機の状態で、汚染物質には、人の健康や環境に影響を与える粒子状物質や有害ガスなどがある

In the short term, air quality around the globe will continue to decline.
短期的には、地球の大気質は低下し続けるでしょう。

acid rain ［名］酸性雨

定義 rainwater with a pH level lower than normal due to the presence of pollutants, such as sulfur dioxide and nitrogen oxide, which can damage the environment
pH レベルが通常より低い雨水のことで、原因は二酸化硫黄や窒素酸化物など環境を破壊する汚染物質の存在

 Stricter regulations on emissions from industries and vehicles will significantly reduce the release of pollutants that cause acid rain.
工業施設や自動車からの排出ガス規制を強化することで、酸性雨の原因となる汚染物質の放出が大幅に削減されるでしょう。

acidification ［名］酸化、酸性化

定義 the process of increasing acidity in an environment, often caused by human activities that release acidic substances into the air, water, or soil
環境の中の酸性度が増加する過程のことで、多くの場合、酸性物質を空気や水、土壌に放出する人間の活動によって引き起こされる

 Ocean acidification will intensify, causing a decrease in pH levels and impacting marine life.
海の酸性化が強まり、pH 値が低下し、海洋生物に影響を与えるでしょう。

aerosol ［名］エアロゾル

定義 a suspension of fine solid particles or liquid droplets in air or another gas, which can affect air quality, climate, and human health
空気または他の気体中の微細な固体粒子または液体の液滴の懸濁液で、大気の質や気候、人間の健康に影響を与える可能性がある

 Increased regulations and international cooperation will aim to minimize the use of harmful aerosols.
規制の強化や国際協力によって、有害なエアロゾルの使用を最小限に抑えることが目標化されるでしょう。

combustion ［名］燃焼

定義 the process of burning a substance in the presence of oxygen, which releases energy and heat, and often produces gases and particulate matter
酸素の存在下で物質を燃やす工程で、エネルギーと熱が放出され、多くの場合、ガスや粒子状物質が発生する

 The widespread adoption of renewable energy sources and electrification will decrease reliance on combustion-based energy generation.
再生可能エネルギーの普及と電化によって、燃焼をベースにしたエネルギー生成への依存度が低下するでしょう。

004

altcoin

［名］オルトコイン、ビットコイン以外の暗号通貨

 解説

Bitcoin may have been the first cryptocurrency to dominate the headlines, but today, thousands of **altcoins** are available for investment and trading. While Bitcoin remains the largest and most well-known cryptocurrency, **altcoins** offer a range of different features and benefits, from enhanced privacy and security to faster transaction times and lower fees.

ビットコインは最初に話題になった暗号通貨かもしれないが、現在では何千ものオルトコインが投資や取引に利用できる。ビットコインは依然として最大かつ最も有名な暗号通貨だが、オルトコインには、プライバシーやセキュリティーの強化、取引時間の短縮、手数料の低減など、さまざまな特徴や利点がある。

定義 any cryptocurrency other than Bitcoin, often created as an alternative or complement to the original cryptocurrency

ビットコイン以外の暗号通貨のことで、たいていが大元の暗号通貨の代替品や補完品として作られたもの

2030 Altcoins will continue to draw attention for their profit potential regardless of whether they're useful.

オルトコインは、役に立つかどうかにかかわらず、その利益の可能性から注目され続けるでしょう。

CBDC [名]中央銀行デジタル通貨

 定義 short for "central bank digital currency," a digital form of a country's fiat currency, issued and regulated by a central bank
「中央銀行デジタル通貨」の頭字語で、ある国の中央銀行が発行し規制するデジタル形式の不換通貨

2030 CBDCs will give governments the utility of cryptocurrency as well as broad surveillance over the flow of money.
中央銀行デジタル通貨は、政府に暗号通貨の有用性とともに、お金の流れに対する幅広い監視機能を提供することになるでしょう。

fiat currency [名]不換通貨

 定義 a type of currency that is not backed by a physical commodity, such as gold or silver, but is instead issued by a government
金や銀などの現物に裏打ちされることなく、政府によって発行される通貨の一種

2030 Fiat won't disappear overnight, but more people will question its value as cryptocurrency adoption increases.
不換通貨が一夜にして消えることはないものの、暗号通貨の普及が進むにつれて、その価値に疑問を持つ人が増えていくでしょう。

stablecoin [名]ステーブルコイン

 定義 a type of cryptocurrency designed to maintain a stable value, often pegged to a reserve of assets, like traditional currencies or commodities
安定した価値を維持するように設計された暗号通貨の一種で、多くの場合、従来の通貨や商品のように、資産の準備に限定されている

2030 Stablecoins will provide an onramp for many people interested in exchanging other cryptocurrencies.
ステーブルコインは、他の暗号通貨との交換に興味を持つ多くの人々にきっかけを与えることになるでしょう。

token [名]トークン、代用貨幣

 定義 a digital asset representing a unit of value, often used within a specific platform, ecosystem, or application
価値の単位を表すデジタル資産で、特定のプラットフォーム、エコシステム、またはアプリケーション内で使用されることが多い

2030 Crypto tokens will become more common as DeFi gains traction.
分散型金融の普及に伴い、暗号代用貨幣はより一般的になっていくでしょう。

005

android

［名］アンドロイド、人造人間

解説

Androids have, for the most part, been limited to places like auto shows and research facilities. But that will soon change. **Androids** will help ease labor shortages, provide care to older adults, and, further down the road, assist in commercial and residential housekeeping. Eventually, **androids** may be as common as pets.

アンドロイドの存在はこれまで、大部分が自動車ショーや研究施設といった場所に限定されていた。しかし、それも間もなく変わるだろう。人手不足を解消し、高齢者の介護を行い、さらにその先には、商業施設や住宅の清掃作業の支援にもアンドロイドが役立つだろう。いずれは、ペットと同じように、アンドロイドが身近な存在になるかもしれない。

定義 a humanoid robot or synthetic organism designed to resemble and imitate human features and behaviors
　　人間の特徴や行動を模倣して設計された人型ロボットまたは合成生物

 Androids will be equipped with highly sophisticated facial recognition technology, allowing them to accurately identify and remember individuals, even in crowded or changing environments.
　　アンドロイドに高度な顔認識技術が導入され、混雑したり変化したりする環境でも個人を正確に識別し、記憶することができるようになるでしょう。

humanoid [形] 人間の形をした、人間に酷似した

 定義 referring to something that has an appearance or character resembling that of a human being
人間に似た外見や特徴を持つ物の

 2030 Humanoid robots will be able to perform complex tasks such as cooking, cleaning, and caregiving.
人間型のロボットが、料理や掃除、介護などの複雑な作業をこなせるようになるでしょう。

biomimetic [形] 生体模倣の

定義 referring to the imitation of natural systems, structures, or processes in engineering, technology, or design
工学やテクノロジー、設計において、自然の仕組みや構造、工程をまねた

 2030 Biomimetic insect-inspired robots will possess flight capabilities similar to real insects such as bees or dragonflies.
生体模倣の昆虫型ロボットが、ハチやトンボなどの実際の昆虫同様の飛行能力を身につけるようになるでしょう。

embodied machine [名] 肉体を持った機械

定義 a robot or AI system with a physical presence, allowing it to interact with and perceive its environment
物理的に存在するロボットや AI システムで、置かれた環境に対応したり、知覚したりできる

 2030 Embodied machines will start to replace human-operated machinery in hazardous environments.
危険な環境では、人間が操作する機械に代わって、肉体を持った機械が使われ始めるでしょう。

sentient [形] 知覚を持った、意識を持った

定義 referring to a being or entity that possesses the capacity for consciousness, self-awareness, or subjective experiences
意識や自己認識、主観的経験を持つ力を備えた存在や実体の

 2030 Whether or not AI achieves sentience, AI will appear to many to have achieved sentience when it has not.
AI が意識を獲得するかどうかにかかわらず、AI は多くの人に、実際にはそうではないのに意識を持っているかのごとく見えるようになるでしょう。

11

anti-aging

[形] アンチエイジングの

006

解説

Scientists are hard at work trying to decipher the mechanisms that control aging. Some aspire to help people live longer. Others strive to enhance people's overall quality of life as they age. One group of researchers has successfully extended the lifespan of old mice through gene therapy. Humans may not be far behind.

科学者たちは、老化を制御するメカニズムの解明に懸命に取り組んでいる。人間がより長生きできるよう願う人もいる一方で、年齢を重ねた人の生活の質を高めることを目指す向きもある。ある研究グループは、遺伝子治療によって老いたマウスの寿命を延ばすことに成功した。人間にもそう遠くなく可能になるかもしれない。

定義 preventing, lessening, or reversing the effects of aging
老化を防止、軽減または回復するような

 Anti-aging will become a more mainstream area of healthcare, with regular treatments or therapies to slow aging being integrated into standard health protocols.
アンチエイジングが占める医療の主流領域が増え、老化を遅らせるための定期的な処置や治療法が、標準的な健康管理の手続きに組み込まれるようになるでしょう。

life expectancy [名]平均余命

 定義 the average number of years a person is expected to live based on factors such as current age, lifestyle, and health
現在の年齢やライフスタイル、健康状態などの要素に基づいた、ある人が生きられであろう平均年数

2030 Life expectancy will decrease in the short term but increase in the long term.
平均余命は、短期的には短くなりそうですが、長期的には延びるでしょう。

longevity [名]寿命、長寿

 定義 the length of time a person or organism lives
人や生物が生きる時間の長さ

2030 Advances in genomics will lead to a greater understanding of the genetic factors that contribute to longevity.
ゲノミクスの進歩により、長寿に寄与する遺伝的要因の解明が進むでしょう。

reanimation [名]蘇生

 定義 the process of bringing someone or something back to life, often used in the context of science fiction or medical research
人や物を生き返らせる過程のことで、SF や医学研究に関する話の中で使われることが多い

2030 Advances in cryotechnology will lead to reduced cellular damage during the freezing process, making reanimation more feasible.
冷凍技術の進歩により、凍結時の細胞へのダメージが軽減され、蘇生がより現実的になるでしょう。

telomere [名]テロメア、染色体末端部位

 定義 a protective structure at the end of a chromosome that shortens with each cell division, eventually leading to cell death or aging
染色体の末端にある保護構造のことで、細胞分裂のたびに短くなり、最終的に細胞死や老化に至る

2030 A greater understanding of telomere biology will lead to more accurate biomarkers of biological age and health.
テロメアの生態の理解が進み、生物学的な年齢や健康状態をより正確に示す生体指標につながるでしょう。

13

authoritarian

007

［形］権威主義的な

解説

Many factors have led to the spread of authoritarianism since the end of the 20th century. One is the explosion in inequality caused by out-of-control capitalism. Another is China's increasing economic and political power challenging the dominance of the West. Meanwhile, Russia's expansionist ambitions have caused some to believe that authoritarianism offers more stability and control in an uncertain world.

20世紀の終わり以降、多くの要因が権威主義の蔓延を招いてきた。一つは、制御不能な資本主義が引き起こした不平等の爆発だ。もう一つは、欧米の支配に対抗する中国の経済力・政治力の増大である。一方、ロシアの拡張政策の野心は、権威主義が不確実な世界により安定した支配をもたらすと考える人々を生み出している。

定義 characterized by a system or style of government that exerts strong centralized control and restricts individual freedoms and civil liberties, often without a democratic process

中央集権的な強い統制を行い、個人の自由や人権を制限し、しばしば民主的なプロセスを経ない、といった政府の仕組みや形態によって特徴づけられた

 Even in democratic countries, a vocal minority will continue to push for authoritarian rule.

民主主義国家でも、少数派が声を上げ、権威主義的な支配を推し進め続けるでしょう。

totalitarian state ［名］全体主義国家

定義 a form of government characterized by absolute control and authority of a single ruling party or leader, suppressing individual freedoms and opposition

単一の与党または指導者による絶対的な支配と権威を特徴とし、個人の自由と反対を抑圧する政府形態

 Totalitarian states will continue to have a significant impact on global politics and the economy.

全体主義国家は、今後も世界の政治や経済に大きな影響を与え続けるでしょう。

Orwellian ［形］ジョージ・オーウェル流（全体主義体制）の

定義 pertaining to or reminiscent of the dystopian society depicted in George Orwell's novel *1984*, characterized by totalitarian control, government surveillance, propaganda, and the suppression of individual freedoms

ジョージ・オーウェルの小説『1984 年』に描かれた、全体主義的支配、政府の監視、プロパガンダ、個人の自由の抑圧を特徴とするディストピア社会に関する、またはそれを連想させるような

 The lessons of Orwell's cautionary tale will be just as relevant as they were in 1949.

オーウェルの警句の教訓は、1949 年当時と同様に適切であり続けるでしょう。

autocrat ［名］独裁者、専制君主

定義 a ruler who has absolute power and authority, often exercising it in an arbitrary and oppressive manner

絶対的な権力や権威を持ち、しばしば恣意的、抑圧的な方法でそれを行使する支配者

 At least a third of the global population will live in an autocracy.

少なくとも世界人口の 3 分の 1 は独裁国家に暮らすことになるでしょう。

Big Brother ［名］ビッグ・ブラザー、支配者

定義 a government or organization that uses surveillance and control to maintain its authority over citizens or members

市民や構成員に対する権威を維持するために、監視や統制を行う政府または組織

 As technology evolves, Big Brother's reach will extend further into our daily lives.

テクノロジーの進化に伴い、ビッグ・ブラザーの手はさらに伸び、私たちの日常生活にまで及ぶでしょう。

008

autonomous

［形］自律性の、自動の

In some parts of the US, you can hail an **autonomous** vehicle and experience a driverless ride to your destination. Delivery robots already bring pizza to people's doors, and delivery drones carry medical supplies to hard-to-reach areas. The **autonomous** age has begun, and soon we'll wonder how people lived without this modern convenience.

米国の一部の地域では、自律走行車を呼び寄せて、目的地まで運転手なしで移動する体験ができる。すでに宅配ロボットがピザを配達し、宅配ドローンが医薬品を行きにくい場所まで運んでいる。自律型の時代が幕を開け、やがては、いったい人々はかつて、今のこの利便性なしでどうやって暮らしていたのだろうとか思うようになるだろう。

定義 referring to something capable of functioning or making decisions independently, without direct human control
人間の直接的なコントロールなしに、独立して機能したり、意思決定したりすることができるような

 Autonomous vehicles will drastically reduce traffic accidents caused by human error.
自律走行車によって、人為的なミスによる交通事故が激減するでしょう。

drone [名]ドローン

定義 a type of aircraft that does not require a human pilot on board, controlled either remotely or autonomously

人間の操縦士を必要としない航空機の一種で、遠隔操作されるか、自律的に制御される

2030 Drones will contribute to a reduction in response times for emergency services, such as fire and rescue missions.

ドローンは、消防や救助活動といった緊急サービスの対応時間の短縮に貢献するでしょう。

ADAS [名]高度運転支援システム

定義 short for "advanced driver assistance systems," electronic systems in vehicles that help drivers with safety and convenience features

「高度運転支援システム」の頭字語で、自動車における電子システム。安全性や利便性の高い機能を持って運転者を支援するもの

2030 All new vehicles will come equipped with ADAS.

すべての新車に高度運転支援システムが搭載されるようになるでしょう。

flying car [名]空飛ぶ車

定義 a type of personal air vehicle that combines the capabilities of a car and an aircraft, enabling both ground and air travel

自動車と航空機の機能を併せ持つ個人用飛行機の一種で、地上と空中の両方を移動することができる

2030 The first commercially available flying cars will serve as taxis in a few major cities.

最初に市販される空飛ぶ車は、いくつかの主要都市でタクシーとして使われることになるでしょう。

robotaxi [名]自動運転タクシー

定義 an autonomous vehicle that provides on-demand transportation services without the need for a human driver

オンデマンドの輸送サービスを提供する自律走行車で、人間の運転手を必要としない

2030 The geofenced areas where robotaxis operate will expand significantly.

自動運転タクシーが営業するジオフェンスエリアが、大幅に拡大するでしょう。

bias

[名] 偏向、先入観

009

解説

In the age of big data and artificial intelligence, recognizing and addressing various forms of **bias** has become increasingly important. **Bias** can lead to skewed results, misinterpretations, and unfair treatment, affecting decision-making processes and the development of technology. Researchers and practitioners have been working on methods to identify and mitigate **bias** in data collection, algorithms, and human interactions.

ビッグデータと人工知能の時代において、さまざまな形の偏向を認識し、対処することがますます重要になってきている。偏向は、歪んだ結果や誤った解釈、不公平な扱いにつながり、意思決定の過程や技術開発に影響を与える。研究者も現場で働く人たちも、データ収集やアルゴリズム、人間の相互作用における偏向を特定し、緩和する方策に取り組んできた。

定義 systematic and unfair prejudices in data or algorithms that result in discrimination based on factors such as race, gender, age, or other protected characteristics

データ、あるいはアルゴリズムにおける体系的かつ不当な偏見のことで、人種や性別、年齢、その他の保護されるべき特性などの要因に基づく差別をもたらすもの

Improved algorithms will mitigate bias in automated decision-making systems such as automated hiring systems.

アルゴリズムの改善によって、自動雇用システムなどの自動意思決定システムにおける偏向が軽減されるでしょう。

algorithmic bias [名] アルゴリズムバイアス

 定義 a systematic error in a computer system that produces unfair or discriminatory outcomes due to biased data, assumptions, or design
コンピューターシステムの体系的なエラーの一つで、偏ったデータや仮定、設計が原因で不公平な、あるいは差別的な結果を生み出すもの

2030 As software expands to pervade every aspect of society, algorithmic bias will occur more frequently.
ソフトウェアが社会のあらゆる場に浸透するにつれて、アルゴリズムバイアスはより頻繁に発生するでしょう。

selection bias [名] 選択バイアス

 定義 a distortion in the results of a study or analysis due to a non-random sample selection or an exclusion of certain groups
研究や分析の結果における歪みの一つで、無作為とは言えないサンプルの選択や集団の除外が原因で生じる

2030 There will be a stronger emphasis on study design to avoid selection bias.
選択バイアスを回避するために研究デザインがより重視されるようになるでしょう。

data bias [名] データバイアス

 定義 a distortion in data resulting from biased data collection, processing, or interpretation methods, leading to inaccurate or misleading conclusions
偏ったデータの収集や処理、解釈方法に起因するデータの歪みの一つで、不正確な、あるいは誤解を招くような結論を導くもの

2030 Improved data collection methods will aim to eliminate bias at the source.
データの収集方法が改善され、情報源にある偏向が排除されるようになるでしょう。

confirmation bias [名] 確証バイアス

 定義 the tendency to search for, interpret, or remember information in a way that confirms one's preconceptions, often leading to incorrect conclusions
自分の先入観を確かめるように情報を探したり解釈したり記憶したりする傾向のことで、多くの場合、誤った結論に至る

2030 In schools, lessons designed to foster critical thinking skills will incorporate discussions of confirmation bias.
学校では、批判的思考力を養うための授業に、確証バイアスの議論が取り入れられるでしょう。

010

biocomputer

[名] バイオコンピューター

解説

Biocomputers offer potential advantages over traditional electronic computers, such as reduced energy consumption, the ability to operate in diverse environments, and improved processing capabilities for certain tasks. Researchers are exploring the development of **biocomputers** using DNA, proteins, and other biological elements, aiming to create a new generation of computational systems that can solve complex problems more efficiently and sustainably.

バイオコンピューターには、エネルギー消費の削減、多様な環境下での動作、特定のタスクに対する処理能力の向上など、従来の電子計算機をしのぐ潜在的な利点がある。研究者たちは、DNAやタンパク質といった生物学的な材料を用いたバイオコンピューターの開発を模索しており、複雑な問題をより効率的かつ持続的に解決できる新世代の計算システムの構築を目指している。

定義 a computing device that uses biological materials, such as DNA or proteins, to perform computational tasks
DNA やタンパク質などの生体物質を用いて演算処理を行う計算装置

 Some biocomputers will make use of evolutionary computing techniques to solve complex problems by mimicking natural processes.
バイオコンピューターの中に、自然のプロセスを模倣して複雑な問題を解決する進化型コンピューティング技術を利用するものが出てくるでしょう。

organoid [名]オルガノイド

 定義 a small, three-dimensional structure of living cells that resembles an organ and is grown in a laboratory for research purposes
生きた細胞でできた小さな3次元の構造体で、臓器に似ており、研究目的で実験室で育てられる

2030 Organoids will be developed from non-human cells, alleviating ethical concerns and supply chain issues.
人以外の細胞からオルガノイドを開発することで、倫理的な問題や供給網の問題が軽減されるでしょう。

biomaterial [名]生体材料

 定義 a natural or synthetic material that interacts with biological systems and is used in medical devices, tissue engineering, and drug delivery systems
天然の、または合成された材料で、生体の仕組みと相互に作用し、医療機器や再生医療、薬物送達システムに使われる

2030 Hydrogel-based biomaterials will be used to create artificial cartilage and joint replacements.
ヒドロゲルを用いた生体材料が、人工軟骨や人工関節の作成に使用されるでしょう。

optogenetics [名]光遺伝学

 定義 a technique that combines genetics and optics to control and monitor the activity of individual neurons in living tissue using light
遺伝学と光学を組み合わせた技術のことで、生きた組織内の個々の神経細胞の活動を光で制御・監視するもの

2030 Optogenetics will be utilized to precisely map and manipulate neural circuits involved in learning and memory.
光遺伝学を活用して、学習や記憶に関わる神経回路の精密なマッピングや操作が行われるでしょう。

synthetic cells [名]合成細胞

 定義 artificially created cells or cell-like structures that mimic the functions of natural cells, designed for research or practical applications
人工的に造られた細胞または細胞に似た構造物のことで、天然の細胞の機能をまねたもの。研究や実用化を目的として設計されている

2030 Researchers will develop synthetic cells capable of replication.
研究者が、複製可能な合成細胞を開発するでしょう。

biodegradable

011

［形］生分解性の

解説

In 2018, Starbucks announced it would phase out plastic straws in favor of paper. This high-profile pledge was a sign that consumer pressure and growing awareness of environmental concerns were having an impact. Now, packaging, personal care products, and even textiles are undergoing a **biodegradable** transformation. Some large companies have even pledged to make their entire product lines **biodegradable**.

2018年に、スターバックス社はプラスチック製ストローを段階的に廃止して紙製に切り替える、と発表した。この注目すべき公約は、消費者の圧力と環境問題への意識の高まりが影響を及ぼしていることを示すものだった。今や、梱包やパーソナルケア製品、布地までもが生分解性へと変貌を遂げつつある。大企業の中には、製品ライン全体を生分解性にすることを約束したところもある。

 capable of being broken down naturally by microorganisms, such as bacteria and fungi, into non-toxic substances that do not harm the environment
細菌や菌類などの微生物によって自然に分解され、環境に害を与えない無害な物質になれる

 The first company to mass produce a sustainable, biodegradable plastic bag alternative will be worth billions of dollars.
持続可能で生分解性を持つレジ袋の代替品を最初に大量生産した企業は、数十億ドルの価値を手にするでしょう。

landfill ［名］埋立地、埋め立てごみ処理場

 定義 a site where waste is disposed of by burying it under layers of soil
廃棄物を土の下に埋めて処分する場所

2030 Many landfills will incorporate waste-to-energy systems, allowing for the generation of clean and renewable energy from the decomposition of organic waste material.
多くの埋立地で廃棄物発電システムが導入され、有機廃棄物の分解からクリーンで再生可能なエネルギーを生成できるようになるでしょう。

microplastic ［名］マイクロプラスチック

定義 tiny particles of plastic, often less than 5 mm in size, which can originate from various sources and pose threats to the environment and human health
プラスチックの微粒子で、多くの場合 5 ミリメートル以下の大きさのもの。さまざまな発生源があり、環境や人の健康に脅威を与える

 2030 Concentrations of microplastic in people's blood will increase.
人の血中マイクロプラスチックの濃度が上昇するでしょう。

compost ［名］堆肥、培養土

定義 a mixture of decomposed organic materials that can be used as a nutrient-rich fertilizer
有機物を分解した混合物で、栄養価の高い肥料として使用できる

 2030 Community composting programs will become more widespread.
地域社会による堆肥化計画がより広まるでしょう。

vermiculture ［名］ミミズ堆肥化

定義 the practice of using earthworms to break down organic waste materials, such as food scraps or agricultural residues, into nutrient-rich vermicompost
ミミズを使って生ゴミや農業残渣などの有機廃棄物を分解し、栄養豊富なミミズ堆肥を作ること

 2030 The use of specialized composting worms will enhance the efficiency of vermiculture systems.
堆肥化に特化したミミズを使うことで、ミミズ堆肥化の効率が上がるでしょう。

blended learning

[名] ブレンディッドラーニング

012

解説

Modern technologies are bringing long overdue changes to the classroom. **Blended learning** provides students with a more personalized, self-paced education while also helping students develop essential technological skills. Meanwhile, teachers are transitioning from being mere repositories of knowledge to becoming guides and facilitators, empowering students to navigate their educational journeys with critical thinking and problem-solving skills.

現代のテクノロジーは、教室に長い間待ち望まれていた変化をもたらしている。ブレンディッドラーニングが生徒に提供するのは、より個人に特化され、自分のペースで行えるような学習であり、さらには、必要なテクノロジー面での技能だ。一方、教師は単なる知識の蓄積者から、生徒が批判的思考と問題解決能力をもって教育の道筋を進めるように導く案内人兼世話人へと移行している。

定義 an educational approach that combines in-person instruction with online learning activities and resources
対面での指導とオンラインでの学習活動やリソースを組み合わせた教育の手法

 2030 Advances in technology will allow blended learning to become more personalized, catering to individual students' needs.
テクノロジーの進化によって、ブレンディッドラーニングはより個々人に特化されたものとなり、生徒一人ひとりのニーズに応るようになるでしょう。

asynchronous learning [名]非同期学習、アシンクロナスラーニング

 定義 a type of online education in which students access course materials, complete assignments, and participate in discussions at their own pace, without real-time interaction with instructors or peers

オンライン教育の一種で、講師と、あるいは生徒間でのリアルタイムのやり取りがなく、生徒が自分のペースで教材にアクセスしたり、課題をこなしたり、ディスカッションに参加したりするもの

2030 The acceptance of remote work and the need for continuous learning will increase the prevalence of asynchronous learning in adult education.

リモートワークの容認や継続的な学習へのニーズから、社会人教育における非同期学習の普及が進むでしょう。

personalized learning [名]個人に特化された学習、パーソナライズドラーニング

 定義 an educational approach that tailors instruction, content, and assessment to meet the individual needs, interests, and abilities of each student

生徒一人ひとりのニーズや興味、能力に合わせて指導、内容、評価を調整する教育手法

2030 Personalized learning will become common with advances in AI and adaptive learning technologies.

AI や適応学習技術の進歩によって、個人に特化された学習が一般的になっていくでしょう。

remote learning [名]遠隔学習、リモートラーニング

 定義 an educational method that allows students to attend classes, access learning materials, and complete assignments from a distance

離れた場所から授業に参加したり、教材を利用したり、課題をこなしたりできる教育手法

2030 XR technologies will make remote learning a more immersive learning experience than a tablet or PC.

クロスリアリティーの技術によって、遠隔学習は、タブレットやパソコンを使うよりも没入感のあるものになるでしょう。

synchronous learning [名]同期学習、シンクロナスラーニング

 定義 a type of online education in which students and instructors engage in real-time interaction through video conferencing, live chat, or other communication tools, allowing for immediate feedback and collaboration

オンライン教育の一種で、生徒と講師がビデオ会議、ライブチャット、その他のコミュニケーションツールを通じてリアルタイムにやり取りし、即時のフィードバックや協働を可能にするもの

2030 Advanced network technologies like 5G and beyond will facilitate smoother, more reliable synchronous online learning experiences.

5G 以降の高度なネットワーク技術によって、よりスムーズで信頼性の高い同期型オンライン学習体験が可能になるでしょう。

bullying

［名］いじめ

013

解説

Social media platforms and online communication have provided new avenues for **bullying**. With the ability to hide behind anonymous usernames and online profiles, cyberbullies can harass their victims at any time and from anywhere. However, there has also been a growing awareness of the impact of **bullying** and increased efforts to combat it through education and intervention programs.

ソーシャルメディアのプラットフォームやオンラインコミュニケーションは、いじめの新しい手段を提供してきた。ユーザー名やオンラインプロフィールの匿名性の陰に隠れられるので、ネットいじめに走る者たちは、いつでも、どこからでも獲物を見つけて嫌がらせをすることが可能だ。しかし、いじめの影響に対する認識も高まり、教育や介入プログラムを通じて、いじめと闘う取り組みが拡大している。

定義 a pattern of aggressive behavior involving the misuse of power to target and harm others physically, emotionally, or psychologically
攻撃的な行動パターンの一つで、支配力を乱用し、他者を身体的、感情的、あるいは心理的に攻撃対象として危害を加えること

2030 AI technology will be implemented in social media platforms and schools to detect and prevent instances of bullying.
AI 技術を SNS プラットフォームや学校に導入し、いじめの事例を検知・防止するようになるでしょう。

disablism [名] 身障者差別

 定義 discrimination or prejudice against individuals with disabilities, often arising from negative stereotypes or misconceptions
障害を持つ人に対する差別や偏見で、多くの場合、否定的な固定観念や誤解に起因する

2030 Accessibility standards will be universally implemented, ensuring that all public spaces, transportation systems, and digital platforms are designed to accommodate individuals with disabilities.
アクセシビリティーの基準が幅広く適用され、すべての公共スペースや交通期間、デジタルプラットフォームが障害者に対応できるように設計されるでしょう。

lookism [名] 容姿による差別、外見的差別

 定義 prejudice or discrimination based on a person's physical appearance, often resulting in unfair treatment or social exclusion
人の外見に基づく偏見や差別のことで、多くの場合、不当な処遇や社会的排除をもたらす

2030 Anti-lookism campaigns and awareness initiatives will gain momentum, challenging the harmful impacts of lookism and promoting body acceptance and self-love.
反ルッキズムのキャンペーンや啓発活動が活発化し、ルッキズムの有害な影響と闘い、ありのままの体を受け入れることや自分をいつくしむ考え方が促進されるでしょう。

body-shame [動] 〜の体形をけなす

 定義 to criticize or humiliate someone based on their body size, shape, or appearance, often causing feelings of embarrassment or unworthiness
体格や体形、外見について人を批判したり侮辱したりする。当人に恥辱や不快感を植え付ける一面がある

2030 Mental health support systems will place greater emphasis on addressing body image concerns.
心の健康をサポートする制度では、体形のイメージへの懸念に対処することがより重視されることになるでしょう。

fat-shame [動] 〜の肥満を辱める

 定義 to criticize or mock someone for their size or weight, promoting negative stereotypes and contributing to body image issues
体格や体重を理由に人を批判したり嘲笑したりする。否定的な固定観念を助長し、身体イメージに関する問題を悪化させる行為。

2030 Societal attitudes toward body size and weight will shift, promoting acceptance and respect for individuals of all body types.
体格や体重に対する社会の捉え方が変わり、あらゆる体形の人が受け入れられ、尊重されるようになるでしょう。

27

Climate Change 気候変動

carbon

［名］炭素

014

解説

Without **carbon**, life as we know it could not exist. But when the delicate balance of **carbon** in our environment is disrupted, it can have far-reaching consequences. **Carbon** in its greenhouse gas form fuels climate change. But other forms, such as **carbon** nanotubes, may help to counteract these negative impacts. The future is tied to **carbon**.

炭素がなければ、私たちが生命と認識しているものは存在し得ない。しかし、私たちの環境における炭素の絶妙なバランスが崩れたとき、それは広範囲にわたる影響を及ぼす可能性がある。温室効果ガスとしての炭素は、気候変動を促進する。しかし、カーボンナノチューブのような別の形態は、このような悪影響を打ち消すのに役立つかもしれない。未来は、炭素と結び付いている。

定義 a chemical element that forms the basis for all known life on Earth, playing a central role in organic compounds and serving as the backbone of complex molecules

地球上のすべての既知の生命の基礎を形成する化学元素で、有機化合物の中心的な役割を果たし、複雑な分子の骨格となる

More countries will implement carbon pricing schemes to incentivize businesses to reduce their carbon footprint.

より多くの国が炭素価格制度を導入し、企業が二酸化炭素の排出量を削減する動機づけを行うでしょう。

carbon accounting [名]炭素勘定

 定義 the systematic process of quantifying, tracking, and managing the amount of carbon dioxide and other greenhouse gas emissions produced by an organization, industry, or activity

組織や企業、活動によって排出される二酸化炭素などの温室効果ガスの量を定量化し、追跡し、管理する体系的な過程

2030 Carbon accounting systems will provide instant and continuous monitoring of carbon emissions.

炭素勘定のシステムによって、炭素排出量を即時かつ継続的に監視することができるようになるでしょう。

carbon dioxide [名]二酸化炭素

 定義 a colorless, odorless gas composed of one carbon atom and two oxygen atoms, which is produced through natural processes, such as respiration, and human activities, such as burning fossil fuels

炭素原子1個と酸素原子2個からなる無色・無臭の気体で、呼吸などの自然な作用と化石燃料の燃焼などの人間の活動によって生成される

2030 Researchers will make progress in converting captured carbon dioxide into useful products, such as synthetic fuels and construction materials.

研究者らの取り組みが前進し、回収した二酸化炭素を合成燃料や建設資材などの有用な製品に変換することができるようになるでしょう。

carbon footprint [名]カーボンフットプリント

定義 the total amount of greenhouse gas emissions, primarily carbon dioxide, generated directly or indirectly by an individual, organization, product, or event

個人や組織、製品、催事などによって直接的または間接的に発生する二酸化炭素を主とする温室効果ガスの総排出量のこと

 2030 "Carbon footprint" labels will be standard on all products and services, informing consumers about the environmental impact of their purchases.

すべての商品やサービスに「カーボンフットプリント」のラベルが標準的に貼付され、消費者が購入時に環境への影響を知ることができるようになるでしょう。

carbon neutrality [名]カーボンニュートラルであること

定義 a state in which the net amount of carbon dioxide and other greenhouse gases emitted by an individual, organization, or country is balanced by equivalent reductions or carbon offsets

個人や組織、国家が排出する二酸化炭素やその他の温室効果ガスの純量が、同等の削減量やカーボンオフセットによって均衡を保っている状態

 2030 Many companies will establish clear roadmaps to carbon neutrality, but some will not follow through with them.

多くの企業がカーボンニュートラルへの明確なロードマップを策定するものの、それを実行に移さない企業も出てくるでしょう。

015

chatbot

［名］チャットボット

解説

Chatbots are revolutionizing everything from customer service to healthcare. Instead of waiting on hold or navigating through complex menus, people can now engage in real-time conversations with **chatbots** to get the information and assistance they need. There are bugs yet to be worked out, but the models that power **chatbots** grow more advanced every day.

チャットボットは、顧客サービスから医療に至るまで、あらゆる分野に革命をもたらしている。待たされたり複雑なメニューを操作したりする代わりに、人々はチャットボットとリアルタイムで会話し、必要な情報や支援を得られるようになった。未解決の問題点もあるが、チャットボットを動かすモデルは日々進化している。

定義 a computer program that simulates human conversation by processing and responding to text or voice inputs from users
ユーザーからの文字または音声での入力を処理し応答することによって、人間の会話を模倣するコンピュータープログラム

Chatbots will play a key role in mental health support services.
チャットボットは、心の健康支援サービスにおいて重要な役割を果たすでしょう。

virtual assistant [名]仮想アシスタント

 AI-powered software that assists users in performing various tasks, such as setting reminders, providing information, and controlling connected devices

AI を搭載したソフトウェアで、さまざまな課題をこなしてユーザーを支援する。リマインダーの設定や情報提供、接続機器の制御などを行う

 Most people will have a virtual assistant with a customized look and accent.

大半の人が、カスタマイズされた外見と話し方を備えた仮想アシスタントを手に入れるでしょう。

intent recognition [名]意図認識

 the process of identifying a user's purpose or goal when interacting with an AI system

AI システムとやり取りする際の、ユーザーの目的や目標を特定する過程

 The software systems people interact with will have a better understanding of what people are trying to accomplish.

人々がやり取りするソフトウェアシステムが、利用者の目的をよりよく理解するようになるでしょう。

context-aware [形]コンテキストを意識した

 referring to a computer system or application that understands and adapts to the situational context of its user, providing more relevant and personalized experiences

ユーザーの状況を理解し適応することで、より適切でパーソナライズされた体験を提供するコンピューターシステムやアプリケーションの

 New sensors and advanced NLP engines will give software systems new insight into people's circumstances.

新しいセンサーと高度な自然言語処理エンジンによって、ソフトウェアシステムが人々の状況に対する新たな判断力を備えるでしょう。

NLP [名]自然言語処理

 short for "natural language processing," a field of artificial intelligence that focuses on enabling computers to understand, interpret, and generate human language

「自然言語処理」の頭字語で、コンピューターが人間の言葉を理解・解釈・生成できるようにすることに焦点を当てた人工知能の分野

 Voice recognition systems will make far fewer mistakes when trying to interpret what people are saying.

音声認識システムが、人の話を解釈する際に犯す誤りが、大幅に減るでしょう。

31

016

clickbait

［名］クリックベイト

解説

Whether online or offline, sensationalism sells. **Clickbait** has become a common strategy used to foster audience engagement in the digital age, similar to how eye-catching headlines are used in traditional print media. However, this practice has also attracted increased scrutiny of media and advertising methods, leading to efforts to promote media literacy and critical thinking skills among consumers.

オンラインであれオフラインであれ、扇情主義は売れる。クリックベイトは、従来の印刷媒体で人目を引く見出しが使われるのと同様に、デジタル時代に閲覧者の関心を高めるために使われる当たり前の戦略となってきた。しかし、このやり方は、メディアや広告の手法に監視の目を向けさせ、消費者のメディアリテラシーや批判的思考力を高める取り組みにつながっている。

定義 sensational, misleading, or attention-grabbing headlines or content designed to attract clicks and drive web traffic
扇情的な、誤解を招きかねない、あるいは注目を集めようという意図を持った見出しやコンテンツのことで、クリックを誘いウェブトラフィックを促進するように考案されている

Clickbait will become increasingly common in free online media.
無料のオンラインメディアでは、クリックベイトがますます一般的になっていくでしょう。

content warning [名]内容警告

 定義 a notice or disclaimer provided before potentially distressing or sensitive material to allow readers or viewers to prepare or avoid it if necessary

痛ましい内容やデリケートな内容の素材について、あらかじめ読者や視聴者が心の準備をしたり必要なら回避したりできるように表示される、告知文または免責事項

2030 AI will enable content warnings to help people avoid specific types of content.

AI によって、特定の種類のコンテンツを回避するための内容警告が可能になるでしょう。

doomscrolling [名]ドゥームスクロール

 定義 the act of compulsively browsing through negative news or social media content, often leading to feelings of anxiety, sadness, or helplessness

悲観的なニュースやソーシャルメディアのコンテンツを強迫的に閲覧する行為のことで、たいてい不安、悲しみ、無力感などの感情を引き起こす

2030 Doomscrolling will be recognized as a potential indicator of underlying anxiety or depression.

ドゥームスクロールは、潜在的な不安やうつ病の指標として捉えられるようになるでしょう。

curiosity gap [名]好奇心のギャップ

 定義 the intentional creation of an information gap in content, designed to pique the reader's curiosity and encourage them to click or engage further

コンテンツを意図的に情報不足なものにすることで、閲覧者の好奇心を刺激し、さらなるクリックや参加を促すこと

2030 A revolt against abusers of the curiosity gap will result in media that aims to provide information without psychological manipulation.

好奇心のギャップを悪用する者への抵抗が起こり、心理操作なしに情報を提供することを目指すメディアが現れるでしょう。

listicle [名]まとめ記事、一覧記事

 定義 an article or piece of content presented in the form of a numbered or bulleted list, often used to simplify complex information or make it more appealing

番号付きリストや箇条書きの形式で提示される記事またはコンテンツのことで、複雑な情報を簡略化したり、より魅力的にするために使われることが多い

2030 Listicles will be taught in school as a presentation technique.

まとめ記事は発表のテクニックの一つとして、学校で教得られることになるでしょう。

33

climate

［名］気候

017

解説

The reports are grim: we are not meeting our **climate** goals. Rising global temperatures, extreme weather events, and the loss of biodiversity are just a few of the alarming signs of our planet's ecological crisis. International cooperation and collective efforts are essential to drive systemic change and create a sustainable future.

報告内容は厳しい。私たちは気候変動に関する目標を達成できていないというのだ。地球の気温上昇、異常気象、生物多様性の喪失は、地球の生態系危機の憂慮すべき兆候のほんの一部である。系統だった変化を促し、持続可能な未来を作り出すには、国際協力と集団的な努力が不可欠だ。

 the long-term patterns and trends of weather conditions in a particular region, including temperature, precipitation, and wind, which can be influenced by natural and human factors

特定の地域における気象条件の長期的なパターンと傾向のことで、気温や降水量、風などが含まれ、自然や人為的な要因の影響を受けることがある

 Changes in precipitation patterns will result in more frequent and severe droughts in some regions, while others will experience heavier rainfall and an increased risk of floods.

降水パターンの変化により、ある地域ではより頻繁で深刻な干ばつが発生する一方、別の地域ではより雨量が増して洪水のリスクが高まることになるでしょう。

carbon cycle [名]炭素サイクル

 定義 the natural process by which carbon atoms are exchanged between the atmosphere, land, oceans, and living organisms, playing a vital role in maintaining the Earth's carbon balance
炭素原子が大気や陸、海、生物の間で交換される自然の過程のことで、地球の炭素のバランスを維持する上で重要な役割を果たす

 2030 The adoption of sustainable agricultural practices will help to balance the carbon cycle.
持続可能な農法が採用され、炭素サイクルのバランスを取る上で助けになるでしょう。

global warming [名]地球温暖化

定義 the long-term increase in Earth's average surface temperature, mainly due to human activities releasing greenhouse gases
地表の平均気温が長期的に上昇することで、主に人間の活動による温室効果ガスの放出が原因

2030 An increase in disease-carrying organisms will highlight the severity of global warming.
病気を媒介する生物が増え、地球温暖化の深刻さが浮き彫りになるでしょう。

greenhouse effect [名]温室効果

 定義 the warming effect observed on Earth due to the trapping of infrared radiation by greenhouse gases, causing an increase in global temperatures and influencing climate patterns
地球上で観測される温暖化現象で、温室効果ガスによる赤外線の捕捉を原因とする。地球全体の気温の上昇を引き起こし、気候パターンに影響を与える

2030 The greenhouse effect will continue to intensify, trapping more heat in the Earth's atmosphere.
温室効果は強まり続け、地球の大気中に多くの熱を閉じ込めていくでしょう。

greenhouse gas [名]温室効果ガス

 定義 a gas that contributes to the greenhouse effect by trapping heat in Earth's atmosphere
地球の大気中に熱を閉じ込め、温室効果をもたらすガス

2030 Home appliances will be designed to operate with significantly lower greenhouse gas emissions.
家電製品が、温室効果ガスの排出量を大幅に削減できるように設計されるようになるでしょう。

Cold War II

［名］第二次冷戦

018

解説

Cold War II refers to the heightened political, social, ideological, informational, and military tensions among global powers in the 21st century. While the original Cold War was waged between the United States and the Soviet Union, **Cold War II** highlights the geopolitical competition among the United States, Russia, and China.

第二次冷戦とは、21世紀における世界の大国間の政治的、社会的、イデオロギー的、情報的、軍事的緊張の高まりを指す。かつての冷戦は米国とソビエト連邦の間で続いたが、第二次冷戦は米国、ロシア、中国の間での地政学的な競合に焦点を当てたものである。

定義 the period of escalating tensions, competition, and conflict between major global powers in the early 2000s
2000年代前半の、大国間での緊張、競争、対立が激化している時期

Countries like China will continue to challenge the last remaining superpower technologically, economically, and in various other strategic domains.
中国のような国々が、技術的、経済的、その他のさまざまな戦略的領域で、最後に残った超大国に挑み続けるでしょう。

proliferation ［名］（核）拡散

 定義 a rapid increase in the number or amount of something, particularly referring to the development and deployment of nuclear or autonomous weapons

何かの数や量が急激に増えることで、特に核兵器や自律型兵器の開発・配備に言及するもの

2030 Autonomous weapons will permanently alter both warfare and politics.

自律型兵器は、戦争と政治のどちらをも永続的に変えるでしょう。

---

bioweapon ［名］生物兵器

 定義 a harmful biological agent, such as a virus or bacteria, that is used as a weapon to cause harm or death

有害な生物学的製剤で、損害や死をもたらす武器として使用されるウイルスやバクテリアなどのこと

2030 Fears of bioweapons will shake people's trust in the Biological Weapons Convention.

生物兵器の恐怖は、生物兵器禁止条約に対する人々の信頼を揺るがすことになるでしょう。

---

autonomous weapons ［名］自立型兵器

 定義 a weapon system that, once activated, can select and engage targets without further human intervention

一旦起動すれば、人間の手を煩わせることなく標的を選択し、交戦することができる兵器システム

2030 Some countries will deploy autonomous weapons for law enforcement purposes.

法の執行を目的に自律型兵器を配備する国もあるでしょう。

---

swarm ［名］兵器の大群、スウォーム

 定義 a group of small, autonomous weapons that work together in a coordinated manner to accomplish a specific objective, such as overwhelming a target or area with firepower

射撃能力を持って目標物や目標区域を制圧するなど、特定の目的を達成するために連携して作動する小型の自律型兵器群

2030 Swarms of autonomous weapons will take out military targets with unparalleled speed, precision, and efficiency.

自律型兵器がまとまれば、比類のない速度、精度、効率で軍事目標を破壊するでしょう。

019

conspiracy

［名］陰謀

解説

Social media platforms have facilitated the spread of countless **conspiracy** theories. They are often shared by users who are unaware of the inaccuracy of the information. Powerful state actors have also invented **conspiracy** theories to influence everything from global politics to human health. High-profile examples include the QAnon **conspiracy** theory and the false claims about the 2020 US presidential election.

ソーシャルメディアは、数え切れないほどの陰謀論を広めるのを後押ししてきた。陰謀論は、情報の不正確さに気づいていないユーザーによって共有されることが多い。また、強大な国家権力が、国際政治から人々の健康に至るまで、あらゆるものに影響を与えるために陰謀論を作り出してきた。よく知られた例に、Qアノンの陰謀論や、2020年の米国大統領選挙に関する誤った主張がある。

定義 a secret plan by a group to do something unlawful or harmful, or the belief in such a plan without evidence
違法または有害なことを行う集団による秘密の計略、あるいは根拠なしにそのような計略を信じること

Social media will continue to make the dissemination of conspiracy theories disturbingly easy.
SNS によって、陰謀論は驚くほど簡単に広まり続けるでしょう。

propaganda ［名］プロパガンダ

 定義 information or material disseminated by an individual, organization, or government with the intention to shape public opinion or manipulate perceptions, often through biased or misleading means
偏向させたり誤解を招いたりするような手段で世論を形成する、あるいは認識を操作する目的の下で、個人や組織、政府によって発信される情報または資料

2030 More individuals will leverage advanced technology to spread propaganda that has a significant impact on global affairs.
より多くの人が先進的なテクノロジーを活用し、世界情勢に大きな影響を与えるプロパガンダを広めることになるでしょう。

misinformation ［名］誤報、虚報、デマ

 定義 false or inaccurate information that is spread without the intent to deceive but which can still result in harm or confusion
人を欺く意図なく流布されたものであっても、危害や混乱をもたらす可能性があるような、虚偽の、あるいは不正確な情報

2030 The long-lasting repercussions of Covid-19 misinformation will become clear.
新型コロナウイルスに関する虚報がもたらす長期的な影響が、明らかになっていくでしょう。

deep state ［名］闇の国家、国家内国家

 定義 a supposed secret network of influential individuals within a government or organization who work to undermine its policies or authority
政府または組織内の影響力のある個人で構成され、その政策や権威を損なうために働く秘密のネットワークとされるもの

2030 Referencing the "deep state" will continue to be a way for conspiracy theorists to propagate baseless claims without any actual evidence.
陰謀論者は、事実無根の主張を広める手段として「闇の国家」を引き合いに出し続けるでしょう。

disinformation ［名］偽情報、虚報、デマ

 定義 false information that is spread, especially by a government, to influence public opinion or obscure the truth
世論を左右したり、真実を隠したりするために、特に政府によって流される偽の情報

2030 It will become increasingly challenging to differentiate between fact and fiction.
事実と架空の話を区別することがますます難しくなるでしょう。

39

cost-of-living crisis

020

［名］生活費の危機

解説

Record corporate profits may bring enormous wealth to CEOs and stockholders, but they can come at the expense of everyday workers who are struggling to pay for basic necessities such as housing, food, and healthcare. The resulting **cost-of-living crisis** has sparked debates around the need for social policies and government interventions to ensure a decent quality of life for all.

企業が記録的な利益を上げると、CEOや株主に莫大な富をもたらすかもしれないが、住宅、食料、医療などの基本的な必需品の支払いに苦労している一般の労働者がその犠牲になることもある。結果として生じる生活費の危機は、すべての人に適切な生活の質を保証するための社会政策や政府の介入の必要性をめぐる議論に火をつけている。

定義 a situation where the costs of essential goods and services increase, making it difficult for people to maintain their living standards
必需品や不可欠なサービスのコストが上昇し、生活水準を維持することが難しくなる状況

 Several countries will witness uprisings as extreme poverty makes life unlivable for many.
極度の貧困によって多くの人が生活できなくなる中、いくつかの国で反乱が起きるでしょう。

childcare [名]保育、小児保育

 定義 the supervision, care, and education of children, often provided by professionals or facilities outside the child's home

子どもを監督したり面倒を見たり、教育したりすることで、多くの場合、専門家や、子どもの自宅以外の施設によって提供される

2030 To combat declining birthrates, some countries will provide free childcare to encourage couples to start families.

少子化対策として、保育サービスを無償で提供し、夫婦が子どもを持つことを奨励する国もあります。

affordable [形]入手可能な、手頃な価格の

 定義 reasonably priced and within the financial means of most people

たいていの人が経済的に手が届く範囲内の手頃な値が付けられた

2030 Real estate ownership will become unaffordable to many.

不動産は、多くの人にとって手の届かないものになるでしょう。

delayed retirement [名]退職の先送り、退職の延期

 定義 the postponement of retirement beyond the traditional retirement age, often due to financial necessity or personal choice

経済的な必要性や個人の選択により、従来の退職年齢を超えて退職を延期すること

2030 Many will not be able to afford to retire until their 70s or 80s.

多くの人が、70代や80代になるまで退職する余裕がなくなるでしょう。

UBI [名]最低所得保障

 定義 short for "universal basic income," a form of social security where all citizens receive a regular, unconditional sum of money from the government

「最低所得保障」の頭字語で、すべての国民が政府から定期的に無条件で金を受け取る社会保障の一形態

2030 More countries will experiment with UBI to offset AI-driven job loss.

AIによる雇用喪失を相殺するために、実験的に最低所得保障制度を取り入れる国が増えるでしょう。

cryosphere

021

［名］氷圏、寒冷圏

解説

Climate change has caused ice sheets, glaciers, and permafrost to melt at alarming rates, leading to rising sea levels and threatening coastal communities. The 2002 collapse of Antarctica's 3,250 square-kilometer Larsen B Ice Shelf shocked scientists, making the vulnerability of the **cryosphere** strikingly apparent. Monitoring and studying the **cryosphere** is crucial for understanding and predicting the impacts of climate change.

気候変動により、氷床や氷河、永久凍土が驚くべき速さで融解し、海面上昇を招き、沿岸地域社会の脅威となっている。2002年に起きた南極大陸のラーセンB棚氷の崩壊は、科学者に衝撃を与え、雪氷圏の脆弱性が顕著になった。気候変動の影響を理解し、予測するためには、雪氷圏の監視と研究が不可欠である。

定義 the Earth's frozen components, including ice sheets, glaciers, snow, and permafrost, which play a critical role in the global climate system
地球上の凍った構成要素のことで、氷床や氷河、雪、永久凍土などを含み、地球全体の気候の仕組みに重要な役割を果たす

The melting of the cryosphere will alter ocean currents.
氷圏の融解は、海流を変えることになるでしょう。

ice calving [名]氷山・氷河の崩壊

 定義 the process in which chunks of ice break off from the edge of a glacier, ice shelf, or iceberg
氷河や棚氷、氷山の端から氷の塊が壊れていく過程

2030 Ice-calving events will become more frequent and larger in scale, leading to increased iceberg production.
氷の崩壊現象がより頻繁かつ大規模になり、より多くの氷山が生まれることにつながるでしょう。

ice cap [名]氷帽

 定義 a thick, dome-shaped mass of ice and snow that covers a highland area or mountain peak
高地や山頂を覆う、厚いドーム状の氷雪の塊

2030 The melting of the polar ice caps will accelerate climate change and vice versa.
極地の氷帽の融解は気候変動を加速させ、その逆も然りとなるでしょう。

permafrost [名]永久凍土（層）

 定義 a layer of soil, rock, or sediment that remains frozen for at least two consecutive years, found in polar and subpolar regions
少なくとも連続 2 年間は凍結したままの土や岩石、堆積物の層で、極地や亜極地に見られる

2030 The melting of the permafrost will result in the release of large amounts of methane.
永久凍土が溶けることで、大量のメタンが放出されるでしょう。

glacial retreat [名]氷河後退

 定義 the process in which a glacier's terminus recedes due to melting or reduced accumulation of snow
氷河の末端が、雪解けや積雪の減少によって後退する過程

2030 Glacial retreat will negatively impact the availability of freshwater resources.
氷河後退は、淡水資源の有効性に悪影響を及ぼすでしょう。

022

cryptocurrency

［名］暗号通貨

解説

Some people praise **cryptocurrencies** for their potential benefits, like making it faster and more cost-effective to send money around the world. Others criticize them for their association with criminal activities, such as money laundering and drug trafficking. While many individuals, companies, and even some countries hold some **cryptocurrencies**, their future remains uncertain.

暗号通貨の潜在的な利点を称賛する人もいる。世界中により速く送金できるし、より費用対効果が高くなる、といった利点があるというのだ。一方、マネーロンダリングや麻薬取引といった犯罪行為との関連で、暗号通貨を批判する人もいる。多くの個人、企業、そして一部の国家さえもが暗号通貨を保有しているが、その将来はいまだ不透明なままだ。

定義 a digital or virtual currency that uses cryptography for security, often decentralized and operating on a blockchain
セキュリティーのために暗号を使用するデジタルすなわち仮想の通貨で、多くの場合、ブロックチェーン上で動作する分散型

 Most people will own some cryptocurrency, and many will use it regularly.
ほとんどの人が何らかの暗号通貨を所有し、多くの人がそれを定期的に使うことになるでしょう。

Bitcoin [名] ビットコイン

 定義 a widely recognized cryptocurrency established in 2009 by an unidentified individual or group using the pseudonym Satoshi Nakamoto

広く知られる暗号通貨で、2009 年にサトシ・ナカモトというハンドルネームを用いて、正体不明の個人あるいは団体によって立ち上げられたもの

2030 The value of a single unit of the currency will rise above one million dollars.

この通貨 1 ユニットの価値が上がって 100 万ドルを超えるでしょう。

Ethereum [名] イーサリアム

 定義 an open-source blockchain platform that enables the creation of decentralized applications and supports its own cryptocurrency, Ether

分散型アプリケーションの作成を可能にし、独自の暗号通貨イーサーをサポートする、オープンソースのブロックチェーン用プラットフォーム

2030 The second-biggest cryptocurrency will achieve a multi-trillion dollar market cap.

この 2 番目に強力な暗号通貨は、数兆ドルの時価総額を達成するでしょう。

virtual currency [名] 仮想通貨

 定義 a digital form of value that can be used for online transactions, sometimes operating independently from a central authority

オンライン取引に使用可能な、通貨価値を持つデジタルな形態のことで、時には中央の管理当局から独立して取引される

2030 Virtual currencies will be used just as frequently as fiat currencies.

仮想通貨は、不換通貨と同じように頻繁に使われるようになるでしょう。

web3 [名] ウェブ3

 定義 a proposed third generation of the Internet, focusing on decentralization, blockchain technology, and increased user control over data

インターネットの第 3 世代として提案されたもののことで、分散化、ブロックチェーン技術、データに対するユーザーのコントロールの強化に焦点が当てられている

2030 Users will wrest control back from large platforms and aggregators making the success of web3 a near certainty.

ユーザーは、大規模なプラットフォームや情報収集サイトの支配から脱却し、ウェブ 3 の成功がほぼ確実なものになるでしょう。

023

cybersecurity

［名］サイバーセキュリティー

解説

Failure to implement **cybersecurity** measures is like going outside naked in a typhoon: you are, in a word, "exposed." Cyberthreats are becoming increasingly sophisticated and prevalent, so people cannot simply rely on software to protect themselves. It is vital to practice good digital hygiene because a successful attack can have devastating consequences.

サイバーセキュリティー対策を怠るというのは、台風の中、裸で外に出るようなものだ。一言で言えば「さらし者」なのだ。サイバー攻撃の脅威はますます高度化し、蔓延してきているため、人々はソフトウェアに頼るだけでは自分を守れない。攻撃が成功すれば壊滅的な結果をもたらすので、上手なデジタル衛生行動を実践することが重要だ。

定義 the protection of computer systems, networks, and data from theft, damage, or unauthorized access
コンピューターシステムやネットワーク、データを、窃盗、破壊、不正利用などから保護すること

 Cybersecurity jobs will be in high demand.
サイバーセキュリティー関係の仕事に、高い需要が見込まれるでしょう。

cyber espionage ［名］サイバースパイ

 the act of using cyber attacks and hacking techniques to obtain sensitive or classified information from individuals, organizations, or governments
サイバー攻撃やハッキング技術を駆使して、個人や組織、政府などから機密情報を入手する行為

2030 Cyber espionage-related attacks will increase exponentially.
サイバースパイ関連の攻撃が飛躍的に増加するでしょう。

cybercrime ［名］サイバー犯罪

 criminal activity that involves computers, networks, or the Internet
コンピューターやネットワーク、インターネットなどに関わる犯罪行為

2030 New AI tools will make BEC (business email compromise) attacks more effective.
新しいAIツールによって、BEC（ビジネスメール詐欺）攻撃がより有効性を増してしまうでしょう。

cyberstalking ［名］サイバーストーキング

 the use of digital communication technologies to harass, intimidate, or threaten someone
デジタル通信技術を使用して、人に嫌がらせや威嚇、脅迫を行うこと

2030 Cyberstalking will continue to be a relatively gender-neutral crime.
サイバーストーキングは、比較的性別不問の犯罪であり続けるでしょう。

cyberwarfare ［名］サイバー戦争

 the use of cyber attacks by one nation or group against another to damage, disrupt, or gain unauthorized access to computer systems and networks
ある国や集団が他の国に対してサイバー攻撃を行うことで、コンピューターシステムやネットワークに損害を与えたり混乱させたり、不正アクセスを行ったりすることが目的

2030 Governments will make substantially larger investments in branches of the military that deal with cyberwarfare.
各国政府が、サイバー戦争に対応する軍部への投資を大幅に拡大するでしょう。

024

cybersickness

［名］サイバー酔い

解説

Despite the numerous benefits that technology brings, it also has the potential to affect our mental and physical health adversely. **Cybersickness** was one of the earliest documented forms of illness related to digital technology. As XR integrates itself into our everyday lives, a range of new disorders will accompany its widespread adoption.

テクノロジーは、それがもたらす数々の恩恵とは裏腹に、私たちの精神的・肉体的な健康に悪影響を及ぼす可能性もはらんでいる。サイバー酔いは、最も早い段階で報告されたデジタル技術に関連する病気の一つだ。クロスリアリティーが私たちの日常生活に溶け込むにつれて、さまざまな新たな障害の発生が予想される。

---

 a form of motion sickness experienced by individuals in virtual reality or immersive digital environments, characterized by symptoms such as nausea, dizziness, and discomfort due to a sensory conflict between visual and vestibular inputs

仮想現実や没入型デジタル環境において人が経験する乗り物酔いの一種で、吐き気やめまい、不快感などの症状が特徴とする。視覚と前庭からの入力の間の感覚的な衝突が原因

 As XR technologies become mainstream, cybersickness will become more widespread.

クロスリアリティーの技術が主流になるにつれて、サイバー酔いはますます広がっていくでしょう。

AR Blindness ［名］AR失明、拡張現実の失明

定義 a condition experienced by individuals using AR technology, where they become visually unaware or "blind" to their physical surroundings

拡張現実の技術を使っている人が経験する状態の一つで、物理的な周囲の環境に視覚的に気づかない、あるいは「失明した」状態になること

 Emergency rooms will see numerous visits every day from people who had accidents due to AR blindness.

救急処置室に、AR失明が原因で事故に遭った人が毎日多数訪れることになるでしょう。

AR Phantasmagoria ［名］AR幻想、拡張現実の幻想

定義 a phenomenon where prolonged use of AR technology leads to a user experiencing persistent visual illusions or hallucinations of AR overlays, even when not using the technology

AR（拡張現実）技術を長時間使用するときに起きる現象の一つで、AR技術を使用していないときでも、ARの重ね合わせ画面の錯視や幻覚が持続すること

 Patients with severe AR phantasmagoria will require medication or cognitive-behavioral therapy.

重度のAR幻想の患者には、薬物療法や認知行動療法が必要になるでしょう。

MR Disassociation ［名］MR分離

定義 a temporary mental state where individuals struggle to distinguish between MR elements and real-world objects, resulting in confusion, disorientation, and impaired judgment

人がMR（複合現実）の要素と現実の物体を区別するのに苦労する一時的な精神状態のことで、混乱や見当識障害、判断力の低下などが起こる

 Some businesses will prohibit the use of XR devices to prevent workplace accidents due to MR disassociation.

MR分離が原因の労働災害を防止するために、XRデバイスの使用を禁止する企業も出てくるでしょう。

Virtual Isolation Syndrome ［名］バーチャル孤立症候群

定義 a psychological condition characterized by social withdrawal and a diminished desire for real-world interactions due to excessive reliance on virtual reality experiences, leading to feelings of loneliness and detachment

引きこもりや現実世界での交流への欲求が減退などを特徴とする心理状態のことで、仮想現実体験への過度の依存が原因。孤独感や離人症につながる

 Prominent medical figures and healthcare organizations will advise children and adolescents to strictly limit their XR use.

著名な医学者や医療機関が、子どもや若者にクロスリアリティーの利用を厳しく制限するよう助言するでしょう。

cyborg

［名］サイボーグ

解説

In perhaps just a few years' time, DNA nanobots will reside inside our brains, enhancing our biological ability to think. Artificial eyes will give us telescopic and microscopic vision, and prosthetic tails will offer us a superhuman ability to balance. Becoming a **cyborg** may seem like science fiction, but the initial research and development is already well underway.

ほんの数年後には、DNAナノボットが私たちの脳の中に入り込み、生物学的な思考能力を高めてくれるだろう。人工の目によって望遠鏡や顕微鏡のような視力を与えられ、人工装具としての尾部を着ければ超人的なバランス感覚が提供されるだろう。サイボーグになるというのはSFのようだが、初期の研究開発はすでに始まっているのだ。

定義 a being with both organic and artificial components, often designed to enhance human capabilities
有機物と人工物の両方を備えた生き物のことで、多くの場合、人間の能力を強化するために設計される

 Biotechnology will enable a closer fusion of humans and machines.
バイオテクノロジーによって、人間と機械がより密接に融合できるようになるでしょう。

brain-computer interface ［名］ブレーンコンピューターインターフェース

 a technology that establishes a direct communication pathway between the brain and an external device, allowing control and information exchange
脳と外部機器の間に直接、通信経路を確立し、制御や情報交換を可能にする技術

2030 Brain-computer interfaces will become common input devices, similar to mice and keyboards.
ブレーンコンピューターインターフェースは、マウスやキーボードと同様に、当たり前の入力装置になるでしょう。

exoskeleton ［名］外骨格

 a wearable external framework that augments a person's strength, mobility, or endurance, often used in medical or industrial settings
人の体力や運動能力、持久力を増強するウェアラブルな外部装着型フレームで、医療や産業の分野でよく使われる

2030 Construction workers will regularly wear exoskeletons on the job.
建設作業員は、業務中に定期的に外骨格を装着するようになるでしょう。

bionic ［形］生体工学の

 referring to the integration of artificial components or systems within a living organism, often to replace or enhance a natural function
生体内に人工的な部品や仕組みを埋め込んだ。多くの場合、自然の機能を代替または強化することが目的

2030 Bionic eyes will restore vision to people with certain kinds of blindness.
生体工学的眼球が、ある種の失明者の視力を回復させることになるでしょう。

neurotechnology ［名］ニューロテクノロジー

 tools, devices, and methods for understanding, monitoring, or manipulating the nervous system and brain functions
神経系および脳機能の理解や監視、操作のための道具や装置、方法のこと

2030 Neurotechnology advances will lead to brain stimulation treatments for depression.
ニューロテクノロジーの進歩によって、うつ病の脳刺激治療が可能になるでしょう。

data science

[名] データサイエンス

026

解説

Data science emerged as a distinct discipline in the early 2000s, and degree programs started popping up soon after. Students in such programs learn statistical analysis, machine learning, data visualization, data mining, and programming languages such as Python and R. And when **data science** majors graduate, they have the potential to secure lucrative positions in a variety of fields.

データサイエンスは2000年代前半に勃興した学問で、その後すぐに学位課程が整い始めた。そうした課程を専攻する学生は、統計解析、機械学習、データ可視化、データマイニング、パイソンやRなどのプログラミング言語などを学ぶ。そして、データサイエンス専攻の学生が卒業すると、さまざまな分野で有利な立場を確保できる可能性が高い。

定義 a multidisciplinary field that combines statistical analysis, programming, and domain expertise to extract insights and knowledge from large and complex datasets

統計解析、プログラミング、ドメインの専門知識を組み合わせて、大規模かつ複雑な集積データから知見を導き出す学際的な分野

The field of data science will expand to include dedicated branches for healthcare and climate science.

データサイエンスの分野は拡大し、医療や気候科学などの専門領域に枝分かれしていくでしょう。

data mining ［名］データマイニング

定義 the process of extracting valuable patterns, insights, or knowledge from large datasets

大規模な集積データから価値あるパターンや知見を導き出す過程

 Data mining of biometric data from wearables will lead to significant advances in personalized healthcare.

ウェアラブル機器から得られる生体情報のデータマイニングが、個別化医療の大きな進歩につながるでしょう。

big data ［名］ビッグデータ

定義 the massive volume of structured and unstructured data that is generated, stored, and analyzed, often requiring specialized tools and techniques

生成、保存、分析された膨大な量の構造化・非構造化データで、通常、取り扱いに専門的なツールや技術を必要とする

 Big data analysis will enable more efficient resource allocation in the healthcare industry, reducing costs.

ビッグデータの解析によって、医療業界ではより効率的な資源の配分が可能となり、コストが削減されるでしょう。

computer vision ［名］コンピュータービジョン

定義 a field of artificial intelligence focused on enabling computers to interpret, understand, and process visual information from the surrounding world

人工知能の一分野で、コンピューターが周囲の世界からの視覚情報を解釈、理解、処理できるようにすることに重点が置かれる

 Advances in computer vision will enable autonomous vehicles to operate in all weather conditions.

コンピュータービジョンの進歩により、自律走行車があらゆる気象条件下で走行できるようになるでしょう。

speech recognition ［名］言語認識、音声認識

定義 the ability of a machine or software to understand, interpret, and convert spoken language into text or commands

機械やソフトウェアが、話し言葉を理解し、解釈し、文字や命令に変換する能力

 Speech recognition will be a standard feature in the majority of smart devices.

言語認識の機能は、大半のスマートデバイスに標準装備されるでしょう。

DeFi

027

［名］DeFi（ディーファイ）、分散型金融

解説

DeFi has emerged as an innovative alternative to traditional financial systems, leveraging the blockchain to create decentralized financial services. **DeFi** technologies enable users to access services like lending, borrowing, and trading without relying on centralized intermediaries such as banks. **DeFi** has the potential to provide greater financial inclusion and accessibility to individuals around the world.

DeFiは、ブロックチェーンを活用して分散型金融サービスを実現する、従来の金融システムに代わる革新的な仕組みとして導入された。DeFiの技術により、ユーザーは銀行などの中央集権的な仲介機関に頼ることなく、貸し借りや取引などのサービスを利用できるようになる。DeFiは、世界中の個人に対して、より大きな金融包摂とアクセシビリティーを提供する可能性を持っている。

定義 a financial ecosystem based on blockchain technology that operates without central authorities, enabling decentralized financial services
ブロックチェーン技術に基づき、中央管理当局を介さずに運用され、分散型の金融サービスを可能にする金融収益構造

TradFi will move into the DeFi space, pushing out many of the new players.
従来型金融が分散型金融の立場に移行し、多くの新規利用者を排除するでしょう。

DAO [名] DAO（ダオ）、分散型自立組織

 定義 short for "decentralized autonomous organization," a digitally-native organization run by rules encoded as smart contracts on a blockchain, with no central authority

「分散型自律組織」の頭字語で、ブロックチェーン上の自動化契約として符号化された規則によって運営される、中央管理当局を持たないデジタルネイティブな組織

2030 Several DAOs will give large groups of people ownership of professional sports teams.

いくつかの分散型自立組織が、大規模な人々の集団にプロスポーツチームの所有権を与えるでしょう。

dApps [名] dApps（ダップス）、分散型アプリケーション

 定義 decentralized applications built on a blockchain or other decentralized network, often utilizing smart contracts to facilitate transactions

ブロックチェーンやその他の分散型ネットワーク上に構築された分散型アプリケーションのことで、多くの場合、自動化契約を利用して取引を促進する

2030 Some of the most popular dApps will be for gambling.

最も人気のあるダップスの中に、ギャンブル用のものが含まれてくるでしょう。

smart contract [名] 自動化契約、スマートコントラクト

 定義 a self-executing digital contract that automatically enforces the terms and conditions written within its code, providing transparency, efficiency, and security in various transactional processes

コード内に書かれた条件を自動的に実行する自己実行型のデジタル契約のことで、さまざまな取引のプロセスにおいて透明性、効率、安全性を提供する

2030 Smart contracts will disrupt the real estate industry.

自動化契約は、不動産業界を崩壊させるでしょう。

multisignature [名] マルチシグネチャー

定義 a type of digital signature scheme requiring multiple parties to sign a transaction, often used to enhance security in cryptocurrency transactions

複数の当事者による署名が必要なデジタル署名方式の一種で、暗号通貨取引のセキュリティー強化によく使われる

 2030 Features like multisignature will help smart contract platforms put some lawyers out of business.

マルチシグネチャーのような機能は、自動化契約のプラットフォームが一部の弁護士を廃業に追い込むのに一役買うでしょう。

depopulation

028

［名］人口減少、過疎化

解説

Low birth rates translate to an inability to sustain a workforce or economic growth. It puts strain on social welfare systems and leads to potential skill shortages. In the long run, however, **depopulation** may not be such a bad thing. Resources can be more efficiently allocated, leading to a higher standard of living and a reduced ecological footprint.

出生率の低下は、労働力の維持や経済成長の妨げになる。社会福祉制度に負担をかけ、潜在的な技能不足につながる。しかし、長い目で見れば、人口減少はそれほど悪いことではないのかもしれない。資源をより効率的に配分することができ、生活水準の向上やエコロジカルフットプリントの低減につながる。

定義 the process of decline in the population of a region
ある地域の人口が減少していく過程

Many countries will debate and begin implementing depopulation measures.
多くの国で過疎化対策が議論され、実行に移されるようになるでしょう。

chromosome ［名］染色体

 定義 a thread-like structure composed of DNA and proteins found in the nucleus of cells, carrying genetic information and transmitting hereditary traits from one generation to another

細胞の核に存在する DNA とタンパク質からなる糸状の構造体で、遺伝情報を運び、遺伝形質をある世代から別の世代に伝達する

2030 Scientists will continue unlocking the secrets of the chromosome, leading to ethical concerns about designer babies.

科学者たちは、染色体の謎を解き明かし続け、それがデザイナーベビーに関する倫理的な懸念につながっていくでしょう。

birth rate ［名］出生率

 定義 the statistical measure of the number of births occurring in a population over a specific period, usually expressed as the number of births per year per thousand individuals

ある集団で特定の期間に発生した出生数を統計的に測定したもので、通常、1,000 人当たりの年間出生数で表される

2030 Despite a growing global population, the birth rate in many developed nations will start to or continue to decline.

世界的な人口増加にもかかわらず、多くの先進国で出生率が減少に転じるか、減少し続けるでしょう。

surrogate ［名］代理母

 定義 a person who carries and gives birth to a child on behalf of another individual or couple, typically as an arrangement facilitated through a legal agreement

別の個人やカップルに代わって子どもを身ごもり、出産する人のことで、通常、法的合意を通じて手続きが進められる

2030 The market for surrogate mothers will increase as more women choose to enter the labor force.

働く女性が増えるに従って、代理母の市場も拡大するでしょう。

genetic diversity ［名］遺伝的多様性

 定義 the variation and range of genetic material within a population, species, or ecosystem

集団や種、生態系の内部での遺伝物質の差異や範囲

2030 The increasing global population will result in an increase in genetic diversity.

世界人口の増加によって、遺伝的多様性が拡大するでしょう。

digital death

［名］デジタルな死、デジタルデス

029

解説

What should happen to our digital assets after we die? One of the main challenges of **digital death** is ensuring that our online presence is managed in a way that respects our privacy and honors our legacy. Another challenge is ensuring that our digital assets are transferred or deleted in a way that complies with legal and ethical guidelines.

私たちが死んだ後、デジタル資産はどうなるのだろうか。デジタルデスの主な課題の一つは、私たちのネット上での存在を、間違いなくプライバシーを尊重し、遺産に敬意を表する方法で管理することだ。もう一つの課題は、法的・倫理的なガイドラインを遵守した方法で、デジタル資産を確実に移譲したり削除したりすることである。

定義 the cessation of a person's digital life and online presence, typically following their physical death, and the management of their digital assets

ある人のデジタル面での生活とネット上での存在を停止することで、通常、その人が身体的な死を迎えた後に行われる。また、同じ人物のデジタル資産を管理すること

 The management of digital assets after death will become a standard component of legal wills.

死後のデジタル資産の管理は、法的な遺言の標準的な構成要素になるでしょう。

suspended animation [名]人工冬眠、仮死状態

 定義 a state of temporary metabolic slowdown or cessation in living organisms, induced by factors such as extreme cold or lack of oxygen, which can prolong life during unfavorable conditions

極寒や酸素不足などの要因によって引き起こされる、生物の一時的な代謝の低下や停止の状態のことで、悪条件下での延命効果がある

2030 Suspended animation will be successfully tested on a mammal, paving the way for potential human trials.

人工冬眠が、ほ乳類での実験に成功し、人での実験につながる可能性が出てくるでしょう。

biostasis [名]バイオステーシス

 定義 the deliberate slowing or cessation of biological functions in living organisms, aiming to extend longevity, enable survival in extreme conditions, or facilitate medical interventions and research

生物の生体機能を意図的に低下させたり停止させたりすることで、その目的は長寿命化、極限状態での生存、医療介入や研究の促進にある

2030 Biostasis will become an option for end-stage patients, extending the boundary of life and redefining death.

バイオステーシスは末期患者の選択肢の一つとなり、生命の境界が広がり、死が再定義されるでしょう。

post-mortem privacy [名]死後のプライバシー

 定義 the protection of an individual's privacy and personal information after their death, including the management of digital assets and sensitive data

個人の死後のプライバシーおよび個人情報の保護のことで、デジタル資産や機密データの管理などが含まれる

2030 Major social media platforms will incorporate automatic privacy protections upon the verified death of a user.

主要な SNS プラットフォームで、ユーザーの死亡が確認された場合、自動的にプライバシー保護が行われるようになるでしょう。

cryogenics [名]低温学

 定義 the study of the behavior of materials at extremely low temperatures, often associated with the preservation of human bodies in the hope of future revival

極低温における物質の挙動に関する研究を指し、多くの場合、将来の蘇生を期待して人体を保存することに関連する

2030 Scientists will develop a process that prevents damaging ice formation during freezing.

科学者たちは、凍結時の有害な氷の形成を防ぐ工程を開発するでしょう。

digital privacy

030

［名］デジタルプライバシー

解説

Digital privacy is a critical concern as people continue to generate vast amounts of personal data through their online activities. The protection and control of this data are crucial for safeguarding individual rights and maintaining trust in the digital ecosystem. As technology advances, the potential for unauthorized access and data breaches increases along with it, making **digital privacy** an imperative.

人々がオンライン活動を通じて膨大な量の個人データを生成し続ける中、デジタルプライバシーは重要な関心事である。こうしたデータの保護と管理は、個人の権利を守り、デジタルエコシステムの信頼を維持するために極めて重要だ。技術の進歩に伴い、不正アクセスやデータ漏洩の可能性が高まっており、デジタルプライバシーの確保は急務だ。

定義　the protection of personal information and data generated through digital activities and the right to control access to and use of that information
デジタル活動を通じて生成された個人情報およびデータの保護と、その情報へのアクセスおよび使用を制御する権利

Many countries will implement or strengthen privacy regulations to enhance their control over personal data.
多くの国がプライバシーに関する規制を実施したり強めたりして、個人データの管理を強化するでしょう。

digital native　[名]デジタルネイティブ

定義 a person who has grown up with digital technology and is familiar with its use, often displaying a high level of comfort and proficiency in navigating digital environments

デジタルテクノロジーとともに成長し、その使用に精通している人のこと。多くの場合、デジタル環境下で物事を進めることに大いに快適さを覚えるとともに長けている

2030 By 2030, digital natives will account for more than half the global population.
2030年には、デジタルネイティブが世界人口の半数以上を占めることになるでしょう。

right to be forgotten　[名]忘れられる権利

定義 a legal concept that allows individuals to request the removal of personal information from search engine results, websites, or databases, particularly when the data is outdated or irrelevant

検索エンジンの検索結果やウェブサイト、データベースなどからの個人情報の削除を要求できる法的概念。特にデータが古びたり当人に無関係になったりした場合に適用される

2030 Governments will enact stricter laws enforcing the right to be forgotten, but technical challenges will prevent online platforms and search engines from fully complying.
各国政府は「忘れられる権利」を強化する法律を制定するでしょうが、技術的な問題から、オンラインプラットフォームや検索エンジンが完全に対応するのは難しいでしょう。

digital remains　[名]デジタル遺品

定義 the digital traces left behind by an individual after their death, including social media profiles, email accounts, and online content

個人の死後に残されたデジタルな痕跡のことで、ソーシャルメディアのプロファイルや、電子メールアカウント、オンラインコンテンツなどが含まれる

2030 Digital remains will give rise to a new industry centered around digital memorials.
デジタル遺品は、デジタル記念行事などを取り巻く新しい産業を生み出すでしょう。

digital footprint　[名]デジタルフットプリント

定義 the data trail created by an individual's online activities, including social media interactions, search history, and website visits, which can be used to build a digital profile or track behavior

個人のオンライン活動によって作成されるデータの痕跡のことで、ソーシャルメディアでのやり取りや検索履歴、ウェブサイトへのアクセス記録などが含まれ、デジタルプロファイルの構築や行動の追跡に使用される可能性がある

2030 It will become nearly impossible to wipe clean a digital footprint.
デジタルフットプリントをすっかり消し去ることは、ほぼ不可能になるでしょう。

61

discrimination

［名］差別

031

解説

People have made progress in addressing **discrimination** in various areas, but many challenges remain. The arrival of new technologies means we must not only police ourselves but also the systems and devices we rely on every day. Fostering digital literacy and ensuring equitable access to technology is essential for combating **discrimination** in the rapidly evolving digital landscape.

人々はさまざまな分野で差別への対処を進めてきたが、多くの課題が残っている。新しいテクノロジーが次々と現れると、私たち自身のみならず、私たちが日々依存しているシステムやデバイスにも目を光らせなければならなくなる。デジタルリテラシーを育み、テクノロジーの公平な利用を確保することは、急速に進化するデジタル環境における差別と闘うために不可欠だ。

定義 the unjust or prejudicial treatment of different categories of people, especially on the grounds of race, age, or sex
特に人種、年齢、性別を根拠にして、異なる世界に属する人々を不当に、あるいは偏見を持って扱うこと

 Many countries will enact or strengthen laws to protect people from discrimination in various aspects of life, including employment, housing, and public services.
多くの国で、雇用や住宅供給、公共サービスなどの生活のさまざまな面で人々を差別から守るための法律が制定・強化されるでしょう。

racism [名] 人種差別（主義）

 定義 prejudice, discrimination, or antagonism directed toward individuals or groups based on their perceived racial or ethnic background
人種的・民族的背景の認識に基づいて個人や集団に向けられる偏見、差別、敵愾心のこと

2030 Demographic shifts in the US will result in a more diverse legislature that will challenge systemic racism.
米国では人口動態の変化によって、より多様な人々からなる議会が誕生し、制度的な人種差別に挑戦することになるでしょう。

institutional racism [名] 制度的人種差別

 定義 a form of discrimination that occurs within the policies, practices, and structures of institutions, resulting in unequal treatment or outcomes for different racial or ethnic groups
差別の一形態で、組織の方針や慣行、構造の中で起こり、異なる人種や民族の集団に対して不平等な扱いや結果をもたらす

2030 Many conservatives in the US will continue to deny the existence of institutional racism.
米国の保守派の多くは、制度的人種差別の存在を否定し続けるでしょう。

intersectionality [名] 交差性、インターセクショナリティー

 定義 a theoretical framework that examines how various social and political identities, such as race, gender, and class, intersect and contribute to unique experiences of oppression or privilege
人種やジェンダー、階級といった、さまざまな社会的・政治的帰属意識がどのように交わり、抑圧や特権に関わる特有の体験に寄与するのかについて考察する上での理論的枠組み

2030 Activist movements will increasingly adopt intersectional frameworks to address the overlapping systems of oppression that affect marginalized individuals and communities.
活動家による運動が、ますます交差的な枠組みを取り入れるようになり、疎外された個人やコミュニティーに影響を与える重層的な抑圧の仕組みに対処しようとするでしょう。

prejudice [名] 先入観、偏見

 定義 a preconceived opinion or judgment about a person or group, often based on stereotypes or biases, and not on reason or actual experience
個人や集団に関する固定観念に基づく考えや判断のことで、多くの場合、理性や実際の経験ではなく、通念や偏向に基づいている

2030 Schools and organizations will implement more anti-bias education programs to challenge prejudice.
学校や組織が実施する、先入観と闘うための反偏見教育プログラムの数が増えるでしょう。

diversity

032

［名］多様性、ダイバーシティー

解説

As globalization progresses, connecting people worldwide, it becomes increasingly crucial to acknowledge and appreciate the inherent value of **diversity**. The richness brought by different cultures and backgrounds not only strengthens communities but also fuels the success of businesses. To foster inclusivity, it is essential to provide platforms that respect and amplify every voice.

グローバル化が進み、世界中の人々がつながるようになると、多様性の価値を認め、評価することがますます重要になる。異なる文化や出自がもたらす豊かさは、社会を強化するだけでなく、ビジネスの成功の原動力ともなる。包括性を育むには、すべての人の声を尊重し、それを広げる基盤を提供することが不可欠だ。

定義 the quality or state of having a range of different elements, particularly relating to the inclusion of people with various backgrounds, identities, and experiences

さまざまな要素を持った性質や状態のことで、特に多様な背景やアイデンティティー、経験を持つ人々を取り込むことに関連するもの

 Organizations will be required to have DEI policies in place.
組織には DEI（多様性、公正、包摂性）ポリシーの策定が義務付けられるでしょう。

neurodiverse　[形] 多様な精神構造を持った、神経多様性の

 referring to a range of neurological variations and conditions present among individuals, including ADHD and dyslexia

ADHD（多動性障害）や失読症など、人々の間に見られる幅広い神経学的な差異や状態についての

2030 Neurodivergent individuals will have more tools and resources available to help them navigate and thrive in society.

多様な精神構造を持った人が社会で活躍するための道具や資源が、より充実するでしょう。

URM　[名] 過小評価されたマイノリティー

 short for "underrepresented minority," racial or ethnic groups that are underrepresented in a particular context, such as education or the workforce

「過小評価されたマイノリティー」の頭字語で、教育や労働力など特定の領域において代表的でない人種や民族の集団のこと

2030 Advances in technology will allow for more opportunities for URMs to access resources, education, and professional growth.

テクノロジーの進歩によって、過小評価されたマイノリティーが資源や教育、職業上の成長を享受する機会がより多く得られるようになるでしょう。

minority　[名] マイノリティー、少数派、少数民族

 a group of people that represents a smaller proportion of a population, often distinguished by race, ethnicity, religion, or culture

人口に占める割合が小さい人々の集団のことで、多くの場合、人種や民族、宗教、文化によって区別される

2030 The concept of "minority" will evolve as demographic shifts result in a more diverse society.

人口動態の変化による社会の多様化に伴って、「マイノリティ」の概念も変化していくでしょう。

third-culture kid　[名] 第三文化の子ども、サードカルチャーキッド

 an individual who has spent a significant part of their developmental years in a culture different from their parents' culture

両親の文化とは異なる文化の中で、発達期のかなりの部分を過ごしてきた人

2030 Technology will make it easier for third-culture kids to stay connected with their cultures of origin, fostering a sense of belonging and identity.

テクノロジーによって、第三文化の子どもたちが、生まれ育った文化とつながり、帰属意識やアイデンティティーを育みやすくなるでしょう。

DIY

033

［名］自分でやること、自家作業

解説

The **DIY** movement has continued to gain popularity thanks in part to social media and video-sharing platforms, which provide countless resources for learning new skills and sharing ideas. Advances in technology, such as 3D printing and affordable, user-friendly tools, have further enabled people to create and customize items in ways that were once out of reach for most.

DIYが人気を博し続けているのは、一つには、ソーシャルメディアや動画共有プラットフォームが、新しい技能を身につけたりアイデアを共有したりするための無数の材料を提供しているからだ。また、3Dプリンターや手頃な価格の使いやすいツールなど、テクノロジーの進歩によって、かつては手の届かなかったアイテムの制作やカスタマイズが可能になってきている。

定義 short for "do it yourself," the activity of doing, creating, or repairing things oneself, without the help of professionals
「自分でやる」の頭字語で、専門家の力を借りずに自分で何かを行ったり、作ったり、修理したりすること

Schools will add DIY-related courses to the curriculum.
学校で、自家作業に関連する科目がカリキュラムに追加されるでしょう。

hackathon [名]ハッカソン

 定義 a time-limited event where participants from various backgrounds collaborate to solve problems through intensive brainstorming, coding, and prototyping
時間限定のイベントの一つで、多様なバックグラウンドを持つ参加者たちが協力して、集中的なブレーンストームやプログラミング、試作などを行いながら問題を解決するもの

2030 Large hackathons will become televised events with many teams getting sponsorship deals.
大規模なハッカソンがテレビ中継されるイベントになり、多くのチームがスポンサー契約を結ぶことになるでしょう。

makerspace [名]メーカースペース

 定義 a collaborative workspace where people can gather to create, learn, and share resources and tools for various DIY projects, such as woodworking, electronics, and 3D printing
共同作業場の一つで、そこでは人々が集まって、木工、電子工作、3D プリントといったさまざまな DIY プロジェクトのためのリソースや道具を作り、学び、分け合うことができる

2030 Most libraries will expand to include makerspaces.
ほとんどの図書館が拡張され、メーカースペースを備えるようになるでしょう。

CNC [名]コンピューター数値制御

 定義 short for "computer numerical control," a technology that uses computers to control machine tools, such as mills, lathes, and routers
「コンピューター数値制御」の頭字語で、コンピューターを使って圧搾機や旋盤、外形加工機などの工作機械を制御する技術のこと

2030 CNC technology will become more common in makerspaces.
コンピューター数値制御の技術は、メーカースペースでより一般的になるでしょう。

design thinking [名]デザイン思考

 定義 a problem-solving approach that encourages collaboration, experimentation, and user feedback to develop user-centered solutions
問題解決方法の一つで、協働や実験、利用者からのフィードバックを推奨し、利用者中心のソリューションを開発する

2030 Design thinking will extend beyond product design and be applied to address broad societal issues.
デザイン思考は、商品設計にとどまらず、広く社会的な問題に取り組むために応用されるでしょう。

dog whistle

034

［名］犬笛、特定の人だちだけが分かるメッセージ

解説

Some politicians don't shy away from making use of **dog whistle** politics. This tactic has allowed politicians to rally support from certain groups while maintaining a veneer of plausible deniability. One notable example is the use of coded language surrounding immigration, such as "border security" and "national sovereignty," which appeals to anti-immigration sentiments without explicitly stating them.

政治家の中には、犬笛政治を利用することをためらわない人がいる。この戦術のおかげで、政治家はうわべだけもっともらしい反証を保ったまま、特定の集団から支持を集めてきた。その顕著な例が移民を巡る暗号化された言葉の使用で、「国境警備」や「国家主権」といったものだ。これらは、はっきり表明せずに移民排斥の感情に訴えかけるものである。

（定義） a political strategy or messaging technique that uses coded language to appeal to specific demographics, playing into existing biases or prejudices without overtly expressing them

暗号化された言葉を用いて特定の層に訴えかける政治戦略あるいはメッセージ伝達方法のことで、あからさまに表現することなく既存の先入観や偏見を利用するもの

Far-right politicians will continue to appeal to their base through dog-whistle politics.

極右の政治家たちは、犬笛政治で自分たちの支持層にアピールし続けるでしょう。

racial profiling [名] 人種的分析、人種による選別

定義 the discriminatory practice of targeting individuals for suspicion of crime based on their race, ethnicity, or national origin

犯罪の疑いがある個人を対象とした差別的な行為のことで、人種、民族、出身国などに基づいて判断される

 Surveillance technologies, facial recognition systems, and predictive policing algorithms will continue to perpetuate racial profiling and disproportionately target marginalized communities.

監視技術や顔認識システム、予測的な取り締まりアルゴリズムが、人種による選別を永続させ、疎外されたコミュニティーを不当に標的にし続けるでしょう。

anti-Semitism [名] 反ユダヤ主義

定義 prejudice, discrimination, or hostility against Jewish people, often rooted in historical stereotypes and biases, which can manifest in various forms

ユダヤ人に対する偏見、差別、敵意のことで、多くの場合、歴史的な先入観や偏見に根ざしており、さまざまな形で現れる可能性がある

 Far-right groups will continue to promote hateful anti-Semitic narratives and conspiracy theories.

極右集団が、憎悪に満ちた反ユダヤ主義的な言説や陰謀論を宣伝し続けるでしょう。

border security [名] 国境警備

定義 the measures, policies, and infrastructure implemented to protect a country's borders, control the movement of people and goods, and prevent unauthorized entry or illegal activities

国境を守り、人や物の移動を管理し、不正な侵入や違法行為を防ぐために設けられる措置、政策、およびインフラのこと

 Border checkpoints will increasingly adopt biometric identification, including facial recognition, iris scanning, and fingerprinting.

国境検問所で、顔認証や虹彩読み取り、指紋認証といった生体認証の導入が進むでしょう。

coded language [名] 暗号的な言葉、遠回しな表現、隠語

定義 language that uses certain words or phrases to imply something different from their traditional meaning, often used to convey hidden messages or to subtly express contentious ideas

特定の語句を使用して、従来の意味とは異なる事柄を暗示する表現のことで、多くの場合、それらを用いて隠れたメッセージを伝えたり、物議を醸すような考え方を巧妙に言い表したりする

 Media companies posing as legitimate news sources will continue using coded language that results in exacerbating the polarization of society.

正規の情報源を装ったメディアが、社会の二極化を激化させるような隠語を使い続けるでしょう。

035

ecology

［名］エコロジー、生態学、生態系

解説

Advances in technology and data science are providing new insight into complex ecological systems. For example, by analyzing high-resolution satellite images over time, researchers can track deforestation, urbanization, and habitat changes, enabling them to develop targeted conservation strategies. Machine learning algorithms also help researchers uncover intricate relationships between species, predict population dynamics, and model the impacts of environmental changes.

テクノロジーやデータサイエンスの進歩は、複雑な生態系に対する新たな洞察をもたらしている。例えば、高解像度の衛星画像を長期にわたって分析することで、研究者は森林伐採や都市化、生息地の変化を追跡し、的を絞った保全戦略を立てることができる。また、機械学習のアルゴリズムは、生物種の間の複雑な関係を明らかにし、生物の生息数の動態を予測し、環境変化の影響をモデル化するのに役立っている。

定義 the scientific study of the relationships between living organisms and their environment, including interactions with other organisms and the physical surroundings
生物と、他の生物や物理的環境との相互作用などを含めた環境の関係についての科学的研究のこと

Ecologists will adopt interdisciplinary approaches to tackle complex ecological challenges.
生態学者たちが学際的な手法を用い、複雑な生態学上の課題に取り組むでしょう。

habitat ［名］生息地、生息環境

定義 the natural environment in which a particular organism lives, providing the necessary resources, such as food, water, and shelter, for survival, growth, and reproduction

特定の生物が生活する自然環境のことで、生存、成長、生殖に必要な、食料や水、すみかといった資源を提供する

 Some species will move to new areas as climate change causes their habitats to shift.

気候変動によって生息環境が変化し、新しい場所へ移動する種も出てくるでしょう。

coral bleaching ［名］サンゴの白化現象

定義 a stress response in which corals expel the symbiotic algae living within their tissues, causing them to turn white and become more susceptible to disease and death

サンゴが組織内に生息する共生藻類を排出するストレス反応のことで、サンゴが白化し、病気にかかったり死にやすくなったりする

 More underwater nurseries to grow new corals will sprout up.

新しいサンゴを育てるための水中養殖場が急増するでしょう。

restoration ［名］回復、修復、復元

定義 the intentional process of returning ecosystems, habitats, or species to their original, undisturbed state, aiming to recreate ecological integrity and functionality

生態系や生息地、生物種を、損傷を受ける前の状態に戻す意図を持った工程のことで、生態系の完全性や機能性の再現を目指すもの

 More educational programs will incorporate restoration projects as part of their curricula.

カリキュラムの一部に環境修復活動を導入する教育プログラムが増えるでしょう。

rehabilitation ［名］復旧、復興

定義 the process of restoring ecosystems, habitats, or species to a functional and healthy state after degradation or damage

劣化、損傷した生態系や生息地、生物種を機能的で健康な状態に回復させる工程

 Collaboration between scientists, conservation organizations, and local communities will drive ecosystem rehabilitation, ensuring the involvement of diverse stakeholders and the integration of traditional ecological knowledge.

科学者、自然保護団体、地域社会が協力し、多様なステークホルダーの参加と伝統的な生態学的知識の統合を確保しながら、生態系の回復を推進します。

71

ecosystem

［名］生態系、エコシステム

036

解説

In 1995, conservations reintroduced wolves into Yellowstone National Park. The wolves preyed on herbivores like elk, causing shifts in their behavior and distribution, subsequently leading to changes in vegetation. As plant communities rebounded, habitat conditions improved for various wildlife species while also reducing overgrazing. Such interventions are vital for restoring and maintaining the balance and health of **ecosystems**.

1995年、イエローストーン国立公園にオオカミを呼び戻すための保護活動が実施された。オオカミはエルクなどの草食動物を捕食し、その行動や分布に変化をもたらし、植生に変化をもたらした。植物群落が回復すると、さまざまな野生生物の生息環境が改善され、過放牧も解消された。生態系のバランスと健全性を回復・維持するためには、このような介入が不可欠なのだ。

定義 a community of living organisms, such as plants, animals, and microbes, interacting with each other and the environment
植物、動物、微生物などの生物が相互に、また環境との間で作用し合う共同体

 Climate change will cause some ecosystems to disappear entirely.
気候変動によって、一部の生態系が完全に消滅してしまうことになるでしょう。

fauna [名]動物相、動物区

 定義 all the animal life in a particular region, habitat, or time period, which interact with each other and their environment as part of an ecosystem
特定の地域、生息地、または時期におけるすべての動物の生態のことで、そこでは動物が相互に、あるいは環境との間で生態系の一部として作用し合う

2030 Some animals will evolve to flourish in response to climate change, while others will go extinct.
気候変動に対応して繁栄するように進化する動物もいれば、絶滅する動物もいます。

flora [名]植物相、植物区

 定義 all the plant life in a particular region, habitat, or time period
特定の地域や生育地、時期におけるすべての植物の生態のこと

2030 Scientists will use genetic engineering to help some plants adapt to climate change.
科学者たちは、遺伝子工学を用いて、一部の植物が気候変動に適応できるようにします。

invasive species [名]侵略的外来種、侵入生物種

 定義 non-native plant, animal, or microorganism species that disrupt ecosystems, spread rapidly, and negatively impact native species, often causing economic or environmental harm
外来種の植物、動物、または微生物で、生態系を乱し、急速に拡散し、在来種に悪影響を及ぼすもの。多くの場合、経済または環境の面で損害を引き起こす

2030 Globalization and climate change will lead to more invasive species.
世の中のグローバル化と気候変動によって、侵略的外来種が増加するでしょう。

microorganism [名]微生物

 定義 a microscopic organism, such as bacteria, viruses, fungi, or algae, which can be found in various environments and play essential roles in ecosystems and human health
細菌、ウイルス、菌類、藻類などの微小な生物のことで、さまざまな環境に存在し、生態系や人の健康に不可欠な役割を果たす

2030 Scientists will discover ways to apply microorganisms to bioremediation.
科学者らが、微生物を生物による環境修復技術に応用する方法を発見するでしょう。

El Niño

037

［名］エルニーニョ（現象）

解説

The **El Niño** cycle has occurred for thousands of years, affecting the far corners of the Earth. Today, as climate change continues its relentless advance, its effects are far more pronounced and deadly. Warmer oceans intensify the **El Niño** cycle, leading to more frequent and severe weather events such as droughts, floods, and storms.

エルニーニョは何千年も前から発生し、地球の隅々まで影響を及ぼしてきた。しかし、気候変動が容赦なく進行している今日、その影響はより顕著で致命的なものとなっている。海が暖かくなるとエルニーニョ現象が強まり、干ばつや洪水、暴風雨などの気象現象がより頻繁かつ、より深刻になる。

定義 a periodic climate phenomenon characterized by unusually warm sea surface temperatures in the equatorial Pacific Ocean, which can have a significant impact on global weather patterns and ecosystems
太平洋赤道域の海面温度が異常に高くなることを特徴とする周期的な気候現象で、地球の気象パターンや生態系に大きな影響を与えることがある

As climate change progresses, the effects of El Niño will become more extreme.
気候変動が進むにつれて、エルニーニョ現象の影響はより極端になっていくでしょう。

flood zone [名]洪水帯

 an area of land that is susceptible to flooding from a nearby water source, such as a river, stream, or coastal area, and often mapped for risk assessment and planning purposes

河川や渓流、海岸などの近隣の水源から浸水しやすい陸の区域で、リスク評価や都市計画などの目的で地図に示されることが多い

2030 Flood zones will expand, causing many coastal areas to become uninhabitable.
洪水帯が広がり、多くの沿岸地域に人が住めなくなるでしょう。

storm surge [名]高潮

 a sudden and often localized rise in sea level caused by strong winds and low atmospheric pressure during a storm

急激で、たいていは局所的な海面上昇のことで、暴風雨の際に強風と低気圧によって引き起こされる

2030 Bays, wetlands, and other areas will be devastated by the saltwater from larger and more powerful storm surges.
湾や湿地帯などが、より大規模で強力な高潮による海水で壊滅的な被害を受けるでしょう。

supercell [名]スーパーセル

 a highly organized and severe thunderstorm characterized by a persistent, rotating updraft, which can produce large hail, damaging winds, and tornadoes

高度に集積化された激しい雷雨で、持続的で回転する上昇気流を特徴とする。大粒のひょうや破壊的な強風、竜巻などを発生させることがある

2030 Global warming will cause more supercells to form.
地球温暖化によって、スーパーセルがより多く形成されるようになるでしょう。

sea level [名]海抜

 the baseline or average level of the ocean's surface, serving as a standard for determining elevations and tidal variations in coastal regions

海面の基本水位または平均水位のことで、沿岸地域の標高や潮位の変化を判断する基準となる

2030 Rising sea levels will have devastating effects on coastal habitats.
海水面の上昇は、沿岸の生息地に壊滅的な影響を及ぼします。

electronic waste

［名］電子（機器）廃棄物

038

解説

The rapid pace of technological advancement, short product lifecycles, and high consumer demand have resulted in a mounting accumulation of **electronic waste**. Improper **electronic waste** disposal leads to toxic substances leaching into soil and water, posing risks to human and ecosystem health. Recycling and responsible management of **electronic waste** are crucial to mitigate these negative impacts.

技術革新のスピードが速く、製品寿命が短く、消費者の需要が高いことから、電子廃棄物が大量に蓄積されている。電子廃棄物の不適切な処理は、有害物質の土壌や水への溶出を招き、人間や生態系の健康にリスクをもたらす。このような悪影響を軽減するには、電子廃棄物のリサイクルや責任を持った管理が重要だ。

定義 discarded electrical or electronic devices, such as computers, smartphones, and appliances
廃棄された、パソコンやスマートフォン、家電製品などの電気・電子機器

The electrical waste management market will become a $70 billion industry.
電子機器廃棄物処理市場は、700 億ドル産業になるでしょう。

battery recycling [名]電池のリサイクル

 定義 the process of collecting, sorting, and reprocessing used batteries to recover valuable materials, reduce environmental impact, and prevent the release of hazardous substances into the environment

使用済み電池を回収、選別し、再処理する工程のことで、貴重な物質を回収したり、環境への負荷の低減したり、有害物質の環境中への排出を防止したりすることが目的

2030 Increasing use of electric vehicles will lead to greater demand for battery recycling.

電気自動車の普及が進むことで、電池のリサイクル需要が高まるでしょう。

rare earth metals [名]稀土類元素

 定義 a group of 17 chemically similar elements often used in electronics and renewable energy systems

化学的に類似した 17 の元素のグループで、電子機器や再生可能エネルギーシステムによく用いられる

2030 As rare earth metals become harder to obtain, their value will skyrocket.

レアアースの入手が困難になるにつれて、その価値が高騰するでしょう。

landfill mining [名]埋立地の採掘

 定義 the process of excavating and extracting materials from existing landfill sites, typically with the aim of recovering valuable resources, reducing waste volume, or remediating environmental impacts

既存の埋立地から材料を発掘・抽出する過程のことで、通常、貴重な資源の回収や廃棄物量の削減、環境への影響の修復が目的

2030 Autonomous robots will assist in landfill mining activities.

自律型ロボットが埋立地での採掘活動を支援するでしょう。

bioleaching [名]生物浸出

 定義 the application of biological agents, such as bacteria or fungi, to extract metals from mineral resources or electronic waste through the process of microbial oxidation and dissolution

細菌や菌類などの生物学的薬剤を応用し、鉱物資源や電子廃棄物から金属を抽出することで、微生物による酸化・溶解の過程を経る

2030 New large-scale bioleaching enterprises will take off.

新興の大規模な生物浸出企業が誕生するでしょう。

equality

[名] 平等

039

解説

Equality is a foundational principle of social justice, but achieving it is an ongoing and arduous endeavor. It is crucial to address the systemic barriers and prejudices that have historically disadvantaged certain groups and implement policies and practices that promote fairness, accessibility, and equal representation. Educating society about the importance of **equality** is essential for creating lasting change.

平等は社会正義の基本原則だが、それを達成するには継続的で困難な努力が要る。歴史的に特定の集団に不利益を与えてきた制度的な障壁や偏見に対処し、公平性や敷居の低さ、平等な表現などを後押しする政策や行動を実践することが極めて重要だ。平等の重要性について社会を教育することは、永続的な変化を生み出すために不可欠なのだ。

定義 the state of being equal, particularly in terms of rights, opportunities, and treatment
物事が等しい状態のことで、特に権利や機会、扱いなどの点で判断される

 Advances in technology will help monitor and promote equality in various sectors of society, such as equal pay in workplaces and equal opportunities in education.
テクノロジーの進歩が、職場における同一賃金や教育における機会均等など、社会のさまざまな分野における平等を監視し、促進することにつながるでしょう。

equal opportunity ［名］機会均等

 ［定義］ the principle of ensuring that all individuals have an equal chance to access resources, benefits, and opportunities

すべての人が、資源や利益、機会を利用する上で平等な可能性を持つことを保証する原則

2030 Technological tools will be used extensively to remove unconscious bias from recruitment processes and create a level playing field.

人材雇用の過程から無意識の偏見を取り除き、公平な土壌を作り出すために、テクノロジーによって開発されたツールが広く使われるでしょう。

representation ［名］代表権、代議制度

 ［定義］ the act of portraying individuals or groups in a way that accurately reflects their diversity and experiences

個人や集団の多様性や経験を正確に反映した形で表現する行為

2030 AI news anchors of different races and genders will allow individuals to experience the world from diverse perspectives.

さまざまな人種や性別の AI ニュースキャスターが登場し、人々が多様な視点から世の中を捉えられるようになるでしょう。

equity ［名］公正、公平、公明正大

 ［定義］ the principle of being fair and impartial, often by acknowledging and addressing the unique needs, circumstances, and barriers faced by different individuals or groups

差別や偏りがないという原則のことで、多くの場合、さまざまな人や集団が抱える固有のニーズ、状況、障壁などを認め、対処することによって実現する

2030 Advanced analytical tools will enable better tracking and measurement of equity, leading to more effective interventions.

高度な分析ツールによって、公平性の追跡や測定がより適切に行われるようになり、より効果的な状況の是正につながるでしょう。

JEDI ［名］公正、公平、多様性、包摂

 ［定義］ short for "justice, equity, diversity, and inclusion," an approach that emphasizes the need to promote social justice alongside diversity, equity, and inclusion efforts in various settings

「公正、公平、多様性、包摂」の頭字語で、さまざまな場面での多様性や公平、包摂の取り組みに沿って、社会正義を推進する必要性を強調するアプローチのこと

2030 JEDI will be a guiding principle in many organizations, with dedicated roles and departments responsible for ensuring these values are upheld.

公正、公平、多様性、包摂は多くの組織で行動の指針となり、これらの価値を確実に守るための専門的な役割や部署が生まれることになるでしょう。

040

Healthcare 医療・健康管理

eugenics

［名］優生学

解説

The concept of **eugenics** has had a troubled history, as it has been associated with unethical practices such as forced sterilizations and racial discrimination. However, advances in genetics and reproductive technologies have opened up new possibilities for addressing genetic disorders and improving reproductive outcomes. The future of the field depends not only on scientific progress but also on ethical considerations.

優生学の概念は、問題の多い過去をはらんでいる。強制不妊手術や人種差別など非倫理的な行為と結びついてきたからだ。しかし、遺伝学や生殖技術の進歩によって、遺伝的疾患への対応や出生率の向上など、新たな可能性が広がっている。この分野の将来は、科学の進歩だけでなく、倫理的な議論にもかかっている。

定義 the improvement of the human species by controlling reproduction to increase the occurrence of desirable heritable traits
生殖をコントロールし、望ましい遺伝的形質の発生を増加させることによって、人間という種を改良すること

Engineering technologies like CRISPR will usher in the era of designer babies.
クリスパーのような工学技術が、デザイナーズベビーの時代を切り開くでしょう。

genetic counseling [名]遺伝カウンセリング、遺伝学相談

 定義 a service that provides guidance and information to individuals and families about the risks, benefits, and implications of genetic tests or conditions
遺伝子検査や病態のリスク、メリット、影響について、個人や家族に説明し情報を提供するサービス

 2030 Genetic counseling will become a routine part of healthcare.
遺伝カウンセリングは、医療の現場で日常的に行われるようになるでしょう。

heredity [名]遺伝

定義 the passage of genetic characteristics or traits from parents to offspring through the transmission of DNA
DNA の伝達を通じて、親から子へ遺伝的特徴や形質が受け継がれること

2030 Mitochondrial replacement therapies will prevent the transmission of certain genetic diseases.
ミトコンドリア置換療法が、ある種の遺伝的疾病が受け継がれることを防いでくれるでしょう。

genotype [名]遺伝子型

 定義 the complete set of genes or genetic information possessed by an organism, which determines its inherited traits and potential characteristics
生物が持つ遺伝子または遺伝情報の完全なまとまりのことで、その遺伝的形質と潜在的特性を決定する

2030 Researchers will gain a greater understanding of how a person's genotype affects their phenotype.
研究者らが、人の遺伝子型が表現型にどのような影響を与えるかについて、さらに解明を進めるでしょう。

polygenic score [名]多遺伝子スコア、遺伝子リスクスコア

定義 a numerical value based on multiple genetic variants that estimates an individual's genetic predisposition for a particular trait or condition
複数の遺伝子変異に基づく数値のことで、特定の形質や状態に対する個人の遺伝的素因を推定するもの

 2030 At-home genetic testing will give people more access to their polygenic scores.
自宅での遺伝子検査によって、人々は自分の多遺伝子スコアをより活用できるようになるでしょう。

EV

041

[名] 電気自動車

解説

The shift toward **EVs** has become increasingly significant in recent years due to concerns over climate change, air pollution, and the need for sustainable transportation. Advances in battery technology, new charging infrastructure, and government incentives have made **EVs** more accessible and practical for everyday use. As a result, automakers are investing heavily in **EV** development.

近年、気候変動や大気汚染への懸念や、持続可能な交通手段への必要性から、電気自動車への転換がますます重要視されている。バッテリー技術の進歩、新しい充電インフラ、政府による優遇措置などにより、電気自動車はより身近で実用的なものとなっている。その結果、自動車メーカーは電気自動車の開発に多額の投資を行っている。

定義 short for "electric vehicle," a vehicle that operates using one or more electric motors, drawing electrical energy from rechargeable batteries
「電気自動車」の頭字語で、充電式電池から電気エネルギーを取り出し、1つ、もしくは複数の電気モーターで走行する車両

 More than 50% of cars sold each year will be EVs.
毎年販売される自動車の 50 パーセント超が電気自動車になるでしょう。

HUD　[名] ヘッドアップディスプレー

定義　short for "head-up display," a system that displays data on a usually transparent screen directly in a user's line of vision
「ヘッドアップディスプレー」を短くした形で、通常、ユーザーの視野の内側にある透明な画面にデータを直接表示する仕組みのこと

　HUDs will become standard in all models of new cars.
ヘッドアップディスプレーは新車の全モデルに標準装備されるようになるでしょう。

frunk　[名] フランク

定義　a storage compartment located in the front of an electric or hybrid vehicle, where a traditional internal combustion engine would typically be located
電気自動車やハイブリッド車の前部にある収納スペースのことで、従来の内燃機関が普通、配置されている場所

　Frunks will serve as a space for multi-purpose functionality, with features like collapsible tables, built-in coolers, or removable compartments.
フランクは、折りたたみ式のテーブルや内蔵クーラー、取り外し可能な小物入れなどを納める多目的スペースとして役立つことになるでしょう。

ignition interlock device　[名] イグニッション連動装置

定義　a device installed in a vehicle that requires the driver to provide a breath sample to test for alcohol before the vehicle can be started
車両に搭載された装置の一つで、車両を発進させる前に、運転者にアルコール検査のための呼気サンプルの提供を求めるもの

　Ignition interlock devices will be able to detect some types of illegal narcotics.
イグニッション連動装置は、ある種の違法な麻薬を検出することができるようになるでしょう。

V2G technology　[名] V2G技術

定義　short for "vehicle-to-grid technology," a system that enables bidirectional energy transfer between electric vehicles and the power grid
「車両から電力網へ送る技術」を短くした形で、電気自動車と電力網の間で双方向のエネルギー伝送を可能にする仕組みのこと

　People will use V2G-equipped EVs to power their homes during blackouts.
人々は、停電時にV2Gを搭載した電気自動車で自宅の電力をまかなうようになるでしょう。

042

fake meat

［名］疑似肉、フェイクミート

解説

Fake meat has gained popularity among individuals looking for more sustainable and ethical food choices, as it typically requires fewer natural resources and produces fewer greenhouse gas emissions compared to traditional meat production. Major food companies and startups have invested in the development of **fake meat** products, resulting in a wide range of options available in grocery stores and restaurants.

疑似肉は、より持続可能で倫理的な食の選択を求める人々の間で人気を博してきた。従来の食肉の生産に比べて、天然資源の使用量や温室効果ガスの排出量が少ないからだ。大手食品会社や新興企業が疑似肉製品の開発に投資した結果、食料品店やレストランでさまざまな選択肢が提供されるようになってきた。

定義 a meat substitute made from plant-based ingredients, designed to imitate the taste, texture, and appearance of meat
植物由来の原料を使用し、食肉の味や食感、外観を模倣するように設計された代替肉

The fake meat industry will take a large bite out of the traditional meat industry, reducing the environmental impact of the agriculture industry.
疑似肉産業は、従来の食肉産業を大幅に代替し、農業の環境負荷を軽減するでしょう。

agriculture [名]農業、農耕

 定義 the practice and science of cultivating land and raising crops, livestock, and other animals for food, fiber, and other products

土地を耕し、作物や家畜などを飼育し、食物や繊維などを生産する活動と科学

2030 New methods and technologies will reduce the carbon footprint of the global agriculture industry.

新しい手法や技術によって、世界の農業の二酸化炭素排出量を削減することになるでしょう。

agricultural waste [名]農業廃棄物

 定義 organic waste material generated from farming activities, including crop residues, animal manure, and discarded produce

農業活動から発生する有機性廃棄物のことで、作物残渣や家畜の糞尿、廃棄農産物などが含まれる

2030 The use of agriculture waste will emerge as a multibillion dollar industry.

農業廃棄物の活用は、数十億ドル規模の産業として浮上することになるでしょう。

lab-grown meat [名]実験室培養肉

 定義 meat produced through cellular agriculture, where animal cells are cultured and grown in a controlled environment

細胞農業によって生産された食肉のことで、動物の細胞を培養し、管理された環境で成長させるもの

2030 Commercial lab-grown meat facilities will compete with vegetable-based fake meat.

商業的な実験室培養肉の生産者は、野菜ベースの疑似肉と競合することになるでしょう。

meat analog [名]ミートアナログ、アナログミート

 定義 a food product that is designed to replicate the taste, texture, and appearance of meat, typically made from plant-based ingredients or lab-grown meat

肉の味、食感、外観を再現するように設計された食品で、通常、植物由来の原料や実験室で育てられた肉から作られている

2030 Meat analogs will be served regularly as part of school lunches.

ミートアナログは、学校給食の一部として定期的に提供されるようになるでしょう。

fascism

043

［名］ファシズム

解説

Fascism is on the rise in countries all over the world. Various factors have led to this shift, including the failure of the neoliberal economic model, the rise of inequality, and the erosion of social safety nets. The alt-right and far-right movements are also playing a significant role as they spread extremist ideologies and promote the suppression of minority groups.

世界中の国々でファシズムが台頭している。新自由主義経済モデルの失敗、格差の拡大、社会的セーフティーネットの侵食など、さまざまな要因がこの変化をもたらしている。また、過激なイデオロギーを広め、少数派の抑圧を進めるオルタナ右翼や極右の動きも大きな役割を果たしている。

定義 a political ideology that seeks to establish a centralized, authoritarian government and emphasizes nationalism and often racism
中央集権主義を志向し、ナショナリズムや人種差別を重視する政治イデオロギー

 Authoritarian tendencies will continue to parallel historical fascist regimes, manifesting in various forms, including attacks on the free press.
権威主義的な傾向は、歴史的なファシスト政権に似て、報道の自由に対する攻撃など、さまざまな形で現れ続けるでしょう。

coup [名]クーデター

 定義 an illegal and forceful attempt by a group, often military or political, to take control of a government by overthrowing its existing leaders

軍事的または政治的な集団が、既存の指導者を打倒することによって政府を支配しようとする、違法かつ強引な試み

2030 Coups will generally involve less bloodshed than in the past.
クーデターは全般的に、かつてほど流血を伴うものにはならないでしょう。

far right [名]極右

定義 the extreme conservative or reactionary section of a political party or system, often associated with nationalist and authoritarian ideologies

政党や政治体制における極端な保守的あるいは反動的な立場のことで、多くの場合、国粋主義者や権威主義的なイデオロギーと関連づけられる

 2030 Far-right groups will continue to push for stricter border controls and nationalist policies.
極右集団は、より厳しい国境管理や民族主義的な政策を引き続き推し進めるでしょう。

alt-right [名]オルタナ右翼、オルトライト

定義 a loosely defined far-right movement that embraces an ideology of white nationalism, racism, and anti-feminism, often using online platforms for organization and communication

白人ナショナリズム、人種差別、反フェミニズムなどのイデオロギーを擁する、定義があいまいな極右運動のことで、組織化やコミュニケーションにオンラインプラットフォームを用いることが多い

 2030 Civil society will continue to push back against the racist ideologies espoused by the alt-right.
市民社会は、オルトライトが信奉する人種差別的なイデオロギーには引き続き背を向けていくでしょう。

mass surveillance [名]大規模監視（活動）

定義 the widespread monitoring and collection of personal information by governments, corporations, or other organizations, often without the knowledge or consent of the subjects

政府、企業、その他の組織によって、しばしば対象者の認知や同意なしに個人情報が広く監視・収集されること

 2030 Governments will continue to expand surveillance programs, compromising privacy under the guise of public safety.
政府は今後も監視制度を拡大し、公共の安全を装ってプライバシーを侵害し続けるでしょう。

food security

044

［名］食糧安全保障

解説

Climate change, population growth, and economic factors all continue to threaten **food security**. The situation is dire for those most affected. Many regions teeter on political instability and famine. New food assistance programs, improved storage and transportation systems, and enhanced agricultural productivity are just some of the measures necessary to alleviate this global emergency.

気候変動、人口増加、経済的要因のすべてが、食糧安全保障を脅かし続けている。最も影響を受ける人々にとっての状況は悲惨なものだ。多くの地域が政情不安と飢餓に瀕している。新しい食糧支援プログラムや、貯蔵・輸送システムの改善、農業生産性の向上などは、この世界的な緊急事態を緩和するために必要な対策のほんの一部だ。

定義 the state of having reliable access to sufficient, safe, and nutritious food to meet dietary needs and preferences
食生活の必要性や嗜好を満たす上で、十分かつ安全で栄養価の高い食品を確実に入手できる状態のこと

 Advances in agricultural technology and practices will increase crop yields.
農業の技術や手法の進歩によって、作物の収穫量が増加するでしょう。

agrihood ［名］アグリフッド

定義 from "agriculture" and "neighborhood," a planned community that integrates agriculture, such as farms or gardens, into residential areas, promoting local food production, sustainability, and a sense of community among residents

agriculture（農業）と neighborhood（住宅地、居住地域）からの造語で、農業を統合した計画居住地域のこと。農場や菜園などを住宅地に統合し、地元の食料生産や持続可能性、住民間のコミュニティー意識などを促進するもの

 Agrihoods will adopt more automated processes.
アグリフッドはより自動化された工程を採用するでしょう。

chronic hunger ［名］慢性的飢餓

定義 a long-term lack of sufficient food, leading to malnutrition, health problems, and reduced quality of life

長期的に十分な食べ物がない状態のことで、栄養失調や健康障害、生活の質の低下を招く

 Political instability will continue to be a leading cause of chronic hunger in certain regions.
政情不安が、特定の地域における慢性的飢餓の主要因であり続けるでしょう。

food assistance ［名］食糧支援、食糧援助

定義 the provision of food or resources to help people in need access food, often through government or nonprofit programs

必要とする人々が食べ物を入手できるよう支援する目的で行われる、食糧や資源の提供のこと。多くの場合、政府か非営利事業を通じて実施される

 Food assistance policies will become more common.
食糧支援政策がより一般的になるでしょう。

instability ［名］不安定、不安定性

定義 a lack of stability or security, often related to political, economic, or environmental factors, which can lead to uncertainty, disruptions, or negative impacts on societies and ecosystems

安定性や安全性の欠如のことで、多くの場合、政治や経済、環境に関わる要因と結び付く。不確実性や混乱、社会や生態系への悪影響をもたらすことがある

 Global power dynamics will continue to shift, leading to changes in political and economic instability.
世界の力関係が変化し続け、政治的・経済的な不安定性の変容につながるでしょう。

gender

［名］ジェンダー、（社会的・文化的）性

解説

Gender is a complex aspect of human identity that encompasses a range of societal roles, behaviors, and expectations associated with femininity and masculinity. As societies evolve and challenge traditional **gender** norms, people must recognize the unique experiences and difficulties faced by different gender groups. Respecting diverse **gender** identities and expressions is essential for fostering inclusivity, empathy, and social harmony.

ジェンダーは、人間のアイデンティティーの複雑な側面であり、女性らしさ、男性らしさに関連するさまざまな社会的な役割や行動、期待を包含している。社会が進化し、伝統的なジェンダーの規範に問題提起する中で、人々はさまざまなジェンダー集団が直面する特有の経験や困難を認識しなければならない。多様なジェンダーのアイデンティティーや表現を尊重することが、包摂、共感、そして社会の調和を育むために不可欠だ。

定義 the socially constructed roles, behaviors, and expectations associated with being male, female, or another identity, which may differ from an individual's biological sex

男性であること、女性であること、または生物学的性別とは異なる別のアイデンティティーを持つことに関連する、社会的に築かれた役割や行動、期待

2030 Healthcare, including mental health services, will become more gender-sensitive.

心の健康に関するサービスを含む医療は、よりジェンダーに配慮したものになるでしょう。

cisgender [形] シスジェンダー

 定義 referring to individuals whose gender identity corresponds with their assigned sex at birth, as opposed to transgender individuals

トランスジェンダーの人とは逆に、個人の性自認が出生時に与えられた性別と一致して

 2030 Cisgender people will play an active role in advocating for the rights of their transgender and non-binary counterparts.

シスジェンダーは、トランスジェンダーやノンバイナリーの人たちの権利を擁護するための積極的な役割を担うでしょう。

genderqueer [形] ジェンダークィア

定義 referring to individuals who do not identify exclusively as male or female

人が、男性または女性のいずれかを特定して自認していない

 2030 Genderqueer individuals will have increased visibility and representation in the media, politics, and other public spheres.

メディアや政治などの公的な領域において、ジェンダークィアの人たちの認知度や露出が高まるでしょう。

pangender [形] パンジェンダー

定義 identifying with multiple or all genders, encompassing a wide range of gender identities and expressions

複数の性別、あるいはすべての性別を自認し、幅広い性自認や表現を包含した

 2030 Community support and resources for pangender individuals will increase, fostering a sense of belonging and creating safe spaces where individuals can connect, share experiences, and find support.

パンジェンダーに対するコミュニティーの支援や資源が増え、帰属意識が育まれるようになり、それによって個人同士がつながったり経験を共有したり支援を受けたりできる安全な場所ができるでしょう。

heteronormative [形] 異性愛を規範とする

定義 describing a viewpoint that expresses heterosexuality as the normal or preferred sexual orientation, often resulting in the marginalization of non-heterosexual identities

往々にして非異性愛のアイデンティティーが疎外される結果を生みながらも、異性愛が正常もしくは好ましい性的指向だとする視座を持って

 2030 Education systems will challenge heteronormative narratives, teaching students about a broad range of sexual orientations and gender identities.

教育現場は、異性愛を規範とする言説に異議を唱え、幅広い性的指向や性自認について生徒に教えるようになるでしょう。

91

gender identity

[名]性自認、ジェンダーアイデンティティー

046

解説

Increased awareness about the complexities of **gender identity** is slowly leading to a growing acceptance of transgender and non-binary individuals in many regions of the world. However, obstacles remain, as many continue to face discrimination, lack of comprehensive legal protections, persistent societal and institutional biases, and limited access to gender-affirming healthcare.

性自認の複雑さについての認識が高まり、世界の多くの地域でトランスジェンダーやノンバイナリーの人々が徐々に受け入れられつつある。しかし、障害は残っている。たくさんの人たちが、依然として差別や包括的な法の保護の欠如、変わらぬ社会的・制度的な偏見、ジェンダーに配慮した医療の利用制限などと向き合い続けているのだ。

 an internal sense of one's own gender, which may be different from the sex assigned at birth

自分自身の性別について抱いている感覚のことで、出生時に与えられた性別とは異なる可能性がある

 Conversations about gender identity will become increasingly common at a young age.

性自認に付いて話し合う機会が、若いうちからどんどん増えていくでしょう。

gender-fluid [形]ジェンダーフルイドの、性自認が流動的な

 referring to individuals whose gender identity fluctuates over time, encompassing a range of gender identities and expressions

人の性自認が、さまざまな性の自覚や表現の間で時間の経過とともに変動して

 Inclusion of gender-fluid people in media and public life will increase.
メディアや公的な場において、性自認が流動的な人々の包摂性が高まるでしょう。

gender-nonconforming [形]ジェンダーノンコンフォーミングの、社会的なジェンダーの規範に異議を唱える

 referring to individuals who do not adhere to societal expectations or norms regarding their gender expression or identity

個人の性別の表現やアイデンティティーに関して、社会的な期待や規範に従わない

 Anti-discrimination laws will robustly protect gender-nonconforming people in workplaces, schools, and other settings.
差別禁止法によって、職場や学校などの環境で、社会的なジェンダーの規範に異議を唱える人々がしっかり保護されるようになるでしょう。

gender expression [名]ジェンダー表現、性別表現

 the way in which an individual communicates their gender identity to others, often through clothing, hairstyle, mannerisms, or other personal choices

ジェンダーアイデンティティーを他者に伝える方法のことで、多くの場合、衣服や髪形、振る舞い方、その他の個人的な選択に表れる

 Gender-neutral language will become more widely used.
ジェンダーニュートラルな表現がより広く使われるようになるでしょう。

greygender [名]グレージェンダー

 individuals who identify outside the traditional gender binary but do not fully embrace a specific non-binary or genderqueer identity

伝統的な性別の二元論にとらわれていはいないものの、特定のノンバイナリーやジェンダークィアの自認を完全に受け入れているわけでもない人

 Greygender representation in politics and leadership positions will increase.
政治の世界や指導層に、グレージェンダーを代表する人たちが増えるでしょう。

generative AI

［名］生成AI

047

解説

Every new technology is a double-edged sword. **Generative AI** allows for the creation of art, music, and literature by anyone with access to the technology, breaking down barriers to artistic expression. However, there are also concerns about the authenticity and ownership of AI-generated content, as well as the potential for the spread of misinformation and deepfakes.

あらゆる新しいテクノロジーは、諸刃の剣である。生成AIによって、当該のテクノロジーを利用できる人なら誰でも美術や音楽、文学を創作でき、芸術表現への障壁を取り払うことができる。しかし、AIが生成したコンテンツの真贋や所有権については、虚報やディープフェイクの拡散の可能性と同様に、懸念材料でもある。

定義 a type of artificial intelligence that learns from data to create new, original content or output

人工知能の一種で、データから学習し、新しい独自のコンテンツや作品を生み出す

 Generative AI will democratize music, art, and other domains.

生成 AI によって、音楽や美術などの創作が大衆化するでしょう。

prompt [名]プロンプト

 a specific instruction or input provided to a generative AI model to guide and influence its output
生成 AI モデルの出力を誘導し、影響を与えるために提供される特定の命令や入力内容

2030 The field of prompt engineering will change drastically as systems gain a better understanding of human intent.
プロンプトエンジニアリングの分野は、システムが人間の意図をより深く理解できるようになるにつれて、大きく変化するでしょう。

emergent behavior [名]創発的振る舞い

 complex and unexpected actions that arise from simple interactions between individual components within a system
システム内の個々の構成要素間の単純な相互作用から生じる、複雑で予期せぬ動作

2030 The ubiquity of AI will result in emergent behaviors manifesting everywhere from autonomous vehicles to large language models.
AI のユビキタス化によって、自律走行車から大規模言語モデルまで、あらゆるところで創発的動作が顕在化するでしょう。

LLM [名]大規模言語モデル

 short for "large language model," a type of AI model designed to understand and generate human-like text based on vast amounts of language data
「大規模言語モデル」の頭字語で、AI モデルの一種。膨大な量の言語データに基づいて、人間が作り出すような文章を理解し、生成するように設計されている

2030 New LLMs will be able to fact-check themselves, surpassing the capabilities of most individuals.
新しい大規模言語モデルは、たいていの人間の能力を上回り、自分で事実確認を行えるようになるでしょう。

hallucination [名]ハルシネーション、幻覚

 an erroneous or false perception generated by an AI system, often resulting from incorrect data interpretation or the introduction of noise into the model's outputs
AI システムによって生成される誤りや誤認。多くの場合、誤ったデータ解釈や、モデルの出力にノイズが混入することに起因する

2030 Hallucination will continue to be a problem, but new software tools will give insight into why specific hallucinations occur.
ハルシネーションは問題であり続けるでしょうが、新しいソフトウェアツールによって、なぜ特定のハルシネーションが起こるのかが分かるようになるでしょう。

geo-engineering

048

［名］地球工学

解説

The problem with **geo-engineering** is that if things don't go according to plan, it could lead to a colossal disaster, perhaps spelling the end of human existence. But some argue that without **geo-engineering**, humankind is already doomed. While both sides try to argue their point, some organizations are throwing caution to the wind and carrying out unauthorized tests.

地球工学の問題点は、計画通りに進まなければ、巨大な災害を引き起こし、へたをすると人類の存亡に関わるかもしれないということだ。しかし、地球工学がなければ人類はすでに滅亡している、と主張する人もいる。両者が主張を闘わせる一方で、無謀にも無認可の実験を行う組織もある。

定義 the deliberate and large-scale intervention in Earth's climate system to counteract or reduce the impacts of climate change
地球の気候の仕組みに意図的かつ大規模な介入を行うことで、気候変動の影響の緩和が目的

 Scientists will consider large-scale geo-engineering projects to combat climate change.
科学者たちは、気候変動に対抗するための大規模な地球工学プロジェクトを検討するでしょう。

terraform [動]〜を地球化する

定義 to modify or alter the physical characteristics of a planet, moon, or other celestial body to make it habitable or suitable for human life
惑星や衛星、その他の天体の物理的特性を修正または変更し、居住可能に、あるいは人間の生活に適したものにする

 Terraforming a planet will be many years away, but the first experiments will take place.
惑星が地球化されるのは何年も先のことですが、最初の実験は行われるでしょう。

exobiology [名]宇宙生物学

定義 the branch of biology that investigates the origin, evolution, and potential existence of life in the universe
生物学の一分野で、宇宙における生命の起源、進化、存在の可能性を調査するもの

 Discoveries on Mars will lead to new insights into exobiology.
火星でのさまざまな発見が、宇宙生物学の新たな知見につながるでしょう。

Fermi paradox [名]フェルミのパラドックス

定義 the apparent contradiction between high estimates of the probability of extraterrestrial life and the lack of evidence or contact with such civilizations
地球外生命体の存在確率を高く見積もることと、証拠やそのような文明との接触がないことの間にある明らかな矛盾

 Many researchers will agree that the Fermi paradox can be explained by civilizations growing too big to sustain themselves.
多くの研究者が、フェルミのパラドックスは、文明が発達しすぎて維持できなくなったことで説明可能だ、という点で合意するでしょう。

extraterrestrial [名]地球外生物、地球外生命体

定義 any object, substance, or phenomenon originating from or existing beyond Earth
地球外を起源とする、あるいは地球外に存在する何らかの物体、物質、または現象

 We will use more advanced tools to search for extraterrestrial life, but we will not be successful in the short term.
私達は、より高度な道具を使って地球外生命体を探そうとするでしょうが、短期間では成功しないでしょう。

governance gap

049

[名] ガバナンスギャップ、統治上の欠陥

解説

Rapid changes caused by globalization and technological advances have made it difficult for governments to respond quickly and effectively to the needs of their citizens. Political polarization and, in some cases, outright corruption have only made the **governance gap** worse. In many cases, citizen engagement in the policy-making process will be essential to bridge this gap.

グローバル化と技術革新による急激な変化によって、政府は市民のニーズに迅速かつ効果的に対応することが難しくなっている。政治的な偏向や、場合によっては、あからさまな腐敗が、ガバナンスギャップをさらに深刻にしている。このギャップを埋めるためには、多くの場合、政策決定プロセスへの市民の参加が不可欠である。

定義　a situation where governments or institutions fail to adequately address the challenges and needs of the societies they serve
政府や組織が、奉仕先である社会の課題やニーズに適切に対応できていない状況のこと

Rapid societal changes will make the governance gap more severe.
急激な社会の変化は、統治上の欠陥をより深刻なものにするでしょう。

Related Words and Phrases
関連語

foreign policy [名]外交政策

 定義 a government's strategy and actions in dealing with other nations, often relating to diplomacy, trade, security, or development
外交、貿易、安全保障、開発などに関連する、他国との取引における政府の戦略や行動

2030 Multinational corporations will exert an even greater influence on foreign policy.
多国籍企業が外交政策に与える影響力はさらに大きくなるでしょう。

free trade [名]自由貿易

 定義 a policy or practice that promotes the exchange of goods and services between countries without significant barriers, such as tariffs, quotas, or excessive regulations, fostering international economic cooperation and growth
関税、ノルマ、過度の規制などの大きな障壁なしに、国家間での商品やサービスの取引を促進し、国際的な経済協力と成長を促進する政策や慣行のこと

2030 Free trade agreements will face increasing challenges due to regional data protection and privacy regulations.
自由貿易協定は、地域のデータ保護やプライバシーの規制のために、いっそう困難に直面するでしょう。

corruption [名]汚職、腐敗

 定義 dishonest or fraudulent conduct by those in power, typically involving bribery or the abuse of authority for personal gain
権力者による不正行為のことで、典型的には贈収賄や私的な利益のための権限の乱用が含まれる

2030 Rampant corruption will continue to erode public trust.
汚職の横行は、国民の信頼を失墜させ続けるでしょう。

policymaker [名]政策立案者、為政者

 定義 an individual or group responsible for creating and implementing policies, typically within a government or organization
通常、政府または組織内で、政策の策定と実施に責任を持つ個人または集団

2030 Calls will grow for greater governmental transparency, ethics reforms, and campaign finance reforms to ensure that policymakers' decisions are made in the public interest.
政策立案者の意思決定が公共の利益にかなうよう、政府の透明性の向上や倫理改革、選挙資金改革などを求める声が高まるでしょう。

050

gut microbiome
［名］腸内細菌、腸管内菌叢_{そう}

解説

The **gut microbiome** has gained significant attention due to its connection to overall health and influence on various bodily functions. Composed of trillions of microorganisms, the **gut microbiome** impacts digestion, the immune system, and even mental health. Balancing the **gut microbiome** through dietary and lifestyle choices is becoming an essential aspect of maintaining well-being.

腸内細菌は、健康全般との関連やさまざまな身体機能への影響から、大きな注目を集めている。数兆個の微生物で構成される腸内細菌は、消化や免疫系、そして精神的な健康にまで影響を及ぼす。食事やライフスタイルの選択によって腸内細菌のバランスを整えることは、健康を維持するために不可欠な要素となっている。

定義 the community of microorganisms, including bacteria, fungi, and viruses, that inhabit the gastrointestinal tract, contributing to digestion and overall health

消化管に生息する細菌、真菌、ウイルスなどの微生物の集合体で、消化や全身の健康に寄与するもの

 Gut microbiome analysis will be a standard part of medical checkups, informing doctors about patients' health and disease risks.

腸内細菌の解析は、健康診断の標準的な項目となり、患者の健康状態や病気のリスクについての情報が医師に伝達されるようになるでしょう。

fecal transplant ［名］糞便移植

 定義 a medical procedure in which fecal matter from a healthy donor is transferred to a patient to restore a balanced gut microbiome

健康なドナーの糞便を患者に移植し、バランスの取れた腸管内細菌叢を回復させる医療手段

2030 Designer fecal transplants with specific microbial compositions will be tailored to patients' needs.

特定の微生物組成を持つデザイナーズ糞便移植が、患者のニーズに応じて行われます。

gut virome ［名］消化管ウイルス集団

 定義 the collection of viruses, particularly bacteriophages, that inhabit the gastrointestinal tract and interact with the gut microbiome

消化管に生息し、腸管内細菌叢と相互作用するウイルス、特にバクテリオファージの集合体

2030 The human gut virome will be recognized as an integral part of personalized medicine.

人の消化管ウイルス集団は、個々人に応じた医療に不可欠な要素として認識されるようになるでしょう。

microbial diversity ［名］微生物多様性

 定義 the variety of different microorganisms, including bacteria, fungi, and viruses, present in a specific environment, such as the gut microbiome

腸管内細菌叢のような、特定の環境に存在する細菌、真菌、ウイルスなどのさまざまな微生物

2030 There will be increased interest in "rewilding" the human microbiome through approaches like exposure to natural environments.

今後は、自然環境にさらすなどの手法によって、人の微生物叢を「再野生化」させることに関心が集まるでしょう。

probiotics ［名］プロバイオティクス

 定義 live microorganisms that are ingested for their health benefits

健康効果を期待して摂取される、生きた微生物

2030 Probiotics will be commonly used in mental health treatment as the gut-brain axis becomes better understood.

プロバイオティクスは、腸脳軸の解明が進むにつれて、心の病の治療にもよく利用されるようになるでしょう。

051

habitat loss

［名］生息地の喪失

解説

Habitat loss is one of the most pressing environmental challenges, as it contributes to the decline of biodiversity. Rapid urbanization, deforestation, and conversion of natural areas for agriculture and infrastructure are among the primary drivers of habitat loss. The consequences are far-reaching, impacting not only wildlife but also the overall functioning and resilience of ecosystems.

生息地の喪失は、生物多様性の減少につながるので、最も緊急な環境問題の一つである。急激な都市化、森林伐採、農業やインフラ整備のための自然地域の転換などが、生息地の喪失の主な要因に含まれる。その影響は広範囲に及び、野生生物だけでなく、生態系全体の機能や回復力にも影響を及ぼしている。

定義 the decline or disappearance of suitable environments essential for the survival and reproduction of various species
さまざまな生物種の生存と繁殖に不可欠な好適環境の減少または消滅

 Despite awareness of the issue, habitat loss will threaten a significant number of species.
問題が認識されているにもかかわらず、生息地の喪失によって相当数の種が脅かされるでしょう。

desertification [名]砂漠化

 定義 the process by which fertile land transforms into arid desert or semi-arid areas due to factors like climate change, deforestation, overgrazing, or improper land management

肥沃な土地が乾燥した砂漠や半乾燥地帯に変化する過程のことで、気候変動や森林伐採、過放牧、不適切な土地管理などが要因

2030 Large parts of Africa, China, and the Western United States will experience accelerating desertification.

アフリカ、中国、米国西部の大部分で砂漠化が加速するでしょう。

urban sprawl [名]スプロール現象

 定義 the uncontrolled and unplanned expansion of urban areas into previously undeveloped or rural lands

以前は未開発だった土地や田園地帯に、都市部が無制限かつ無計画に拡大すること

2030 Urban sprawl will continue unchecked, especially in developing countries.

特に発展途上国では、スプロール現象が野放図に続くでしょう。

savannization [名]サバナイゼーション、サバンナ化

 定義 the process of transforming a forested ecosystem into a savanna-like environment, often as a result of human activities such as deforestation, agricultural expansion, or climate change

森林生態系がサバンナのような環境に変化する過程のことで、多くの場合、森林伐採や農業の拡大、気候変動といった人間の活動の結果である

2030 Savannization of the Amazon will impact a variety of wildlife.

アマゾンのサバナイゼーションが、さまざまな野生生物に影響を与えるでしょう。

deforestation [名]森林伐採

 定義 the clearing or removal of forests, usually for agricultural, logging, or urban development purposes, which can lead to habitat loss, biodiversity decline, and increased greenhouse gas emissions

森林の伐採または除去のことで、通常、農業や木材の切り出し、都市開発などが目的。生息地の損失や生物多様性の低下、温室効果ガス排出の増加につながる

2030 Deforestation will contribute to the spread of infectious diseases as more animals lose their habitats and come into contact with humans.

森林破壊は、より多くの動物が生息地を失い、人間と接触するようになるため、感染症の蔓延を助長するでしょう。

052

hate speech

[名] ヘイトスピーチ

解説

Navigating **hate speech** in the modern world is complex, balancing freedom of expression with the imperative to protect individuals from harm. While digital platforms have democratized speech, they've also amplified **hate speech**, fostering division and violence. The challenge lies in creating robust, equitable policies that combat **hate speech** while preserving diverse discourse.

現代社会におけるヘイトスピーチの扱いは複雑で、表現の自由と個人を被害から守る必要性とのバランスを取る必要がある。デジタルプラットフォームは言論を民主化した一方で、ヘイトスピーチを増幅させ、分裂や暴力を助長してきた。課題は、多様な言説を守りながらヘイトスピーチと闘う、強固で公平な方向性を打ち出すことにある。

定義 speech, writing, or non-verbal communication that promotes or incites violence, discrimination, or hostility based on attributes such as race, religion, ethnicity, gender, sexual orientation, or other protected characteristics

スピーチや文章、あるいは非言語的コミュニケーションのうち、人種や宗教、民族、性別、性的指向、その他の保護されるべき属性に基づいて、暴力、差別、敵意などを促したり扇動したりすること

Technology companies will leverage AI and other tools to identify and curb hate speech on their platforms more effectively.

テクノロジー関連企業は、AI などのツールを活用して、自社のプラットフォーム上のヘイトスピーチをより効果的に特定し、抑制していくでしょう。

microaggression [名]自覚なき差別、マイクロアグレッション

 定義 a subtle, often unintentional form of discrimination or prejudice that can manifest in seemingly harmless comments or actions but can have a cumulative negative impact on the targeted individual or group

微妙な、たいていは意図しない差別や偏見の形態のことで、一見無害に見える発言や行動の中に表れる可能性があり、対象となる人や集団に累積的な悪影響を及ぼしがちである

2030 Training programs will increase awareness about microaggressions, leading to more respectful interpersonal interactions.

研修プログラムによって、マイクロアグレッションについての認識が深まり、より敬意あふれる対人関係が築かれるようになるでしょう。

stereotype [名]固定観念、通念

 定義 a widely held, oversimplified, and often inaccurate belief or assumption about a particular group of people, which can lead to prejudiced attitudes and actions

特定の人々に関する、広く流布しており、単純化されすぎた、たいていは不正確な信念や仮定のことで、偏見に満ちた態度や行動につながりかねないもの

2030 Media representation will become more diverse, contributing to a reduction in stereotyping.

メディアでの表現内容がより多様化し、固定観念の低減に貢献するでしょう。

victim blaming [名]被害者たたき

 定義 the practice of holding the victim of a crime, abuse, or other harmful act responsible for their own suffering, rather than focusing on the actions of the perpetrator

犯罪や虐待、その他の有害な行為を、加害者の行為に目を向けずに、被害者自身の責任にすること

2030 Education about consent, personal boundaries, and respect for autonomy will help reduce the culture of victim blaming.

共感や人の限界、自主性の尊重などについての教育が、被害者たたきの慣行を減らすことにつながるでしょう。

slander [名]誹謗中傷

 定義 the act of making false and damaging statements about someone with the intention of harming their reputation or causing them distress

誰かに虚偽で傷つけるような発言を向けることで、相手の名誉を傷つけたり苦痛を与えたりする意図に基づくもの

2030 Legal mechanisms will strengthen to provide victims of slander with easier pathways for seeking justice.

法的な仕組みが強化され、誹謗中傷を受けた被害者が法的手段を取りやすくなるでしょう。

Climate Change 気候変動

heat exhaustion

［名］熱中症、熱性疲労

 解説

As the world continues to get warmer, **heat exhaustion** and heat-related illnesses are becoming a pressing concern. Vulnerable populations, including the elderly, children, and those with pre-existing medical conditions, are particularly susceptible to the adverse effects of heat. And even otherwise healthy people can succumb to the heat if they fail to take necessary precautions.

世界の気温が上昇するにつれて、熱中症や熱に関連した疾病が喫緊の課題となってきている。高齢者や子ども、持病のある人など、脆弱な層の人たちは、特に暑さの悪影響を受けやすい。また、健康な人でも暑さ対策を怠れば、熱中症にかかる可能性がある。

定義 a heat-related illness caused by excessive exposure to high temperatures, resulting in symptoms such as dizziness, weakness, and nausea
高温に過度にさらされることで起こる熱に関わる疾病で、めまいや脱力感、吐き気などの症状が出る

 Cooling systems will be installed in places that traditionally lacked them to prevent heat exhaustion.
熱中症を予防するために、従来はなかった場所に冷房設備が設置されるようになるでしょう。

heatstroke ［名］熱射病、熱中症

定義 a potentially life-threatening heat-related illness caused by the body's inability to cool itself

生命を脅かす危険性をはらんだ熱に関わる疾病で、体を冷やせないことが原因

 Tens of thousands of people will die each year from heatstroke.

熱射病による死者が、年間数万人に上るようになるでしょう。

heat index ［名］熱指数

定義 a measure that combines air temperature and relative humidity to estimate the perceived temperature or "feels-like" temperature, which indicates the level of heat stress experienced by the human body

気温と相対湿度を組み合わせた尺度で、感知される温度、つまり「体感温度」を推定するためのもの。人体が経験する熱ストレスのレベルを示す

 The heat index will reach dangerous levels for larger parts of each year.

一年のうち、熱指数が危険な水準に到達する期間が長くなるでしょう。

heat island ［名］ヒートアイランド、都市高温帯域

定義 an urban area characterized by significantly higher temperatures compared to its surrounding rural areas, primarily due to the concentration of buildings, roads, and other heat-absorbing surfaces

周辺の農村部と比較して著しく高い気温を特徴とする都市部のことで、主に建物や道路といった熱を吸収する面が集中している

 Cities will add more green spaces to reduce urban heat islands.

自治体は、都市部のヒートアイランドを減らすために緑地を増やしていくでしょう。

thermoregulation ［名］体温調節

定義 the process by which an organism maintains its internal body temperature within an optimal range through physiological and behavioral adaptations

生物が体内温度を最適な範囲に維持する過程のことで、生理的および行動の順応によるもの

 New clothing technology will assist people in thermoregulation.

新しい衣料の技術が、人々の体温調節をサポートするでしょう。

hydrogen economy

054

［名］水素経済

解説

The **hydrogen economy** is a potential solution for decarbonizing transportation. It promotes the use of hydrogen fuel cells in vehicles, which produce electricity through a chemical reaction between hydrogen and oxygen, emitting only water vapor as a byproduct. Additionally, hydrogen can be used in industrial applications such as steel production, chemical manufacturing, and energy storage.

水素経済は、交通機関の脱炭素化を実現するための解決策の一つである。水素と酸素の化学反応によって電気を作り、副産物として水蒸気だけを排出する水素燃料電池の自動車への搭載を推進するものだ。さらに、水素は鉄鋼、化学工業、エネルギーの貯蔵などの産業用途にも利用できる。

定義 an energy system in which hydrogen is the primary carrier and storage medium for power
水素を、電力の主要な伝達手段および貯蔵媒体とするエネルギーシステム

 Transcontinental hydrogen pipelines will be established.
大陸横断的な水素パイプラインが整備されることになるでしょう。

electrolysis　[名]電気分解、電解

 定義　a chemical process that uses an electric current to separate water into its constituent elements, hydrogen and oxygen, which can then be collected and used
電流を利用して水を構成元素である水素と酸素に分離し、それを回収して利用する化学的工程

2030 Commercial-scale high-temperature electrolysis (HTE) will increase the efficiency of hydrogen production.
商業規模の高温電気分解（HTE）で、水素の製造効率が上がるでしょう。

fuel cell　[形]燃料電池

 定義　an electrochemical device that converts the chemical energy of a fuel, such as hydrogen, and an oxidizing agent, such as oxygen, into electricity
水素などの燃料と酸素などの酸化剤の化学エネルギーを電気に変換する電気化学装置

2030 Gas stations will function as hydrogen refueling stations as well.
ガソリンスタンドが、水素補充所としての役割も担うようになるでしょう。

green hydrogen　[名]グリーン水素

 定義　hydrogen gas produced through the process of electrolysis, using renewable energy sources such as wind or solar power, resulting in a low-carbon and environmentally friendly fuel
電気分解の工程を経て製造される水素ガスのこと。風力や太陽光などの再生可能エネルギー源を利用して作られ、低炭素で環境に優しい燃料となる

2030 Green hydrogen production will increase, making hydrogen as a fuel source more environmentally friendly.
グリーン水素の生産量が増え、燃料としての水素がより環境に優しいものになるでしょう。

power-to-gas technology　[名]パワートゥーガス技術

 定義　a process that involves converting surplus electricity generated from renewable energy sources into gases such as hydrogen or methane
再生可能エネルギーで発電した際の余剰電力を、水素やメタンなどのガスに変換する工程

2030 Power-to-gas facilities will capture and convert CO_2 emissions from large-scale industrial processes.
パワートゥーガス施設が、大規模な工業工程で排出される CO_2 を回収し、変換処理を行うようになるでしょう。

identity theft

055

［名］個人情報の窃盗、成り済まし（犯罪）

解説

Identity theft poses a significant threat in the digital age, affecting countless individuals worldwide. New technologies provide new avenues for perpetrators to exploit their victims, leveraging vulnerabilities in online systems and utilizing sophisticated methods to gain unauthorized access to personal information. While no one is entirely safe, some measures exist to help people increase the security of their data.

成り済ましは、デジタル時代における重大な脅威であり、世界中で数え切れないほどの人々が被害に遭っている。いくつもの新技術が加害者に、被害者に付け込むすべを与えてしまっているのだ。彼らはオンラインシステムの脆弱性をてこにしたり、個人情報に不正にアクセスする巧妙な方法を用いる。一方で、誰もが完全に安全でいられるというわけにはいかないものの、データの保安性を高めるための対策は存在する。

定義 the fraudulent acquisition and use of another person's personal information, typically for financial gain or other criminal purposes
他人の個人情報を不正に取得・利用する行為のことで、通常、金銭的利益やその他の犯罪が目的

 Victims of identity theft will have more trouble reclaiming their digital lives.
個人情報盗難の被害者は、デジタルライフを取り戻すのがより困難になります。

social engineering ［名］ソーシャルエンジニアリング

定義 the manipulation of individuals or groups into divulging confidential information or performing certain actions for illegitimate reasons
違法な理由で個人や集団を操作して機密情報を漏らしたり、特定の行動を取らせたりすること

 Social engineering attacks will increase, and the victims will primarily be older.
ソーシャルエンジニアリングによる攻撃が増加し、被害者は主に高齢者になるでしょう。

phishing ［名］フィッシング（詐欺）

定義 a type of cyberattack in which fraudulent emails, text messages, or websites are used to deceive individuals into providing sensitive information, such as login credentials, credit card numbers, or personal data
サイバー攻撃の一種で、不正な電子メールやテキストメッセージ、ウェブサイトを使用して個人を欺き、ログイン情報、クレジットカード番号、個人データなどの機密情報を教えさせようとする

 Phishing attacks will become increasingly sophisticated, using AI tools to tailor messages to targets.
フィッシング攻撃は、AI ツールを使ってターゲットに合わせたメッセージを送るなど、ますます高度化するでしょう。

vishing ［名］ビッシング

定義 the act of using telephone systems or voice over IP (VoIP) to trick individuals into revealing private information, often used for identity theft or financial gain
電話やボイスオーバー IP（VoIP）を使って個人情報をだまし取る行為のことで、たいてい個人情報の窃盗や金銭的な利益のために用いられる

 Vishing attacks using deepfake voices will become common.
ディープフェイクボイスを利用したビッシング攻撃が一般化することでしょう。

2FA ［名］2 要素認証、2 ファクター認証

定義 short for "two-factor authentication," a method of confirming a user's claimed identity by utilizing a combination of two different identification components, such as a password and a unique code sent to a device
「二要素認証」の頭字語で、2 つの異なる識別要素の組み合わせを利用してユーザーの身元を確認する方法。パスワードと、デバイスに送信される固有の暗号などを使う

 Most forms of 2FA will involve some sort of biometric identification.
2FA のほとんどの形態では、何らかの生体認証が行われます。

inflation

056

［名］インフレ、通貨膨張、物価上昇

解説

Inflation isn't just technical jargon reserved for economists and business journals. When **inflation** spirals out of control, it can have real-world consequences. For example, record-setting **inflation** in the early 2020s made food, gas, and housing too expensive for many to afford. If left unchecked, **inflation** can lead to economic instability and social unrest.

インフレは単に、経済学者やビジネス雑誌のための専門用語ではない。インフレが制御不能に陥ると、現実の世界に影響を及ぼす可能性がある。例えば、2020年代初頭の記録的なインフレでは、食料やガソリン、住宅が高くなりすぎて、多くの人が手を出せなくなった。インフレを放置すれば、経済が不安定になり、社会不安が生じかねない。

定義　the rate at which the general price level of goods and services in an economy increases over time

ある経済圏における商品やサービスの一般的な価格水準が、時間の経過とともに上昇する割合

Cryptocurrencies will act as a hedge against inflation.
暗号通貨はインフレの保険として機能するでしょう。

interest rate [名]利率、金利

定義 the percentage at which interest is paid by a borrower to a lender or earned on deposited funds, typically expressed on an annual basis

借り手から貸し手へ支払われる利息、または預けた資金に対して得られる利息の率のことで、通常、年単位で表される

 Interest rates will rise as banks attempt to discourage people from moving money into cryptocurrencies.

銀行が暗号通貨への資金の移動を抑制しようとするので、金利は上昇するでしょう。

recession [名]景気後退、不況、不景気

定義 a period of negative economic growth that lasts for at least two consecutive quarters, characterized by reduced economic activity, higher unemployment, and lower consumer spending

経済活動の低下、失業率の上昇、個人消費の減少を特徴とする、少なくとも2四半期連続で経済成長がマイナスになっている状況

 The world will recover from the global recession of the mid 2020s, but another one will soon follow.

世界は、2020年代半ばの世界同時不況から回復するものの、すぐに次の不況が来るでしょう。

shrinkflation [名]シュリンクフレーション

定義 the practice of reducing the size or quantity of a product while maintaining or increasing its price, resulting in a hidden form of inflation

製品の価格を維持または上昇させながら、そのサイズや量を縮小することで、隠れた形のインフレをもたらすこと

 Some companies will face extreme backlash as shrinkflation erodes consumer trust.

シュリンクフレーションが消費者の信頼を奪い、極端な反動を受ける企業が出てくるでしょう。

supply chain [名]サプライチェーン、供給網

定義 the interconnected network of organizations, people, resources, and processes involved in producing and delivering goods or services from suppliers to end customers

供給者から最終消費者に至る流れの中の、商品またはサービスの生産および供給に関する、組織、人、資源、工程の相互に結び付いたネットワーク

 Supply chain disruptions will become less frequent as more companies adopt blockchain technology.

ブロックチェーン技術の導入企業が増えれば、サプライチェーンの混乱は減るでしょう。

influencer

［名］インフルエンサー

057

解説

Social media **influencers** emerged alongside the rise of social media platforms, and brands swiftly recognized the potential for collaboration. Today, the **influencer** marketing industry is worth billions of dollars, and it's still growing. **Influencers'** ability to connect with their followers on a personal level has enabled brands to tap into highly engaged audiences and leverage their influence for effective promotion.

ソーシャルメディアのプラットフォームの台頭とともに、SNSインフルエンサーが登場し、企業はコラボレーションの潜在的可能性の大きさに一早く気づいた。現在、インフルエンサーマーケティング業界は数十億ドルの規模を誇り、なおも成長を続けている。インフルエンサーは、フォロワーと個人的なつながりを持つことができるため、企業は関与の度合いの高い顧客層を獲得するとともに、彼らの影響力を活用して効果的な販促活動を行えるようになってきた。

定義 a person with a significant online following who utilizes their platform to shape opinions, trends, and consumer behavior
ネット上に多くの支持者を持った人物のことで、自分のプラットフォームを活用し、意見を発信したり、トレンドや消費者行動を形作ったりする

 Some actors who began as influencers will earn Emmy and Oscar nominations.
インフルエンサーとして世に出た俳優の中から、エミー賞やアカデミー賞にノミネートされる人が現れるでしょう。

earned media ［名］アーンドメディア

 定義 publicity gained by a brand, organization, or individual through unpaid or organic means, such as positive press coverage, social media mentions, or word-of-mouth referrals

ブランド、組織、または個人が獲得する評判のことで、無報酬または手の込んでいない手段を通じて得られるもの。この手段には、例えば好意的な報道、ソーシャルメディアでの言及、口コミによる紹介などがある

2030 Earned media will rely on building brand advocates and fostering active community engagement.

アーンドメディアは、ブランドの支持者を集められるか、コミュニティーとの積極的な関わりを育てられるかにかかってくるでしょう。

sharent ［名］シェアレント

 定義 a parent who actively uses social media platforms to document and share their child's experiences, achievements, and challenges, blurring the line between personal and public aspects of their family life

SNS プラットフォームを積極的に利用する親のことで、自分の子どもの経験や成果、奮闘ぶりなどを記録したり共有したりして、自らの家庭生活の公私を混同している

2030 Sharents will face severe backlash from their children who never gave them consent.

シェアレントは、同意していない子どもたちから厳しい反発を受けるでしょう。

streamer ［名］ストリーマー、実況主

 定義 an individual who broadcasts live video content, typically sharing gameplay, creative activities, or personal experiences with an online audience that can interact through chat or comments

ライブ動画コンテンツを配信する個人のことで、通常はゲームの実況プレーや創作活動、個人的な体験などを、チャットやコメントを使ってやり取りできるネット視聴者と共有する

2030 The most popular streamers will stream XR media.
最も人気の高いストリーマーたちは、クロスリアリティーメディアを配信するでしょう。

instafamous ［形］インスタフェーマス、インスタグラム上で有名な

 定義 pertaining to someone who has gained a significant amount of fame and influence on the social media platform Instagram

ソーシャルメディアのインスタグラムで大きな名声と影響力を獲得した人に関する

2030 More micro-influencers, people who have highly engaged followings within specific communities, will become instafamous.

特定のコミュニティー内に熱心な支持者を抱えるマイクロインフルエンサーの中に、インスタグラム上で有名になる人が増えるでしょう。

information bubble

058

［名］フィルターバブル

解説

Social media and search engine algorithms significantly contribute to the formation of **information bubbles** prevalent in the digital age. As these businesses need more financial incentives to change their practices, it is often left to users to avoid **information bubbles** by limiting the personalized and tailored aspects of their online activities.

ソーシャルメディアや検索エンジンのアルゴリズムは、デジタル時代に蔓延するフィルターバブルの形成に大きく寄与している。これらのビジネスの担い手たちは、より大きな財務上の動機づけがない限りは自分たちの活動内容を変えないので、多くの場合、フィルターバブルの回避はユーザー側に任される。自分のネットの利用行動のうち、個人の嗜好や事情に合わせて調整された部分を減らすしかないのだ。

定義 a situation in which individuals are exposed only to news, opinions, and information that align with their existing beliefs, resulting in limited exposure to diverse perspectives

人が今抱いている信条に沿ったニュースや意見、情報ばかりに触れている状況のことで、結果として、多様なものの見方に接する機会が限られてしまう

2030 The algorithms that choose which content to show people will grow more advanced, making the information bubble increasingly insular and reinforcing existing biases.

人々にどんなコンテンツを見せるか選択するアルゴリズムが、いっそう高度化し、フィルターバブルはますます偏狭なものとなり、既存の偏向を後押しすることになるでしょう。

algorithm　［名］アルゴリズム

定義 a set of ordered instructions designed to solve a specific problem or perform a particular task, often used in computer programming or mathematical calculations

特定の問題を解決したり、特定のタスクを実行するために設計された規則的な指示のまとまりのことで、コンピュータープログラミングや数学の計算でよく使われる

 AI will play an increasing role in developing the algorithms used to analyze and interpret vast amounts of data.

AI は、膨大なデータを分析・解釈するためのアルゴリズムの開発において、ますます大きな役割を果たすでしょう。

echo chamber　［名］エコーチェンバー現象

定義 a social or digital bubble where individuals are surrounded by information, discussions, and interactions that validate and reinforce their own beliefs, contributing to polarization and lack of diverse perspectives

社会的あるいはデジタル領域でのバブル現象の一つで、人が自分の信条を正当化し強化するような情報、議論、やり取りに囲まれ、二極化や、多様な視点の欠如を作り出してしまう

 The rise of personalized news platforms and content curation services will further enhance the echo chamber effect.

パーソナル化されたニュースプラットフォームやコンテンツのまとめサービスの台頭によって、エコーチェンバー現象がいっそう顕著になるでしょう。

groupthink　［名］グループシンク、集団浅慮

定義 a situation in which group members, seeking consensus, minimize conflict by refusing to critically test, analyze, or evaluate ideas and assumptions

集団の構成員たちが、合意を得ようとして、対立を最小化する状況のことで、アイデアや仮説を批判的に調査、分析、評価することを拒否してしまう

 The increasing emphasis on consensus-driven decision-making in politics and business will perpetuate groupthink.

政治やビジネスにおいて、合意形成に基づく意思決定が重視されるようになり、集団浅慮が続いていくでしょう。

tribalism　［名］部族主義

定義 a social phenomenon characterized by strong loyalty to one's own social or political group, often leading to hostility or discrimination toward other groups, and prioritizing the interests of the in-group over broader societal concerns

自分の社会的または政治的集団への強い忠誠心を特徴とする社会現象の一つで、しばしば他の集団に対する敵意や差別につながり、より広い社会的関心事よりも同集団の利益が優先される

 The erosion of trust in traditional institutions and the rise of populist movements will further fuel tribalism.

伝統的な制度に対する信頼の低下とポピュリスト運動の台頭が、部族主義をさらに助長することになるでしょう。

interstellar

059

[形] 星間の

解説

Space exploration technology, such as the Voyager probes and the New Horizons mission, has provided valuable insights into the outer reaches of our solar system. These achievements have fueled the ongoing search for exoplanets and potential extraterrestrial life, raising questions about the possibility of human colonization of other star systems.

ボイジャー探査機やニュー・ホライズンズ計画などにおける宇宙探査技術は、太陽系外縁部に関する貴重な知見を提供してくれた。これらの成果は、太陽系外惑星や地球外生命体の探索を促進し、人類が他の星系を植民地化する可能性について疑問を投げかけている。

定義 located or occurring between the stars
星の間に位置する、または発生する

 New propulsion technology will enable space probes to blast past Voyager I into the interstellar medium.
新しい推進技術により、宇宙探査機が、ボイジャー1号を追い抜いて、星間空間に突入するでしょう。

exoplanet ［名］太陽系外惑星

定義 a planet that orbits a star outside the solar system
太陽系外の恒星を周回する惑星

 The Nancy Grace Roman Space Telescope will power the discovery of thousands of potentially habitable exoplanets.
ナンシー・グレース・ローマン宇宙望遠鏡が、何千もの居住可能な太陽系外惑星を発見するための動力源となるでしょう。

dark matter ［名］ダークマター

定義 hypothetical matter that does not emit, absorb, or reflect light, comprising a significant portion of the total matter in the universe
光を発することも、吸収することも、反射することもない仮説上の物質で、宇宙の全物質のかなりの部分を占める

 Physicists will continue to make progress understanding the composition of dark matter.
物理学者たちが、ダークマターの組成の解明を継続して進めるでしょう。

Cubesat ［名］キューブサット

定義 a small, standardized satellite consisting of one or more cube-shaped units, typically measuring 10 cm on each side, used for various space missions and scientific research
1個以上の立方体でできた小型の規格化された衛星で、通常、一辺が10センチメートル。さまざまな宇宙計画や科学研究のために使用される

 Constellations of Cubesats will be put into orbit around Earth and other celestial bodies, providing scientists with unprecedented opportunities for space exploration and data collection.
地球や天体を周回する多数のキューブサットが、科学者に宇宙探査やデータ収集に関わる前例のない機会を提供するでしょう。

LEO ［名］低地球軌道、低周回軌道

定義 short for "low-earth orbit," an orbit around Earth with a period of 128 minutes or less
「低地球軌道」を短くした形で、周期が128分以下の、地球を周回する軌道

 LEO will become dangerously congested, resulting in a stark increase in satellite collisions.
低地球軌道は危険なほど混雑し、人工衛星の衝突が激増するでしょう。

060

IoT

［名］IoT、モノのインターネット

解説

Today, you can find **IoT** devices everywhere. They monitor energy consumption in homes, provide data on soil moisture levels and weather conditions, and even track patients' vital signs. But the convenience comes at a cost. Many devices are left unsecured, giving hackers a dangerous level of access to our homes and businesses.

今日、いたるところでIoT装置を見かける。それらは、家庭のエネルギー消費を監視し、土壌の水分量や天候のデータを提供し、さらには患者のバイタルサインを追跡する。しかし、その便利さには代償が伴う。多くの装置がセキュリティーを保護されずに放置され、ハッカーが私たちの家庭や職場に危険なレベルでアクセスできるようになっている。

定義 short for "Internet of Things," a network of interconnected physical devices, sensors, and software that collect and exchange data, enabling communication between objects and their environment
「モノのインターネット」の頭字語で、データを収集し交換する物理的な装置とセンサー、ソフトウェアが相互に接続されたネットワークのこと。物とその環境の間のやり取りを可能にする

By 2030, an average of 50 IoT devices will be found in every home.
2030年には、各家庭に平均50台のIoT機器が設置されるようになるでしょう。

wireless charging ［名］無線充電

 ［定義］ a method of transferring electrical power to devices without the need for physical connectors or cables, typically using electromagnetic fields

電力を機器に供給する方法の一つで、物理的なコネクターやケーブルを必要とせず、通常、電磁界を利用する

2030 Wireless charging networks for electric vehicles will emerge in major cities.

電気自動車用の無線充電ネットワークが大都市に出現するでしょう。

smart city ［名］スマートシティー

 ［定義］ an urban area that uses advanced technology and data analysis to optimize resources, infrastructure, and services for the benefit of its inhabitants and the environment

高度な技術とデータ分析を用いて、住民と環境のために資源やインフラ、サービスが最適化される都市圏

2030 More urban centers will adopt smart features to attract new residents dissatisfied with outdated dwellings.

より多くの都心地区でハイテク機能の充実が図られ、時代遅れの住宅に不満を持つ住民を新たに呼び込もうとするでしょう。

home automation ［名］ホームオートメーション

［定義］ the use of technology to control and automate various household settings, such as lighting, temperature, and security

家庭内のさまざまな設定を制御、自動化するためにテクノロジーを利用することで、照明や室温、防犯などを管理する

 2030 Voice recognition technology will be the primary method of interaction with home automation systems.

音声認識技術が、ホームオートメーションのシステムとやり取りする上での主要な方法となるでしょう。

distributed system ［名］分散システム

［定義］ a network of computers or devices that work together to perform tasks, share resources, and communicate with one another, often to enhance reliability and performance

コンピューターやさまざまな機器のネットワークの一つで、相互に連携してタスクを実行したり、リソースを共有したり、通信したりするもの

 2030 Blockchain-based distributed systems will manage a significant portion of global financial transactions.

ブロックチェーンを用いた分散システムが、世界の金融取引のかなりの部分を管理することになるでしょう。

job loss

061

［名］雇用の喪失、失業

解説

The World Economic Forum's 2023 report suggested that some 23% of jobs could be disrupted before the end of the decade, partly due to AI and automation. While new fields will emerge as technology advances, the world will ultimately have to grapple with the idea of whether employment is necessary in the first place.

世界経済フォーラムの2023年の報告によると、AIや自動化の影響もあり、2020年代の終りまでに約23パーセントの雇用が失われる可能性があるという。技術の進歩に伴い新たな職種が生まれる一方で、そもそも雇用は必要なのかという考え方に、世界は最終的に取り組まなければならないだろう。

定義 the reduction or elimination of employment opportunities, leading to unemployment or underemployment
失業または不完全雇用につながる雇用機会の減少、あるいは停止

Job loss will be exacerbated by ever more powerful AI systems.
雇用の喪失は、これまで以上に強力な AI システムによって、悪化するでしょう。

outsource [動]（〜を）外注する

 定義 to delegate tasks, functions, or projects to an external party, often to save costs or access specialized expertise

通例、コストを削減したり専門技術・知識を利用したりしながら、業務、職務、プロジェクトを外部に委ねる

2030 Outsourcing to companies in other countries will grow less common as people turn to AI.

AIへの移行に伴い、国外企業への外注は減っていくでしょう。

side hustle [名]副業、サイドビジネス

 定義 a part-time job or freelance work that an individual engages in outside of their primary employment, often to earn extra income

本業とは別に、副収入を得るために従事するアルバイトやフリーランスの仕事

2030 Many people will pick up a side hustle either to make ends meet or to supplement UBI cash payments.

多くの人が、生活のやりくりや最低所得保障の現金給与を補うために、副業を始めるようになるでしょう。

job market [名]求人市場、労働市場

 定義 the economic environment or sector that encompasses job openings, labor demand, and job search activities, shaping the employment landscape and determining opportunities and conditions for employment

求人、労働需要、求職活動などを含み、雇用環境を形成したり、雇用の機会や条件を決定したりする経済の環境または領域

2030 Around 10% of the job market will involve work that has not existed in the past.

求人市場の10パーセント程度が、過去に存在しなかった職で占められるでしょう。

unemployment [名]失業

 定義 the state in which individuals capable of working are currently jobless, reflecting a mismatch between the number of people seeking employment and the number of available job positions in the labor market

就労可能な個人が目下失業している状態のことで、労働市場における求職者数と求人数のズレを反映している

2030 Global unemployment will reach record highs.

世界の失業率が過去最高を記録するでしょう。

light pollution

062

［名］光害

解説

Excessive and poorly directed artificial light disrupts people's sleep patterns and circadian rhythms. It also affects wildlife, as many species rely on darkness for critical activities such as foraging, reproduction, and migration. Furthermore, it hinders astronomical observations by reducing the visibility of stars and other astronomical phenomena. We must shine a light on the problem of **light pollution**.

人工光は、明るすぎたり誤った方向を照らしたりすると、人の睡眠パターンや概日リズムを乱す。また、多くの生物種が採食や繁殖、移動などの重要な活動を暗闇に依存しているため、野生生物にも影響を与える。さらに、星やその他の天文現象が見えにくくなるため、天体観測にも支障をきたす。私たちは、光害の問題に光を当てなければならない。

定義 the unwanted or excessive artificial illumination of the night sky, resulting in reduced visibility of stars and astronomical phenomena
夜空を照らす不要な、あるいは過剰な人工光。星や天文現象の視認性を低下させることにつながる

The increase in urbanization will lead to cities producing more light pollution.
都市化が進むことで、都市部での光害が悪化するでしょう。

skyglow [名] 夜空の明るさ

 定義 the brightening of the night sky caused by the scattering of artificial light by the atmosphere, which reduces the visibility of stars and other celestial objects

大気による人工光の散乱によって夜空が明るくなることで、星などの天体の視認性を低下させる

2030 Skyglow will become such a serious issue that legislation will be considered, particularly in areas near astronomical observatories.

特に天文台の近辺で夜空の明るさが深刻な問題となり、法整備が検討されることになるでしょう。

glare reduction [名] グレア低減

 定義 techniques and strategies to minimize the discomfort or visibility issues caused by excessive or poorly directed artificial light

明るすぎたり不適切な方向を照らしたりする人工光による不快感や視認性の問題を、最小限に抑えるための技術や戦略

2030 Policymakers will discuss regulations that require citizens to incorporate glare reduction strategies in their outdoor lighting designs.

政策立案者らが規制案を議論し、屋外照明の設計にグレア低減策を取り入れることを民間に求めるでしょう。

light trespass [名] 光の不法侵入

 定義 the spillover of unwanted or excessive artificial light onto neighboring properties, which can cause annoyance, disrupt sleep, and contribute to light pollution

不要な、または過剰な人工光が近隣の土地に漏れることで、迷惑や睡眠妨害、光害の一因につながり得る

2030 Urban design will increasingly take light trespass into account to improve quality of life and sleep quality.

生活の質や睡眠の質を向上させるために、光の不法侵入を考慮した都市設計がますます進むでしょう。

dark sky [名] 光害のない空

 定義 an area, often designated for conservation or astronomical purposes, where efforts are made to minimize artificial light pollution and preserve the natural night sky

環境保全や天文観測のために指定されることの多い地域で、そこでは人工的な光害を最小限に抑え、自然な夜空を守る努力が行われる

2030 Astronomical tourism will increase, driven by interest in dark sky preserves.

光害のない空の保護への関心がきっかけとなって、天文観光が盛んになるでしょう。

machine learning

063

［名］機械学習

In 1952, Arthur Samuel developed one of the first **machine learning** programs: the Samuel Checkers-Playing Program. He believed that teaching computers to play games was important for developing strategies that could be applied to general problems. Today, AI dominates not only many classic board games and video games but also entire industries.

1952年、アーサー・サミュエルは、最初の機械学習プログラムの1つである「サミュエル・チェッカーズ・プレーイング・プログラム」を開発した。彼は、コンピューターにゲームを教えることが、一般的な問題に適用できる戦略の開発に重要だと考えたのである。今日、AIは多くの古典的なボードゲームやビデオゲームだけでなく、産業界全体を支配している。

定義 a branch of AI focusing on creating algorithms that allow computers to learn from and make decisions based on data

アルゴリズムの作成に焦点を当てた AI の一分野で、コンピューターがデータから学習し、データに基づいて意思決定できるようにする

Quantum machine learning will efficiently solve optimization problems like route planning.

量子機械学習が、経路探索のような最適化に関わる問題を効率的に解決するでしょう。

deep learning [名]ディープラーニング

 定義 a branch of artificial intelligence that focuses on training artificial neural networks with multiple layers

人工知能の一分野で、複数の層を持つ人工ニューラルネットワークを訓練することに重点が置かれている

2030 New techniques will enable deep learning models to learn effectively with only a few examples.

新技術によって、ディープラーニングのモデルはわずかな例で効果的に学習できるようになるでしょう。

diffusion model [名]拡散モデル

 定義 an image generation technique utilizing probabilistic generative models that transform random noise into representative and realistic data samples

確率的生成モデルを利用した画像生成技術で、ランダムノイズを代表的で現実的なデータサンプルに変換する

2030 Diffusion models will generate images of people that are impossible to distinguish from real photographs.

拡散モデルによって、実際の写真と見分けがつかないような人物の画像が生成されるようになるでしょう。

neural network [名]ニューラルネットワーク

 定義 a computer system inspired by the human brain, consisting of interconnected nodes or artificial neurons designed to recognize patterns and make decisions

人間の脳にヒントを得たコンピューターシステムで、相互接続されたノードまたは人工ニューロンで構成されており、パターンを認識し意思決定を行う

2030 Neural networks will possess better generalization capabilities, being able to apply learned knowledge to unfamiliar situations with greater accuracy and reliability.

ニューラルネットワークは、より優れた汎化能力を持つようになり、学習した知識を未知の状況に適用する際の正確性と信頼性が格段に向上するでしょう。

Turing test [名]チューリングテスト

 定義 a test introduced by Alan Turing that evaluates a machine's ability to exhibit intelligent behavior indistinguishable from that of a human

アラン・チューリングが提唱したテストのことで、人間と区別がつかないような知的振る舞いを見せる機械の能力を評価するもの

2030 The Turing test will evolve to include not only textual interactions but also incorporate other modalities such as speech, vision, and physical embodiment, allowing for more comprehensive evaluations of machine intelligence.

チューリングテストは進化して、文字のやり取りだけでなく音声や視覚、体感など、他の感覚を取り入れることで、機械の知能をより総合的に評価できるようになるでしょう。

marginalized

064

［形］社会的に無視された、社会の隅に追いやられた

解説

Examining the ways in which various groups are **marginalized**, whether due to race, gender, socioeconomic status, or other factors, sheds light on the systemic issues that perpetuate inequality and exclusion. The unbanked, for example, are predominantly from low-income racial and ethnic minority groups. This exclusion from basic financial services not only perpetuates poverty but also hinders economic mobility.

人種や性別、社会経済的地位といった要因によるものか否かにかかわらず、さまざまな集団がどのようにして社会的に疎外されるのかを検討することは、不平等や排除を永続させてしまう構造的な問題に光を当てることになる。例えば、銀行口座を持たない人々の多くが、低所得の人種や民族のマイノリティー集団に属している。このような基本的な金融サービスからの排除は、貧困を永続させてしまうばかりか、経済的な流動の妨げになる。

定義　referring to individuals or groups that are excluded or treated as unimportant, often due to factors such as race, gender, or social class
たいていは人種、性別、社会的階級などの要因で、個人や集団が排除されたり重要でないものとして扱われたりする

 Marginalized communities will gain significant political representation, leading to legislation that directly addresses their needs and concerns.
社会的に疎外されたコミュニティーが大きく政治的な表舞台に現れるようになることによって、彼らのニーズや懸念に直接対応する法律が生まれるでしょう。

unbanked [形] 銀行口座を持たない

 　referring to individuals who do not have access to formal banking services, often due to factors such as low income, lack of documentation, or geographic isolation

低所得や書類の不足、地理的な孤立などの要因で、正式な銀行サービスを受けられない

 　The spread of mobile banking and digital financial services will dramatically decrease the number of unbanked individuals.

モバイルバンキングやデジタル金融サービスの普及によって、銀行口座を持たない人の数が劇的に減少するでしょう。

redlining [名] 金融機関による線引き

 　a discriminatory practice in which banks or other financial institutions deny loans or insurance to residents of specific neighborhoods

銀行などの金融機関が、特定の地域の住民に対して融資や保険契約を拒否する差別的な行為のこと

 　Data-driven approaches will play a significant role in identifying and dismantling redlining practices.

データ主導の手法が、金融機関による線引きの慣習をあぶり出し、それらを廃止する上で重要な役割を果たすでしょう。

underbanked [形] 銀行口座を利用しない

 　referring to individuals who have limited access to mainstream financial services, often relying on alternative financial services such as check cashing or payday loans

たいてい小切手や給料日ローンなどの代替金融サービスに頼る個人が、主流の金融サービスの利用を制限されて

 　Microcredit and peer-to-peer lending platforms will become more popular.

少額短期融資やピア・ツー・ピア融資のプラットフォームが普及していくでしょう。

mortgage discrimination [名] 住宅ローン差別

 　the unfair treatment of applicants for home loans based on factors such as race, gender, or other protected characteristics, resulting in unequal access to home-ownership opportunities

人種や性別、その他の保護された特性などに基づいた、住宅ローンの申込者に対する不当な扱いのことで、結果として住宅を所有する機会が不平等になる

 　Consumer awareness and education about mortgage rights and processes will rise, making it harder for discriminatory practices to go unnoticed.

住宅ローンの権利や手続きに関する消費者の意識の高まりや教育の充実によって、差別的な行為が見過ごされにくくなるでしょう。

mental health

065

［名］メンタルヘルス、心の健康

解説

As the stigma surrounding mental illness erodes, more people openly discuss their experiences and seek help, leading to increased awareness and access to **mental health** resources. The growing emphases on mindfulness and self-care have also empowered people to take an active role in managing their mental well-being. Digital approaches to therapy have made getting support more convenient than ever.

精神疾患に対する偏見が薄れるにつれ、より多くの人々が自分の経験について率直に語り、助けを求めるようになり、精神衛生に関する情報・手段の認識や利用の向上につながっている。また、マインドフルネスやセルフケアが重視れるようになったことで、人々は積極的に自分で自分の心の健康を管理するようになった。デジタルな手法で治療に手が届くようになり、かつてよりも便利にサポートを利用できるようになってきた。

定義 a person's emotional, psychological, and social well-being, influencing their thoughts, feelings, and behaviors
人の感情的、心理的、社会的な幸福のことで、思考や感性、行動に影響を与えるもの

Mental healthcare will receive priority and recognition equal to physical healthcare.
心の医療は、体の医療と同等の優先順位と評価を受けることになるでしょう。

mental illness [名]精神疾患、心の病

定義 a wide range of psychological disorders or conditions that affect a person's mood, thinking, and behavior, often requiring professional treatment

人の気分や思考、行動に影響を与えるさまざまな心理的な障害や状態のことで、多くの場合、専門的な治療を必要とする

 Mental illnesses will be detected earlier due to advances in predictive algorithms and an increase in genetic testing.

予測アルゴリズムの進歩や遺伝子検査の増加によって、精神疾患の早期発見が実現するでしょう。

mindfulness [名]マインドフルネス

定義 the state of being fully present and engaged in the current moment, intentionally focusing one's attention on thoughts, feelings, bodily sensations, and the surrounding environment, without judgment

今この瞬間に完全に存在し、関与している状態で、評価を下すことなく、意図的に自分の思考や感情、身体感覚、周囲の環境に注意を向けること

 Mindfulness practices will become commonplace in various settings, including schools, workplaces, and at home.

学校、職場、家庭など、さまざまな場面でマインドフルネスの実践が当たり前になるでしょう。

self-care [名]セルフケア、自己療法

定義 the practice of taking intentional actions to maintain or improve one's own physical, emotional, and mental well-being

自分の身体的、感情的、精神的な幸福を維持または改善するために、意図的に取る行動

 Self-care will be widely acknowledged as crucial for overall health, encouraging increased dedication of time and resources to the pursuit.

セルフケアが健康維持に重要であることが広く認識され、そのための時間や資源の確保が促進されるでしょう。

self-compassion [名]セルフコンパッション、自己への慈しみ

定義 the act of treating oneself with kindness, understanding, and empathy, particularly during times of personal suffering or perceived failure

優しさや、理解、共感を持って自分に接する行為のことで、特に個人的な苦しみや失敗を認識したような場合に取る行動

 More therapeutic approaches will incorporate techniques to cultivate self-compassion in patients.

患者のセルフコンパッションを育む技術を取り入れた治療法がより導入されるでしょう。

131

metamaterial

066

［名］メタ物質

解説

Metamaterials may one day bring science fiction to life by enabling people to manipulate light, sound, and other waves in extraordinary ways. But today, they're already more common than many might think. For example, the antennas in wireless communication devices, like smartphones and Wi-Fi routers, rely on **metamaterials** to help enhance signal strength and reception.

メタ物質は、いずれSFを現実に変えるかもしれない。光や音などの波動が並外れた方法で操れるようになるかもしれないからだ。とはいえ現在、すでにメタ物質は、多くの人が考えている以上に一般的になっている。例えば、スマートフォンやWi-Fiルーターなどの無線通信機器のアンテナは、メタ物質を利用して信号の強度や受信状況を向上させている。

定義 a synthetic material with properties not found in nature, engineered to have specific characteristics and abilities, such as manipulating electromagnetic waves or light

自然界に存在しない特性を持つ合成物質のことで、電磁波や光を操作するなど、特定の特性や能力を持つように設計される

 Seismic metamaterials will reduce the impact of earthquakes on buildings.
耐震メタ物質を使って、地震が建物に与える衝撃を軽減させるようになるでしょう。

carbon nanotube [名]カーボンナノチューブ

 定義 a cylindrical, nanoscale structure made of carbon atoms, known for its exceptional strength, electrical conductivity, and thermal properties

炭素原子でできた円筒形のナノスケールの構造物で、優れた強度と電気伝導性、熱特性を持つことで知られている

2030 Carbon nanotube-based water filters will provide clean drinking water for millions.

カーボンナノチューブを使った水フィルターが、何百万人もの人々にきれいな飲料水を提供するでしょう。

graphene [名]グラフェン

 定義 a single layer of carbon atoms arranged in a two-dimensional hexagonal lattice, known for its remarkable strength, flexibility, and electrical conductivity

2次元の六角形格子状に配列された炭素原子の単層のことで、優れた強度や柔軟性、電気伝導性を持つことで知られている

2030 Graphene batteries with twice the capacity of lithium-ion batteries will become commercially available.

リチウムイオン電池の2倍の容量を持つグラフェン電池が実用化されることになるでしょう。

aerogel [名]エーロゲル、エアロジェル

 定義 a lightweight, porous material with an extremely low density, derived from a gel through a process in which the liquid component is replaced with gas, resulting in a solid material that is mostly composed of air

極めて密度が低く軽量な多孔質材料のこと。ゲル状物質から液体成分を気体で置換する工程を経て、大部分が空気で構成された固形物質ができる

2030 Aerogel-infused concrete will increase the durability of new construction projects.

エーロゲルを練り込んだコンクリートによって、新築の造造物の耐久性が高められるようになるでしょう。

supercapacitor [名]スーパーキャパシター

 定義 an energy storage device that can rapidly charge and discharge electricity, offering higher power density and longer lifespans than traditional batteries

急速な充放電が可能な蓄電デバイスで、従来の電池よりも高い出力密度と長い寿命を持つ

2030 Supercapacitors will improve the range and charge time of EVs.

スーパーキャパシターによって、電気自動車の航続距離と充電時間が向上するでしょう。

metaverse

067

[名]メタバース

解説

The term "**metaverse**" was coined by Neal Stephenson in his 1992 science fiction novel *Snow Crash*. In the book, the **metaverse** refers to a virtual reality-based successor to the Internet, where users can interact with each other and explore digital environments. Today, several companies are hard at work turning science fiction into reality.

「メタバース」という言葉は、ニール・スティーブンソンが1992年に発表したSF小説『スノー・クラッシュ』の中で使われた造語である。同書では、メタバースとは、仮想現実をベースとしたインターネットを後継するもののことで、ユーザーが互いにやり取りしながらデジタル環境を探索できる。今日、いくつかの企業が懸命にこれに取り組み、SFを現実にしようとしている。

定義　a shared, immersive, persistent virtual space in which people can interact with virtual objects, avatars, or other simulations

人々に共有され、没入感のある、永続的な仮想空間のことで、利用者は仮想の物体やアバターなどの模擬物とやり取りできる

 Access to the metaverse will be considered a fundamental human right.
メタバースの利用が、基本的人権の一つと見なされるようになるでしょう。

liminal space [名]リミナルスペース

 定義 a type of venue that incorporates both physical and virtual elements
物理的な要素と仮想的な要素の両方が組み込まれた空間の一種

2030 People will spend the majority of each day in liminal space.
人々が一日の大半をリミナルスペースで過ごすようになるでしょう。

meatspace [名]現実世界、物質界

 定義 the physical world
物理的な世界

2030 Many older adults will reject meatspace for the sense of freedom provided by the metaverse.
多くの高齢者が、メタバースのもたらす自由な感覚を求めて、現実世界を拒絶するようになるでしょう。

digital twin [名]デジタルツイン

定義 a virtual replica of a physical object, process, or system, used for simulation, analysis, and optimization purposes
物体や工程、システムの仮想的な複製のことで、シミュレーションや分析、最適化などの目的で使われる

 2030 Digital twins will help doctors prescribe personalized medicine.
デジタルツインは、医師が個別化された医薬品を処方する際の助けになるでしょう。

avatar [名]アバター

定義 a digital representation of a user within a virtual or online environment, often used for communication and interaction
仮想環境やオンライン環境内におけるユーザーのデジタルな代役のことで、通常、コミュニケーションややり取りに使われる

 2030 A multibillion-dollar market will grow around avatar apparel and accessories.
アバターの衣料品やアクセサリーなどに関する、数十億ドル規模の市場が形成されるでしょう。

nanomedicine

068

［名］ナノメディシン、ナノ医療

解説

Nanomedicine is helping to revolutionize diagnostics and treatment options. Researchers are developing innovative drug delivery systems, such as nanobodies and designer proteins, that offer targeted and precise therapies. These breakthroughs enable improved efficacy and reduced side effects compared to traditional approaches. Additionally, the development of nanoscale medical devices opens up new possibilities for minimally invasive procedures and personalized treatments.

ナノメディシンは、診断や治療の選択肢を大きく変えるのに一役買っている。研究者たちは、ナノボディーや人工設計タンパク質などの革新的な薬物送達システムを開発し、標的を絞った精密な治療法を提供している。これらの画期的な技術により、従来の治療法と比較して、治療効果の向上と副作用の低減が実現した。さらに、ナノスケールの医療機器の開発によって、低侵襲治療や個別化治療の新たな可能性が広がっている。

---

 the medical application of nanotechnology, involving the use of nanoparticles and other nanoscale materials for diagnosis, treatment, and prevention of diseases

ナノテクノロジーの医学的応用のことで、ナノ粒子やその他のナノスケール素材を病気の診断や治療、予防に利用するもの

 Nanoscaffolds will play a crucial role in tissue engineering and regenerative medicine.

ナノスキャフォールドが、組織工学や再生医療で重要な役割を果たすでしょう。

nanobody [名]ナノボディー

 定義 a small antibody fragment derived from camelid antibodies, used in biomedical applications for its compact size and high binding specificity to target molecules
ラクダ科の動物の抗体に由来する小さな抗体断片のことで、コンパクトなサイズと標的分子への高い結合特異性から、バイオメディカルへの応用の目的で利用される

2030 Multifunctional nanobodies will simultaneously target multiple disease-related proteins.
多機能ナノボディーが、複数の疾患関連タンパク質を同時に狙えるようになるでしょう。

nanoparticle therapy [名]ナノ粒子治療

 定義 a treatment method that uses nanoparticles to deliver drugs or other therapeutic agents to specific cells or tissues, improving effectiveness and reducing side effects
ナノ粒子を用いて薬物などの治療薬を特定の細胞や組織に送達し、有効性を高めつつ副作用を低減する治療方法

2030 Novel nanoparticle designs will enable theranostics, simultaneous diagnostic imaging and therapeutic interventions.
革新的なナノ粒子の設計によって、画像診断と治療介入を同時に行うセラノスティックスを実現するでしょう。

designer protein [名]人工設計タンパク質

 定義 a protein engineered through computational or experimental methods to have specific functions, structures, or interactions, often used in research and biotechnology applications
コンピューターを使った方法や実験的手法を通じて設計されたタンパク質のことで、特定の機能や構造、相互作用を持ち、通常、研究やバイオテクノロジーへの応用に使われる

2030 Designer proteins will enable precise tuning of drug characteristics for improved effectiveness and safety.
人工設計タンパク質によって、薬物の特性が正確に調整できるようになり、効果や安全性が向上するでしょう。

synthetic antibody [名]合成抗体

 定義 an antibody molecule engineered through laboratory methods, designed to mimic or improve upon the functions of natural antibodies in the immune system
実験室的手法で作られた抗体分子のことで、免疫系における天然抗体の機能を模倣、あるいは改善するように設計されている

2030 The development of synthetic antibodies will accelerate the response to new disease threats.
合成抗体の開発は、新たな病気の脅威への対応を加速させるでしょう。

natural resources

069

［名］天然資源

解説

The world is gradually transitioning from fossil fuels to renewable sources of energy to the benefit of the planet. However, there are some **natural resources** that have no alternatives. Diminishing freshwater supplies are exacerbating a global water crisis, and five million hectares of forest are lost to deforestation each year. Conservation practices will have to change drastically.

世の中は、地球の利益を考えて、化石燃料から再生可能なエネルギー源へと徐々に移行している。しかし、代替のきかない天然資源もある。淡水の減少が地球規模での水の危機を悪化させ、毎年500万ヘクタールの森林が伐採によって失われている。保全活動は抜本的に変わらざるを得ないだろう。

定義 materials and substances, such as water, minerals, and timber, that occur in nature and can be utilized by living organisms for their survival and well-being

水や鉱物、木材などの素材や物質で、自然界に存在し、生物の生存や繁栄のために利用可能なもの

 Extraction of many natural resources will become more difficult due to depletion.

多くの天然資源が枯渇し、採掘が困難になるでしょう。

photovoltaic ［形］光起電性の、太陽光発電の

定義 referring to the conversion of sunlight into electricity through the use of solar cells, which generate a flow of electrons when exposed to light

光が当たると電子の流れが発生する太陽電池を使って、太陽光を電気に変換する

 The efficiency of photovoltaic cells will improve, reducing the cost of solar energy.
太陽電池の効率が向上し、太陽光発電のコストが削減されるでしょう。

thermohaline ［形］熱塩の

定義 referring to the combined effects of temperature and salinity on the circulation and movement of ocean waters, which influence global climate patterns and marine ecosystems

海水の循環と移動に温度と塩分が複合的に影響し、地球の気候パターンや海洋生態系に影響を与えるような

 Climate change will disrupt the thermohaline circulation, causing a significant impact on global climate patterns.
気候変動が熱塩の循環を破壊し、地球の気候パターンに大きな影響を与えるでしょう。

fossil fuel ［名］化石燃料

定義 a non-renewable energy source derived from the remains of ancient plants and animals, such as coal, oil, and natural gas, that releases greenhouse gases when burned

再生不可能なエネルギー源で、太古の動植物の遺骸から得られるもの。石炭、石油、天然ガスなどがあり、燃えると温室効果ガスを発する

 Regulations and public opinion will increasingly turn against the use of fossil fuels due to their environmental impact.
環境への影響の問題から、規制や世論がますます化石燃料の使用を抑え込む方向へ進むでしょう。

reforestation ［名］森林再生

定義 the process of replanting and reestablishing forests in areas where they have been depleted or destroyed, often for ecological restoration, carbon sequestration, and habitat recovery

森林が枯渇したり破壊されたりした地域に再植林し、森林を再建する工程。多くの場合、生態系の回復や二酸化炭素の吸収、生息地の回復が目的

 Reforestation activities will increasingly rely on drones.
森林再生活動は、ますますドローンに依存するでしょう。

net-zero

［名］正味ゼロ

070

解説

There is growing evidence **net-zero** policies help companies make out better in the long run. Research has shown that companies with strong environmental, social, and governance (ESG) performance have better risk management, improved operational efficiency, higher innovation capacity, and enhanced brand reputation. Furthermore, investors and consumers increasingly favor companies that demonstrate a commitment to sustainability.

正味ゼロ政策が、長期的に企業の利益向上に寄与することが、ますます裏付けられるようになっている。調査によると、環境・社会・ガバナンス（ESG）のパフォーマンスが高い企業は、リスク管理に優れており、業務効率が向上し、イノベーション能力が高く、ブランド評価が高いことが分かっている。さらに、投資家や消費者は、持続可能性への関与を示す企業をますます支持するようになっている。

定義 a state where the amount of greenhouse gas emissions produced is balanced by the amount of emissions removed from the atmosphere, resulting in no net contribution to global warming

温室効果ガスの排出量と大気から除去される排出量が均衡している状態のことで、地球温暖化への正味の寄与がなくなる

Net-zero progress will fall short of what scientists deem necessary.
正味ゼロが進展しても、科学者が必要と考えるレベルには達しないでしょう。

carbon offset ［名］カーボンオフセット

定義 a reduction, removal, or avoidance of greenhouse gas emissions in one location, used to compensate for or "offset" an equivalent amount of emissions produced elsewhere

ある場所での温室効果ガスの排出の削減、除去、または回避のことで、他の場所で発生する同量の排出を補償または「相殺」するために用いられる

 Several carbon-offset programs will be eliminated for being ineffective and others will take their place.

いくつかのカーボンオフセットの制度は、効果がないとして廃止され、他の制度に代替されるでしょう。

carbon sequestration ［名］炭素隔離

定義 the long-term removal and storage of carbon dioxide through biological, geological, or technological means, preventing its release into the atmosphere and helping to offset the accumulation of greenhouse gases

生物学的、地質学的、技術的な手段によって二酸化炭素を長期的に除去・貯蔵することで、大気中への放出を防ぐとともに、温室効果ガスの蓄積を相殺する

 Large-scale geologic carbon sequestration will take place.
大規模な地中での炭素隔離が行われるようになるでしょう。

carbon sink ［名］二酸化炭素吸収源

定義 a natural or artificial reservoir that absorbs and stores more carbon dioxide from the atmosphere than it releases, such as forests, oceans, or carbon capture and storage facilities

大気中の二酸化炭素を放出する量よりも多く吸収・貯留する天然または人工のため池で、森林や海洋、二酸化炭素回収・貯留施設などがある

 Large newly planted forests will help serve as carbon sinks.
大規模な新規の植林地が、二酸化炭素吸収源として機能するようになるでしょう。

emissions ［名］排出物、排出量、排出

定義 the release of gases, particles, or other substances into the atmosphere, often as a byproduct of human activities, such as burning fossil fuels, industrial processes, or transportation

大気中に放出されたガスや粒子、その他の物質のことで、化石燃料の燃焼や工業的処理、輸送などの人間の活動の副産物

 Coal production will gradually fall, resulting in a decrease in greenhouse gas emissions.

石炭の生産量が徐々に減少し、その結果、温室効果ガスの排出量が減少するでしょう。

neurotypical

071

［形］神経が標準的な、神経学的機能が正常な

解説

The modern world increasingly recognizes the spectrum of neurodiversity, honoring both **neurotypical** and neurodivergent individuals. While there has been progress in challenging stigmas and offering support for neuro-divergent individuals, systemic barriers and prejudices persist. Embracing neurodiversity necessitates societal shifts in perception, promoting inclusivity in all aspects of life, including education, employment, and public discourse.

現代社会では、神経多様性の範囲についていっそう認識が高まり、神経が標準的な人と多様な人の両方が尊重されている。しかし、汚名をすすぎ、神経多様性を抱える人への支援を提供するという点では進歩が見られるものの、制度的な障壁や偏見は依然として残っている。神経多様性を受け入れるには、社会的な認識の転換が必要であり、教育や雇用、公の場での議論といった生活のあらゆる側面で、包摂性を促進する必要がある。

定義 referring to individuals whose cognitive development and functioning are consistent with societal norms and expectations
人の認知の発達や機能が社会的な規範や期待に合致して

 Education systems will adjust to better cater to all learners, not just those who are neurotypical.
教育制度が、神経学的機能が正常な人たちだけでなく、すべての学習者に対応できるように調整されるでしょう。

normie [名] 普通の人、一般人、平凡な人

定義 a person who is perceived as conforming to mainstream culture, interests, or trends, often used in a derogatory or mocking manner

世の中の主流の文化や興味、傾向に適合していると見なされる人。たいてい、侮蔑的または嘲笑的な意味合いでこう呼ばれる

 The term "normie" will lose its derogatory connotation due to the mainstream acceptance and adoption of Internet culture.

インターネット文化の本流が受け入れられ、選ばれることによって、「普通の人」という言葉は蔑称的な意味合いを失っていくでしょう。

sensory [形] 感覚の、知覚の

定義 relating to the senses or the perception of sensory stimuli

感覚、あるいは感覚刺激の知覚に関連する

 Sensory-friendly environments will become standard in public spaces to accommodate people with sensory processing disorders.

公共の場において、知覚処理障害を持つ人に配慮した知覚に優しい環境が標準的なものになるでしょう。

stigma [名] 汚点、汚名

定義 a mark of disgrace or discredit, often arising from society's disapproval or judgment toward certain behaviors, characteristics, or conditions

不名誉や不信の印で、多くの場合、特定の行動や特性、状況に対する社会の非難や懲罰から生じる

 Greater emphasis on empathy in education will lead to a generation less likely to stigmatize others based on differences.

教育において共感力をより重視することで、違いを理由に他者に汚名を着せることの少ない世代が生まれるでしょう。

neurodivergent [形] 神経多様性の、神経的に多様な

定義 referring to individuals whose cognitive development and functioning differ from societal norms and expectations, often associated with conditions such as autism, ADHD, or dyslexia

人の認知の発達や機能が社会的な規範や期待とは異なって。しばしば自閉症、ADHD、失読症などの状態に関連して用いられる

 New technologies will provide better tools for neurodivergent individuals, allowing for improved communication, learning, and social interaction.

新しいテクノロジーは、コミュニケーションや学習、社会的相互作用の改善を可能にし、神経的に多様な人々にとってより良いツールを提供することになるでしょう。

non-binary

［形］（性自認が）ノンバイナリーの

072

解説

Identifying as **non-binary** in a predominantly binary-gendered society carries unique challenges. Public spaces, such as restrooms and changing rooms, are typically organized around a binary gender system, which can create discomfort and safety concerns for **non-binary** individuals. Language, too, has not caught up to the diverse spectrum of gender identities, often reinforcing a binary understanding of gender.

二元的な性別が主流の社会で、ノンバイナリーであることを認識するには、特有の課題を伴う。トイレや更衣室などの公共空間は、一般的に二元的な性別のシステムに基づいているため、ノンバイナリーな人にとっては不快感や安全上の懸念が生じる可能性がある。また、言語も多様な性自認に対応できておらず、多くの場合、二元的なジェンダーの理解を補強する結果となってしまっている。

定義 referring to individuals whose gender identity does not exclusively align with male or female categories, often existing outside or between these binary definitions
人の性自認が男性または女性の枠に限定されず、たいてい、その二元的な定義の外や中間に位置した

 All-gender bathrooms will make it easier for non-binary individuals to navigate public spaces.
オールジェンダー向けのトイレによって、ノンバイナリーの人たちが公共の場を歩き回りやすくなるでしょう。

queer ［形］クィアの

 ［定義］ referring to a wide range of non-heterosexual, non-cisgender identities and experiences
非異性愛者、非シスジェンダーなどの広範な性自認や経験に関する

 The term "queer" will continue to be reclaimed and used positively within the LGBTQIA+ community and beyond.
「クィア」という言葉は、LGBTQIA+ コミュニティー内外で磨き上げられ、ポジティブな意味合いで使われていくでしょう。

LGBT ［形］LGBT

［定義］ short for "lesbian, gay, bisexual, and transgender," referring to individuals or communities whose sexual orientation or gender identity falls under these categories
「レズビアン、ゲイ、バイセクシャル、トランスジェンダー」の頭字語。人や集団の性的指向や性自認がこれらの枠組みに該当した

 Contributions of past LGBT artists will become more widely recognized.
過去の LGBT アーティストたちの貢献がより広く認知されるようになるでしょう。

LGBTQIA+ ［形］LGBTQIA+

［定義］ referring to the broader spectrum of sexual orientations and gender identities by expanding upon LGBT to include queer, intersex, and asexual individuals
LGBT をクィア、インターセックス、アセクシャルに拡大することで、より幅広い性的指向や性自認に関連した

 The LGBTQIA+ acronym will continue to evolve to be more inclusive of all identities within the community.
LGBTQIA+ という頭字語は進化を続け、世の中のあらゆる性自認を包含するまでになるでしょう。

out ［動］〜を暴露する、〜をアウティングする

［定義］ to reveal someone's sexual orientation or gender identity to others, often done without consent
ある人の性的指向や性自認を、たいていは同意なしに他人に明かす

 Coming out stories will be more common and diversified in media.
カミングアウトに関わるエピソードが、メディアでより一般的かつ多様化して伝えられるようになるでしょう。

073

off-grid

［形］オフグリッドな、送電線網に依存しない

解説

As the global population becomes increasingly concentrated in dense urban centers, there are those who choose to reject modern comforts by adopting **off-grid** living. Some seek only to escape the bustle of the city. Others consider it their responsibility to pursue a more sustainable existence by reducing their ecological footprint and reconnecting with nature.

世界の人口がますます都心部に集中する中で、現代的な快適さを求めずに、オフグリッドな暮らしを選ぶ人たちがいる。単に都会の喧騒から逃れようとする人もいる。他方で、エコロジカルフットプリントを減らし、自然とのつながりを取り戻すことで、より持続可能な生活を追求するのが自分の責務だと考える人もいる。

定義 referring to a lifestyle or mode of living that emphasizes self-sufficiency in electricity generation, often achieved through the use of renewable energy sources and off-grid power systems

自給自足を重視するライフスタイルや生活様式に関連するような。こうした様式は、再生可能エネルギー源やオフグリッド電力システムの利用によって実現されることが多い

 Renewable technologies will enable more people to live off-grid, even in environments where the grid is readily available.

再生可能エネルギーの技術によって、送電線が容易に利用できる環境でも、より多くの人がオフグリッドな生活を送ることが可能になるでしょう。

Related Words and Phrases
関連語

cord-cutter [名]コードカッター、ケーブルテレビを解約してインターネットの動画視聴を選択する人

 定義 an individual who has chosen to cancel or forgo traditional cable or satellite television subscriptions in favor of alternative media sources, such as streaming services, online content, or over-the-air broadcasts

従来のケーブルテレビや衛星放送の受信契約を解除または見送った人のこと。代わりにストリーミングサービスやオンラインコンテンツ、地上波放送などの代替メディアを選択する

2030 The majority of people will be cord-cutters.
大半の人がコードカッターになるでしょう。

digital nomad [名]ノマドワーカー、デジタル遊牧民

 定義 a person who leverages technology to work remotely while traveling or living in different locations, often utilizing Internet connectivity and portable devices to maintain their career and lifestyle

テクノロジーを活用して、旅をしながら、あるいは転居を繰り返しながらリモートで仕事をする人のことで、多くの場合、インターネット接続と携帯端末を利用しながらキャリアとライフスタイルを維持している

2030 Worldwide Internet availability will enable more people to embrace a digital nomad lifestyle.
インターネットの世界的普及によって、より多くの人々がデジタルノマド生活を楽しめるようになるでしょう。

telework [名]テレワーク、リモートワーク

 定義 a work arrangement in which employees perform their job duties remotely, often from home, using communication technologies to stay connected with colleagues, clients, or supervisors

従業員が通信技術を使って同僚や顧客、上司と連絡を取り合いながら、多くの場合、自宅から遠隔で職務を遂行する労務形態のこと

2030 XR technologies will improve the ability for people to collaborate at a distance, making telework more palatable to corporations.
クロスリアリティーの技術によって、離れた場所での協働が可能となり、企業にとってテレワークがより身近なものになるでしょう。

expatriate [名]国外居住者

 定義 a person who lives outside their native country
母国の外で暮らす人

2030 The ease with which people can work remotely will encourage many to try living abroad.
リモートワークが容易になり、皆が国外に住んでみようという気になるでしょう。

147

open-source

［形］オープンソースの

解説

More than 95% of the top one million web servers use the Linux operating system. It is thanks to the contributions of countless developers and the collaborative nature of **open-source** software that Linux has become the backbone of the Internet. Its reliability, scalability, and extensive customization options have made it the preferred choice for businesses and organizations worldwide.

上位100万台のウェブサーバーの95パーセント以上で、リナックスOSが使用されている。リナックスがインターネットのバックボーンとなったのは、無数の開発者による貢献と、オープンソースのソフトウェアとしての共同開発の土壌のおかげである。その信頼性と拡張性、豊富なカスタマイズの選択肢によって、リナックスは世界中の企業や組織に選ばれてきたのだ。

定義 referring to a collaborative approach where users can freely view, modify, and share the source code or design of a product
ユーザーが製品のソースコードや設計を自由に閲覧、修正、共有できる共同作業的手法の

 Viable open-source options will force many major commercial software producers to change their business models.
有効性の高いオープンソースの選択肢が広がり、多くの大手商用ソフトウェアメーカーがビジネスモデルの変更を迫られるでしょう。

open access [名]オープンアクセス、自由な利用

定義 a movement that makes research publications and data freely available online without restrictions, promoting knowledge sharing
研究発表やデータをオンラインで制限なく自由に利用できるようにして、知識の共有を促進する動き

 Open access will become the norm, making scholarly research and scientific knowledge freely accessible to all.
オープンアクセスが当たり前になり、学術研究や科学的知識を誰でも自由に活用できるようになるでしょう。

Linux [名]リナックス

定義 a widely used open-source operating system (OS) based on the UNIX operating system and developed by Linus Torvalds
広く使われているオープンソースの基本ソフト（OS）で、UNIX OS をベースにリーナス・トーバルズによって開発された

 As the number of electronic devices increases in people's homes, so will the number of operating systems.
人々の家庭に電子機器が増えるほど、基本ソフトの数も増えていくでしょう。

operating system [名]基本ソフト、OS

定義 a software component that manages and controls computer hardware and software resources, providing a platform for applications to run and enabling users to interact with the computer system
コンピューターのハードウェアとソフトウェアのリソースを管理・制御し、アプリケーションの実行プラットフォームを提供し、ユーザーがコンピューターシステムと対話することを可能にするソフトウェアコンポーネント

 All major operating systems will provide for seamless integration among multiple devices.
主要な OS はどれも、複数の機器の間のシームレスな統合を実現するでしょう。

platform [名]プラットフォーム、基盤

定義 a base technology or framework on which software applications are developed and run, often including an operating system and other components
ソフトウェアアプリケーションを開発・実行するための基本技術や枠組みのことで、基本ソフトやその他のコンポーネントを含むことが多い

 Preferred online platforms will prioritize privacy and security, implementing robust encryption and data protection measures.
望ましいオンラインプラットフォームは、プライバシーやセキュリティーを優先し、強固な暗号化およびデータ保護対策を実施するものになるでしょう。

075

organic

［形］有機的な、オーガニックな

解説

The nutritional value of produce has been declining since the mid-20th century. Many fruits and vegetables have less protein, calcium, vitamin C, and other essential nutrients. While **organic** produce can be healthier than conventionally grown produce for a number of reasons, agriculture practices will have to change to restore the nutritional integrity of our crops.

20世紀半ば以降、農産物の栄養価は低下している。多くの果物や野菜に含まれるタンパク質やカルシウム、ビタミンCなどの必須栄養素の量が、減っているのだ。有機農産物は、さまざまな理由で、従来の方法で栽培された農産物よりも健康的だと言えるが、その一方で、農産物の栄養面での完全性を回復させるためには、農業のやり方を変えなければならないだろう。

---

 referring to agricultural methods that prioritize natural processes, avoiding synthetic chemicals and promoting ecological balance
自然のプロセスを優先し、合成化学物質を避け、生態系のバランスを促進する農法の

 Organic food producers will face increased scrutiny to ensure that products adhere to safe and healthy production methods.
有機食品の生産者は、製品が安全で健康的な生産方法を遵守して作られたかどうかを、いっそう監視されることになるでしょう。

aquaponics　［名］アクアポニックス

 a sustainable farming system that combines aquaculture with hydroponics in a symbiotic environment, where fish waste provides nutrients for plants, and plants filter and purify the water for the fish
共生型の環境で養殖と水耕栽培を組み合わせた、持続可能な農業システムで、魚の排泄物が植物の栄養分となり、植物は魚のために水をろ過して浄化する

Large-scale aquaponics systems will supply major cities with produce and seafood.
大規模なアクアポニックスのシステムが、主要都市に農産物や魚介類を供給することになるでしょう。

blue food　［名］ブルーフード

 edible aquatic organisms, such as fish, shellfish, and algae
魚介類や藻類など、食用の水生生物

The salmon aquaculture industry will grow significantly.
サケの養殖産業が大きく成長するでしょう。

hydroponics　［名］水耕法

 a method of growing plants in a nutrient-rich water solution without soil
土を使わずに栄養豊富な水で植物を栽培する方法

The global hydroponics industry will exceed $10 billion.
世界の水耕法産業は 100 億ドル規模を超えるでしょう。

vertical farm　［名］垂直農法

 a farming method in which crops are grown in vertically stacked layers, often using hydroponic or aeroponic systems, to optimize space, resources, and production in urban environments
作物を垂直に積み重ねた層で栽培する農法で、多くの場合、水耕栽培や空中栽培の仕組みが使われる。都市環境において、スペースや資源、生産を最適化することが目的

Large-scale vertical farms will appear in many major metropolitan areas.
大規模な垂直農場が、大都市圏に多数出現することになるでしょう。

overexploitation

076

［名］乱獲、乱開発

Regulations can only do so much to prevent **overexploitation**. Some organizations ignore them, prioritizing short-term profits over long-term sustainability. But in cases where communities rely on activities like fishing or mining as their source of livelihood, the need for immediate survival may take precedence over conservation efforts and catch limits. There is no simple solution.

規制によって過剰な開発を防ぐのには限界がある。組織によってはルールを無視して、長期的な持続可能性よりも短期的な利益を優先する。一方で、地域社会が漁業や採掘などの活動に生計を依存している場合、目先の生活維持の必要性が、保全努力や漁獲制限より優先されることもある。単純な解決策はない。

定義 the excessive use or extraction of natural resources, such as minerals, water, or timber, at a rate that exceeds their capacity for regeneration or renewal

天然資源を過度に使用または採取すること。鉱物や水、木材などが対象で、それらの再生能力を超える割合で採取される

Overexploitation will result in the loss of a significant portion of the Amazon rainforest.

乱開発により、アマゾンの熱帯雨林のかなりの部分が失われてしまうでしょう。

catch limit [名]漁獲量制限

 a regulatory measure that sets the maximum amount of fish or other marine species that can be caught within a specific time period or area to prevent overfishing

特定の時期や地域内で獲得できる魚などの海洋生物の最大量を設定する規制措置のことで、乱獲の防止が目的

 New technologies will enable real-time monitoring of catch limits, reducing overfishing violations.

新しい技術によって、漁獲量制限のリアルタイムの監視が可能となり、魚の乱獲が減少するでしょう。

marine protected area [名]海洋保護区域

 a designated region of the ocean or coastal waters that is managed for the conservation of its natural resources, biodiversity, and ecosystem services

海洋や沿岸水域の指定された区域のことで、天然資源や生物の多様性、生態系サービスの保全のために管理されている

The global surface area covered by marine protected areas will double.

地球の表面のうち、海洋保護区域の占める割合が倍増するでしょう。

overfishing [名]魚の乱獲

 the practice of catching fish at a rate that exceeds their ability to reproduce and maintain sustainable populations

魚の繁殖能力や持続可能な個体数を維持する能力を超える割合で、魚を捕獲すること

Overfishing of apex predators will lead to a trophic cascade, increasing jellyfish populations in affected areas.

頂点捕食魚の乱獲が栄養カスケードを引き起こし、影響を受けた地域のクラゲの個体数を増加させるでしょう。

aquatic conservation [名]水環境の保全

 the systematic and deliberate efforts aimed at protecting, preserving, and restoring the health, biodiversity, and integrity of aquatic ecosystems, including freshwater and marine environments

淡水および海洋の環境を含む水生生態系の健全性や生物多様性、完全性などの保護・保全・回復を目的とした体系的で意図的な取り組み

A wave of global initiatives like the SDGs will bring further attention to aquatic conservation activities.

SDGs のような世界的な取り組みの波が、水環境の保全活動へのさらなる注目を集めるでしょう。

planetary defense

077

[名] 惑星防衛

解説

On September 26, 2022, NASA successfully carried out its Double Asteroid Redirection Test (DART), using a kinetic impact to knock an asteroid off its course. But the true mission has only just begun. Scientists will continue to collect and analyze data from the impact to determine what lessons they can apply to deflecting other asteroids.

2022年9月26日、NASAは、運動衝撃を利用して小惑星を軌道から外す「ダブル・アステロイド・リディレクション・テスト（DART）」に成功した。しかし、真のミッションはまだ始まったばかりだ。科学者たちは、この衝撃から得られたデータの収集・分析を続け、他の小惑星の軌道変更にどのような教訓を生かせるかを見極めるだろう。

定義 the collective efforts and strategies aimed at protecting Earth from potential impacts by near-Earth objects, such as asteroids or comets, through methods including detection, tracking, and mitigation

小惑星や彗星などの地球近傍天体による潜在的な影響から地球を守ることを目的とした、総合的な取り組みや戦略のことで、検出、追跡、緩和などの方法を通じて実行される

As our ability to detect potential threats improves, so will our measures to defend against them.

潜在的な脅威を防ぐ能力が向上するにつれて、脅威を防御するための対策も向上するでしょう。

asteroid mining [名]アステロイドマイニング、小惑星での採鉱

[定義] the exploitation of raw materials from asteroids and other minor planets, including near-Earth objects
小惑星や地球近傍天体を含む小惑星から原料物質を採取すること

 The asteroid mining industry won't take off for decades, but private and government organizations will start conducting tests.
小惑星での採掘事業が本格化するのは数十年後でしょうが、民間企業や政府機関が実験を開始するでしょう。

asteroid redirection [名]小惑星方向転換、小惑星軌道変更

[定義] the act of altering the course of an asteroid to prevent a collision with Earth
小惑星の進路を変更することで、地球への衝突を防ぐことが目的

 Space agencies will test a number of methods for preventing asteroids from colliding with Earth.
宇宙機関は、小惑星の地球への衝突を防ぐためのさまざまな方策を検証するでしょう。

moonbase [名]ムーンベース

[定義] a base on the surface of the moon
月面の基地

 NASA will begin laying the groundwork for the first moonbase.
NASA が最初の月面基地の土台作りを開始するでしょう。

planetbase [名]プラネットベース

[定義] a settlement or base established on another planet, with the aim of supporting human habitation or scientific exploration
他の惑星に確立された入植地や基地のことで、人間の居住や科学的な探査の支援が目的

 The first manned trip to Mars will occur in the 2030s, and the first planetbase on Mars will be built before 2050.
2030 年代に最初の有人火星旅行が実現し、2050 年までには火星に最初のプラネットベースが建設されるでしょう。

pollution

078

［名］汚染

解説

Air pollution is the world's biggest killer, claiming millions of lives per year. It also negatively impacts ecosystems, leading to biodiversity loss and ecological imbalances. Efforts to reduce air **pollution** and improve air quality are crucial for safeguarding human health, protecting the environment, and ensuring a sustainable future for generations to come.

大気汚染は世界最大の殺し屋であり、年間数百万人の命を奪っている。また、生態系にも悪影響を及ぼし、生物多様性の損失や生態系の不均衡を引き起こしている。大気汚染を減らし、空気の質を改善する取り組みは、人の健康を守り、環境を保護し、次の世代のために持続可能な未来を確保するために極めて重要である。

定義 the presence or introduction of harmful or toxic substances, such as chemicals, waste, or noise, into the environment
化学物質や廃棄物、騒音などの有害、あるいは有毒な要素が環境の中に存在すること、または導入されること

Pollution will lead to the deaths of more than 10 million people per year.
汚染によって年間 1,000 万人を超える死者が出るでしょう。

atmosphere [名]大気

 定義 the layer of gases surrounding a planet
惑星を取り囲む気体の層

2030 The concentration of carbon in the atmosphere will continue to increase, although not as quickly.
大気中の二酸化炭素の濃度が、さほど急速ではないとしても、高まり続けるでしょう。

biodiversity loss [名]生物多様性の喪失

 定義 the decline in the variety and abundance of plant and animal species within an ecosystem
生態系内の動植物種の種類や量が減少すること

2030 The EU and various nations will establish legal frameworks and implement various strategies to combat biodiversity loss.
EU をはじめとするいくつかの国が、生物多様性の喪失をくい止めるための法的枠組みを確立し、さまざまな戦略を実施するでしょう。

biome [名]生物群系

 定義 a large, naturally occurring community of plants and animals occupying a major habitat, such as a forest, grassland, or desert, defined by its distinctive climate, flora, and fauna
自然に発生する大規模な動植物の群集で、森林や草原、砂漠などの主要な生息地を占めている。特有の気候や植物相、動物相によって定義される

2030 The melting permafrost, wildfires, and other natural disasters will lead to significant changes to the Arctic biome.
永久凍土の融解や山火事などの自然災害は、北極圏の生物群系に大きな変化をもたらすでしょう。

decarbonize [動]～を脱炭素化する、～から炭素を除去する

 定義 to reduce or eliminate carbon dioxide emissions from various sources, such as energy production, transportation, and industry, in order to mitigate the effects of climate change
エネルギー生産や輸送、工業といったさまざまな源から排出される二酸化炭素を削減または除去する。気候変動の影響を緩和することが目的

2030 Commercial incentives to decarbonize transportation, manufacturing, and other industries will increase.
輸送業や製造業などの産業が脱炭素化するための商業的動機づけが高まるでしょう。

preferred pronouns

079

［名］本人が望む代名詞

解説

Preferred pronouns have become an important aspect of personal identity and respectful communication as society becomes more aware of diverse gender identities. Many institutions, educational settings, and workplaces now encourage the sharing of **preferred pronouns** during introductions or in email signatures to promote a more respectful atmosphere and broader inclusivity.

社会が多様なジェンダーアイデンティティーを認識するようになるにつれ、本人が望む代名詞は、個人のアイデンティティーや敬意を払ってコミュニケーションを取る上で重要な一面を担うようになっている。現在、多くの組織や教育現場、職場で、より尊重された雰囲気といっそうの包摂性を促進するために、自己紹介やメールに署名を入れる際に自分が望む代名詞を共有することを奨励している。

定義 the pronouns that an individual identifies with and wants others to use when referring to them, such as "they," "she," or "he"

人が自分を識別したり、他人が自分を指すときに使ってほしい代名詞。例えば「彼ら」「彼女」「彼」など

 Preferred pronouns will be universally recognized and respected, leading to their normal use in all forms of communication.

本人が望む代名詞は、それが広く認識され、尊重されることによって、あらゆるコミュニケーションの場で当たり前に使われるようになるでしょう。

folx [名]人々、皆

 定義 an alternative and inclusive spelling of "folks," often used to emphasize diversity and inclusivity among a group of people, especially within LGBTQIA+ and other marginalized communities

folks（人々、皆）の代替的かつ包摂的な綴りで、特に LGBTQIA+ やその他の隅に追いやられたコミュニティーにおいて、人の集団の多様性と包摂性を強調するためによく使われる

2030 With the increased use of inclusive language, there will be a move toward creating new words to better represent diverse communities.

包摂的な言葉の使用が増えるにつれて、多様なコミュニティーをより適切に表現するための新しい言葉を作り出す動きが出てくるでしょう。

microaffirmation [名]マイクロアファーメーション

 定義 a subtle, positive action or expression that supports and validates someone's experiences or identity

誰かの経験やアイデンティティーを支持し、正当化する、目立たないポジティブな行動や表現のこと

2030 As understanding of the impact of microaffirmations grows, they will become a standard part of interpersonal communication.

マイクロアファーメーションは、その効果が理解されるにつれて、対人コミュニケーションの当たり前の一要素になるでしょう。

Mx. [名]ミクス

 定義 a gender-neutral title used as an alternative to gender-specific titles like Mr., Mrs., or Ms., often preferred by non-binary, genderqueer, or other individuals who do not identify with the traditional binary genders

ミスター、ミセス、ミズのような性別に特化した称号の代りに使用される、性別にとらわれない称号で、たいていは従来の二元的な性を自認しないノンバイナリー、ジェンダークィア、その他の人に好まれる

2030 "Mx." will be commonly used in TV programs and movies.

「ミクス」は、テレビ番組や映画などでよく使われるようになるでしょう。

y'all [名]あなたたち全員、皆

 定義 a contraction of "you all," commonly used in the Southern US as a plural, informal, and gender-neutral form of address that encompasses everyone within a group

you all（あなたたち全員、皆）の縮約形で、アメリカ南部でよく使われる。ある集団内の全員を包含する複数形であり、インフォーマルで性別にとらわれない形

2030 "Y'all" will be recognized as a gender-neutral, plural second-person pronoun in formal English language use.

「皆」は、正式な英語の用法において、性別にとらわれない二人称代名詞の複数形として認められるようになるでしょう。

radicalization

[名] 急進化、先鋭化、過激化

080

解説

Radicalization can happen in any country. It can take many forms, ranging from religious extremism to far-right or far-left political ideologies. The increasing use of online platforms and social media has made it easier for extremist groups to spread their messages and recruit new members. In countries where guns are easily accessible, **radicalization** can have especially dire consequences.

急進化はどこの国でも起こり得ることだ。宗教的な急進主義から極右や極左の政治的なイデオロギーまで、さまざまな形態を取り得る。オンラインプラットフォームやソーシャルメディアの利用が増えたことで、過激派グループが自分たちのメッセージを広め、新しいメンバーを募ることが容易になっている。銃が容易に手に入る国では、急進化が特に悲惨な結果をもたらす可能性がある。

定義 the process by which individuals or groups adopt increasingly extreme beliefs, often leading to support for or engagement in violent actions
個人または集団が次第に極端な信念を持つようになり、しばしば暴力的な行動を支持したり関与したりするようになる過程

Social media and online forums will lead to more radicalization of citizens of democratic countries.
SNS やオンラインフォーラムが、民主主義国の国民のさらなる過激化につながるでしょう。

indoctrination [名]洗脳、教化

 定義 the process of teaching someone to accept a set of beliefs uncritically, often through systematic instruction or propaganda
ある信念を無批判に受け入れるよう誰かに教える過程のことで、多くの場合、体系的な指導やプロパガンダを通じて行われる

2030 Extremist groups, cults, and ideological movements will continue to use online platforms to recruit and indoctrinate followers.
過激派集団やカルト、イデオロギー運動などが、今後もオンラインプラットフォームを使って支持者を募集し、教化していくでしょう。

mass shooting [名]銃乱射事件

 定義 an incident involving multiple victims of gun violence, typically occurring in a public place or at a gathering
複数名の被害者を出す銃による暴力事件のことで、通常、公共の場や集会で発生する

2030 The eventual passing of stricter gun laws will reduce the frequency of mass shootings in the US.
最終的に厳格な銃規制法が成立すれば、米国での銃乱射事件の発生頻度は低下するでしょう。

domestic terrorism [名]国内テロ

 定義 acts of terrorism or violence committed by individuals or groups within their own country, targeting civilians or infrastructure
自国内の個人または集団が、民間人やインフラを標的にして行うテロ行為、または暴力行為

2030 Domestic terrorist plots will predominantly stem from individuals aligned with the right side of the political spectrum.
国内のテロ計画は、政治的に右派に属する個人が主体となるでしょう。

separatist [名]分離主義者、分離派

 定義 an individual or group advocating for the separation or independence of a region or group from a larger political entity
ある地域や集団がより大きな政治体制から分離・独立することを主張する、個人または集団

2030 Hardline policies by several major economies will inadvertently stoke the radicalization of the separatist movements they are trying to suppress.
いくつかの主要経済国による強硬な政策は、そうした国々が抑え込もうとしている分離主義運動の過激化を不用意にあおることになるでしょう。

161

regenerative medicine

081

［名］再生医療

解説

Scientists have made significant strides in harnessing stem cells to treat a wide range of conditions, from cardiovascular diseases to neurodegenerative disorders. Tissue engineering, another key aspect of **regenerative medicine**, involves creating artificial organs, scaffolds, and biomaterials to facilitate tissue repair and regeneration. 3D bioprinting and organoids have opened new avenues for creating complex tissues and organs in the lab.

科学者たちは、心血管疾患から神経変性疾患まで、幅広い疾患の治療に幹細胞を利用することで大きな進歩を遂げました。組織工学は、再生医療のもう一つの重要な側面であり、組織の修復や再生を促進するために、人工臓器、足場、生体材料を作ることです。3Dバイオプリンティングとオルガノイドは、研究室で複雑な組織や臓器を作るための新たな道を開いています。

---

 a field of medical research focused on the repair, replacement, or regeneration of cells, tissues, and organs to restore or establish normal function
正常な機能を回復または確立するために、細胞、組織、および臓器の修復、置換、または再生に焦点を当てた医学研究の一分野

 The creation of complex organ systems will lead to a significant decrease in organ donation waitlists.
複合臓器システムの構築が、臓器提供の待機者の大幅な減少につながるでしょう。

gene editing [名] 遺伝子編集

 a technique that enables scientists to modify an organism's genetic material by adding, deleting, or altering specific genes to achieve a desired outcome
遺伝子の追加、削除、変更によって生物の遺伝物質を改変し、望ましい結果を得る技術

2030 Gene editing will move beyond treatment to prevention, with early life-stage interventions becoming more common to eliminate genetic diseases before symptoms appear.
遺伝子編集は、治療から予防へと進み、症状が出る前に遺伝的疾病をなくすために、早い段階から介入することが一般的になるでしょう。

stem cell [名] 幹細胞

 a type of undifferentiated cell that possesses the ability to self-renew and differentiate into specialized cell types, forming the foundation for the growth, development, and repair of various tissues and organs in the body
未分化な細胞の一種で、自己複製能力や特殊な細胞への分化能力を持ち、体内のさまざまな組織や臓器の成長、発達、修復の基礎を形成する

2030 Patients' stem cells will be used for custom organ regeneration.
患者の幹細胞が、個別の臓器再生に使われるようになるでしょう。

CRISPR [名] クリスパー

 a gene editing technology that uses a specific enzyme, Cas9, to target and modify specific DNA sequences within the genome of an organism
遺伝子編集技術の一つで、Cas9 という特定の酵素を用いて、生物のゲノム内の特定の DNA 配列を狙って改変するもの

2030 CRISPR will extend beyond healthcare to producing disease-resistant crops.
クリスパーは、医療だけでなく、病気に強い農作物の生産にまで広がっていくでしょう。

cloning [名] クローン作成、クローニング

 the process of creating a genetically identical copy of an organism or a cell
遺伝的に同一の生物または細胞の複製を作成する工程

2030 Cloning will help produce genetically compatible organs for transplantation without the risk of rejection.
クローニングによって、拒絶反応のない、遺伝的に適合した移植用臓器が作られるでしょう。

082

renewable energy

［名］再生可能エネルギー

The transition to **renewable energy** is picking up steam. For nine hours on May 16, 2023, **renewable energy** met 100% of Spain's electricity demands, and such milestones are becoming frequent. The adoption of electric vehicles and energy-efficient appliances is also helping to support the shift toward **renewable energy**. A greener future is on the horizon.

再生可能エネルギーへの移行が加速している。2023年5月16日の9時間、再生可能エネルギーがスペインの電力需要の100パーセントを満たした。そして、こうした節目となる出来事の頻繁が高まってきている。電気自動車や省エネ家電の普及も、再生可能エネルギーへの移行を後押ししている。環境にやさしい未来は、すぐそこまで来ている。

定義　energy derived from resources that are naturally replenished, such as sunlight, wind, water, and geothermal heat
太陽光や風力、水力、地熱など、自然に補充される源から得られるエネルギー

2030　Around two-thirds of all energy needs will be satisfied by renewable energy by 2030.
2030年までには、全エネルギー需要の約3分の2が再生可能エネルギーでまかなわれるようになるでしょう。

hydropower [名]水力発電

定義 the generation of electricity by harnessing the energy of moving water, typically through the use of dams or other infrastructure that captures and channels water flow

水流のエネルギーを利用した発電のことで、一般的には、ダムをはじめ、水流を捕まえて他へ送り出すようなインフラを使用する

2030 Hydropower will account for around 20% of the world's total electricity generation.

水力発電は、世界の総発電量の約 20 パーセントを占めることになるでしょう。

nuclear fusion [名]核融合

定義 a nuclear reaction in which atomic nuclei combine to form heavier nuclei, releasing a large amount of energy

原子核が結合してより重い原子核を形成し、大量のエネルギーを放出する核反応

2030 Scientists will achieve more nuclear fusion milestones, but the technology won't be widely used for decades to come.

科学者たちは核融合の一里塚をさらに築いていくでしょうが、この技術が広く使われるようになるのは数十年先のことでしょう。

geothermal [形]地熱の

定義 referring to the heat energy stored within Earth's interior, which can be harnessed for electricity generation, heating, and cooling

地球の内部に蓄積された、発電や冷暖房に利用可能な熱エネルギーの

2030 Geothermal heating and cooling systems will be integrated with smart home technology.

地熱を利用した冷暖房システムが、スマートホームの技術と融合するでしょう。

solar park [名]ソーラーパーク

定義 a large-scale installation of solar panels, often covering many acres, that generates electricity by capturing sunlight and converting it into electrical energy through photovoltaic cells

大規模なソーラーパネルの設置施設で、多くの場合、何エーカーにも及ぶ。そこでは、太陽光を取り込み、光電池を通して電気エネルギーに変換することで発電を行う

2030 Solar park growth will accelerate, reaching a market size of more than $250 billion.

ソーラーパークの成長は加速し、2,500 億ドルを超える市場規模に達するでしょう。

security vulnerability

083

［名］セキュリティーの脆弱性

解説

The digital world is made of Swiss cheese. Skilled hackers, whether lone warriors or state-backed organizations, are always looking for new—and sometimes old—**security vulnerabilities** to exploit. And no system is ever 100% secure. People must consider the best practices to follow with regard to privacy and digital security in light of this reality.

デジタル社会は、スイスチーズのように穴だらけだ。熟練したハッカーは、一匹狼であろうと国家の支援を受けた組織であろうと、常に新たな——時には古い——セキュリティーの脆弱性を探し、つけ込もうとしている。しかも、100パーセント安全なシステムなど存在しない。人々は、こうした現実を踏まえて、プライバシーとデジタルセキュリティーに関して取るべき最善策を考えなければならない。

---

 a weakness or flaw in a computer system, network, or software that an attacker can exploit to gain unauthorized access, compromise data, or cause other harm

コンピューターシステムやネットワーク、ソフトウェアの弱点または欠陥のこと。攻撃者はこれを悪用して、不正アクセスやデータの漏洩などの損害を与える

 Blockchain technology will be used to secure critical infrastructure, significantly reducing security vulnerabilities.

ブロックチェーン技術が、重要なインフラの保安に活用され、セキュリティーの脆弱性を大幅に低減するでしょう。

ransomware　[名]ランサムウェア、身代金要求型不正プログラム

[定義] a type of malicious software that encrypts a victim's files, preventing access until a ransom is paid, often in the form of cryptocurrency
悪意のあるソフトウェアの一種で、被害者のファイルを暗号化し、身代金を支払うまでアクセスできないようにする。多くの場合、身代金は暗号通貨の形で支払われる

 Ransomware attacks on IoT devices will increase.
IoT 機器へのランサムウェア攻撃が増加するでしょう。

malware　[名]マルウェア、悪意のあるソフトウェア

[定義] software designed to disrupt a computer's normal operation
コンピューターの正常な動作を妨害するように設計されたソフトウェア

 Malware will become increasingly AI-driven.
マルウェアは、ますます AI を活用したものになっていくでしょう。

spyware　[名]スパイウェア

[定義] malicious software that secretly monitors and collects information about a user's activities, often for the purpose of identity theft, fraud, or targeted advertising
ユーザーの行動を密かに監視し、情報を収集する悪意のあるソフトウェアのことで、多くの場合、個人情報の窃盗や詐欺、ターゲット広告を目的としている

 Spyware attacks on wearable devices will result in people carrying spyware wherever they go.
ウェアラブルデバイスへのスパイウェア攻撃によって、結果的に人々がどこへ行くにもスパイウェアを持ち歩くことになってしまうでしょう。

zero-day　[形]ゼロデイの、セキュリティー対策が講じられる前日の

[定義] referring to a security vulnerability that is unknown to the software developer or security researchers, making it particularly dangerous as there may be no existing defenses or patches to prevent exploitation
ソフトウェア開発者やセキュリティー研究者が知らないセキュリティー脆弱性の。悪用を防ぐための防御策やパッチが存在しない可能性があるので、特に危険性が高い

 Zero-day exploits will regularly take parts of the metaverse offline.
ゼロデイの脆弱性のせいで、メタバースの一部が定期的につながらなくなるでしょう。

sex positivity

[名]セックスポジティブ運動

084

解説

Sex positivity encompasses a broad range of issues and perspectives, including LGBTQIA+ rights, reproductive rights, body positivity, kink and BDSM, sex education reform, and the destigmatization of sexual topics and practices. It aims to create a more inclusive, equitable, and sex-positive society that values sexual diversity, pleasure, and well-being. It does not endorse or promote harmful or non-consensual behavior.

セックスポジティブ運動は幅広い問題や視点を包含しており、そこには LGBTQIA+の権利、女性の生殖権、ボディーポジティブ運動、性倒錯や BDSM、性教育改革、性的な話題や性的行為の汚名返上などがある。これが目指しているのは、性の多様性や喜び、幸福を大切にする、より包括的で公平な、セックスに対してポジティブな社会の実現だ。有害な、あるいは非合理的な行為を推奨したり促進したりするものではない。

定義 a social and cultural movement advocating for open and non-judgmental attitudes toward sexuality, emphasizing consent, safety, and respect for individual preferences

セックス・性的指向に対して開かれた、偏見のない態度を提唱する社会的・文化的な運動のことで、同意、安全、個人的嗜好の尊重に重きが置かれている

2030 Sex education will become a more divisive topic as some schools embrace an increasingly sex-positive approach.

性教育は、一部の学校がセックスポジティブな考え方を取り入れることによって、より議論の分かれるテーマとなるでしょう。

body positivity ［名］ボディーポジティブ運動

定義 a movement that encourages individuals to accept and celebrate their bodies, regardless of size, shape, or appearance, promoting self-love and challenging societal beauty standards

自分の体を受け入れ、祝福することを奨励する運動のことで、体の大きさや形、外見に関係なく自己への愛情を促し、世の中の美の基準に異議を唱えるもの。

 Body positivity will extend beyond size and weight, embracing diverse body types, shapes, and appearances.

ボディーポジティブ運動は、体の大きさや体重だけでなく、多様な体形や体格、外見を受け入れるものになるでしょう。

emotional intelligence ［名］感情的知性、心の知能指数

定義 the ability to recognize, understand, and manage one's emotions and the emotions of others, allowing for improved communication, empathy, and interpersonal relationships

自分の感情や他人の感情を認識、理解、管理する能力のことで、コミュニケーションや共感、対人関係の改善を可能にするもの

 Emotional intelligence will be highly valued and taught in educational settings, workplaces, and homes.

心の知能指数は、教育現場た職場、家庭で高く評価され、教えられるようになるでしょう

asexual ［形］他者に性的魅力を感じない、セックスに興味のない

定義 referring to individuals who do not experience sexual attraction to others

人が他人に性的魅力を感じない

 There will be more widespread understanding and acceptance of what's estimated to be 1% of the global population.

世界人口の１パーセントと見積もられるようなことが、より広く理解され、受け入れられていくでしょう。

consent ［名］承諾、同意

定義 the voluntary, informed, and ongoing agreement between individuals to engage in a specific activity, particularly in sexual contexts, emphasizing respect and communication

個人間での自発的で、十分な情報を得た、継続的な合意のことで、特定の行為への関与を目的とし、特にセックスについて敬意と意思疎通を重視するもの

 Consent will be a standard part of education, promoting a culture of respect and understanding in interpersonal relationships.

合意が教育の当前の一面となり、対人関係において尊敬や理解の文化を促進するでしょう。

smartphone addiction

085

[名] スマホ中毒

解説

Constant connectivity and endless streams of information and entertainment provided by smartphones have changed the way people interact with the world and with each other. With the rise in mental health issues potentially linked to excessive device usage, there has been a push for viable solutions. Digital detoxes and self-imposed screen time limits are just a few that have emerged.

スマートフォンがもたらす絶え間のない接続性や、情報と娯楽の無限の流入は、人々の社会や他者との関わり方を変えてきた。スマホの使いすぎは精神的な問題につながる可能性があるため、その現実的な解決策を模索する動きが出てきた。デジタルデトックスやスクリーンタイムの自己制限は、そのようにして現れた例のほんの一部だ。

定義 compulsive and excessive use of smartphones, resulting in negative consequences to an individual's mental, emotional, and physical well-being
スマートフォンの強迫的かつ過剰な使用のことで、結果として人の精神的、感情的、身体的な幸福に対する否定的な影響をもたらす

 New regulations will be established to manage and reduce smartphone use, particularly among children and adolescents.
特に子どもや若者のスマートフォンの利用を管理・削減するための新たな規制が設けられるでしょう。

depression [名]うつ、うつ病、抑うつ症

定義 a mental disorder characterized by persistent sadness, loss of interest, and negative changes in thoughts, emotions, and behaviors

持続的な悲しみ、興味の喪失、思考・感情・行動の負の変化を特徴とする精神障害のこと

 Doctors will commonly prescribe psychedelic substances to treat severe depression.

医師は、重度のうつ病を治療するために、幻覚作用を持つ物質を普通に処方するようになるでしょう。

myopia [名]近視、近眼

定義 also known as nearsightedness, a visual condition in which close objects appear clearly, but distant objects appear blurred

nearsightedness とも呼ばれる、近くのものははっきり見えるが遠くのものはぼやけて見える視覚の状態のこと

 Digital screen usage will drive a shift in eye care toward myopia prevention, emphasizing interventions like outdoor time.

デジタル画面の使用によって、目の健康に関する重点が近視予防に移行し、屋外で過ごす時間などを取り入れることが重視されるでしょう。

social isolation [名]社会的孤立、社会的隔離

定義 a lack of social interaction or support, often resulting in feelings of loneliness and detachment from other people

社会的な交流や支援が不足していることで、結果として、孤独感を感じたり、他人から離れたりすることが多い

 Companion robots and virtual beings will offer company and interaction for those experiencing social isolation.

コンパニオンロボットや仮想人間が、社会的孤立を経験する人たちに他社との交流の機会を提供するでしょう。

text neck [名]スマホ首、テキストネック

定義 the strain on the neck and spine caused by constantly looking down at a smartphone or other electronic device

スマートフォンなどの電子機器を見続けることによる、首や背骨への負担

 Many people will experience permanent nerve damage due to years of suffering from text neck.

多くの人が、何年間もスマホ首に悩まされた末に、慢性的な神経疾患を抱えるでしょう。

social justice

［名］社会正義

086

解説

From the labor movements that arose during the Industrial Revolution to the US civil rights movement in the mid-20th century, various historical events and struggles have shaped the trajectory of **social justice**. Over time, **social justice** has expanded to encompass broader issues, including gender equality, LGBTQIA+ rights, environmental justice, and economic disparities.

産業革命期に起こった労働運動から20世紀半ばの米国の公民権運動まで、さまざまな歴史的出来事や闘争が社会正義の軌跡を形作ってきた。時を経て、社会正義は男女平等、LGBTQIA+の権利、環境正義、経済格差など、より広い問題を包含するまでに拡大した。

定義 the fair distribution of opportunities, resources, and rights within society, often associated with efforts to address systemic inequalities and empower marginalized communities

社会における機会、資源、権利の公正な配分のことで、多くの場合、制度的不平等に対処したり、疎外されたコミュニティーを強化したりする取り組みに関わる

Social justice issues will become more globalized, uniting people across countries and continents in pursuit of equality and fairness.

社会正義の問題はよりグローバル化し、平等と公平を追求するために国や大陸を越えて人々が団結するようになるでしょう。

BLM ［名］ブラック・ライブズ・マター運動、「黒人の命は大切だ」運動

 定義 short for "Black Lives Matter," a grassroots movement advocating for the rights and equality of Black individuals, addressing issues such as police brutality, racial profiling, and systemic racism

「黒人の命は大切だ」の頭字語で、黒人の権利と平等を主張する草の根運動のこと。警察の残虐行為、人種による選別や制度的人種差別などの問題に取り組むもの

2030 The success of BLM will inspire the creation of more movements advocating for marginalized groups.

ブラック・ライブズ・マター運動の成功によって、疎外された集団を擁護する、より多くの運動が生まれるでしょう。

---

code switch ［動］コードスイッチする、言説を変える

 定義 to alter one's speech, behavior, or appearance to conform to different social or cultural contexts

異なる社会的または文化的文脈に適合するように、自分の言動や外見を変える

2030 Social movements will challenge the necessity of code-switching, pushing for acceptance of all linguistic styles and dialects in all spaces.

社会運動によって、コードスイッチの必要性に異議が唱えられ、あらゆる場所であらゆる言葉や方言が受け入れられるように変わっていくでしょう。

---

empower ［動］〜を力づける、〜に自信を持たせる

 定義 to give someone the confidence, resources, or authority to take control of their own life, often associated with efforts to uplift marginalized communities and promote self-determination

自分自身の人生をコントロールする自信や能力、権限を誰かに与える。多くの場合、社会的に疎外されたコミュニティーを支援し、人々の自己決定を促進するような取り組みに関連する

2030 The idea of empowerment will shift from individual gain to collective upliftment, fostering communal support and mutual growth.

権限付与の考え方は、個人の利益から集団の向上へと移り、コミュニティーの支援や相互の成長を育むでしょう。

---

acculturation ［名］文化変容

 定義 the process by which individuals or groups adopt the cultural traits, values, and behaviors of another culture, often as a result of immigration, globalization, or extended exposure

個人または集団が他の地域や国の文化的特徴や価値感、行動を採用する過程のことで、多くの場合、移民やグローバル化、長期的な文化接触の結果である

2030 There will be a greater emphasis on reciprocal acculturation, where both newcomers and host cultures adapt and grow from the interaction.

互恵的な文化変容がより重視されるようになり、そこでは新たな文化に溶け込もうとする人たちと、それを受け入れる側の両者が互いに適応・成長し合うことになるでしょう。

Economy 経済

social welfare

［名］社会福祉

087

解説

Technology has the power to change **social welfare** in a variety of ways. Online tools can improve access to information and services, such as telemedicine. Data analytics can also help make welfare programs more efficient. However, as technology may also cause widespread job loss, it is important to consider how big a safety net is necessary.

テクノロジーは、さまざまな形で社会福祉を変える力を持っている。オンラインツールは、遠隔医療など、情報やサービスへのアクセスを改善することができる。また、データ分析によって、福祉プログラムをより効率化することが可能だ。しかし、テクノロジーは広く雇用の喪失を引き起こす可能性もはらんでいるため、どの程度の規模のセーフティーネットが必要なのかを考えることが重要だ。

定義 government programs and policies designed to support the well-being of citizens, particularly those facing financial or social difficulties
政府のプログラムおよび政策のうち、特に経済的な、あるいは社会的な困難に直面している市民の幸福を支援する目的で考案されたもの

 The US will start making much-needed progress supporting social welfare programs as more progressive youth reach voting age.
米国では、より多くの進歩的な若者が選挙権を持つ年齢に達するので、社会福祉制度の支援に不可欠な前進が始まるでしょう。

pension reform [名]年金改革

 定義 changes made to pension systems to address issues like sustainability, adequacy, and fairness for current and future retirees
現在および将来の退職者のための持続可能性、妥当性、公平性などの問題に対処するために、年金制度に加えられた変更

2030 Protests like those seen in France in 2023 will be held against controversial pension reform plans.
2023 年にフランスで見られたような抗議活動が、問題の多い年金改革計画に対して行われるでしょう。

pay gap [形]賃金格差

 定義 the difference in pay between two groups, often referring to the disparity between the earnings of men and women or different ethnic groups
2 つの集団の間の賃金の差のことで、多くの場合、男女または異なる民族間での収入の格差を指す

2030 AI and machine learning will be extensively used to evaluate pay equity.
賃金の公平性を評価するために、AI や機械学習が広範囲に活用されるようになるでしょう。

minimum wage [名]最低賃金

 定義 the lowest hourly wage that employers are required by law to pay to workers
雇用者が労働者に支払うことが法律で義務付けられている、最低の時間当たりの賃金

2030 A global economic shift will lead to the establishment of minimum income guarantees in several major economies.
世界経済の変化によって、いくつかの主要経済大国で最低所得保障が確立されるでしょう。

affordable housing [名]手頃な価格の住宅

 定義 housing that is reasonably priced, allowing individuals and families with low to moderate incomes to meet their basic needs without financial strain
合理的に値付けされた住宅のことで、低所得者から中程度の所得者とその家族が経済的負担なく基本的なニーズを満たせるもの

2030 Modular and 3D-printed homes will decrease the cost of housing construction.
モジュール式あるいは 3D プリント式の住宅が、住宅の建築コストを低下させることになるでしょう。

088

space race

［名］宇宙（開発）競争

解説

The **space race** of the mid-20th century culminated in the first moon landing on July 16, 1969. But new technologies have ignited a renewed push for the stars. A lunar moonbase and a Martian planetbase are already in the works. These projects will help lay the foundation for galactic exploration and colonization.

20世紀半ばの宇宙開発競争は、1969年7月16日の月面着陸を頂点に終結した。しかし、新しい技術によって、再び星を目指す動きが活発化している。月面基地や火星の惑星基地は、すでに準備段階に入っている。これらのプロジェクトは、銀河系の探査と植民地化のための基礎作りに役立つだろう。

定義 intense competition in the 2020s and 2030s among nations and corporations to achieve dominance in space exploration and technology
2020年代から2030年代にかけての、宇宙開発や技術の覇権を巡る国家や企業の激しい競争

Astronauts will regularly set foot on the moon.
宇宙飛行士が定期的に月に降り立つようになるでしょう。

space probe ［名］宇宙探査機

 an unmanned spacecraft designed to explore and gather information about celestial bodies, such as planets, moons, asteroids, or comets
惑星や月、小惑星、彗星などの天体を探査し、情報を収集するために設計された無人宇宙船

2030 A space probe will leave Earth and return with a sample from Ceres.
宇宙探査機が地球を離れ、ケレスからサンプルを採取して戻ってくるでしょう。

satellite ［名］人工衛星

 an artificial object that orbits a celestial body, typically used for communication, navigation, or remote sensing purposes
天体を周回する人工物体で、通常、通信や航行、遠隔測定などの目的で使用される

2030 More than ten thousand satellites will be in orbit around Earth.
地球を周回する人工衛星が 1 万機を超えるでしょう。

space station ［名］宇宙ステーション

 a large, habitable structure in space that serves as a long-term base for scientific research, technology development, and human habitation
宇宙空間に置かれた居住可能な大型構造物のことで、科学的研究や技術開発、人間の居住などの目的で長期的な拠点として機能する

2030 At least five space stations will orbit the Earth or the moon.
少なくとも 5 つの宇宙ステーションが地球や月を周回することになるでしょう。

propulsion ［名］推進力

 the act or process of generating thrust to propel spacecraft or satellites through space
宇宙船や衛星を宇宙空間に推進させるために推力を発生させる動きやその過程

2030 New propulsion technologies will achieve more than a 100% increase in speed over conventional chemical rockets.
新しい推進技術により、従来の化学ロケットの速度を 100 パーセント以上しのぐ高速化が実現されるでしょう。

student-centered learning

089

［名］生徒主体の学習

解説

Student-centered learning offers several advantages over traditional teacher-centered approaches. It caters to individual student needs and interests, allowing for personalized learning experiences. It fosters critical thinking, problem-solving, and decision-making skills by providing opportunities for students to explore, analyze, and reflect. And it cultivates collaboration and communication skills as students engage in group projects and discussions.

生徒主体の学習には、従来の教師中心の手法に比べて、いくつかの利点がある。生徒一人ひとりのニーズや関心に対応し、個人に合わせた学習体験を可能にする。生徒に探求、分析、考察する機会を提供することで、批判的思考、問題解決、意思決定の技能を養わせることが可能だ。また、生徒はグループ課題やディスカッションに参加することで、協調性やコミュニケーション能力を身につける。

定義 an educational approach that focuses on the individual needs, interests, and abilities of students, encouraging them to take an active role in their own learning

生徒一人ひとりのニーズや興味、能力に焦点を当て、生徒が自分の学習に積極的に参加するよう促す教育手法

 Advances in AI and data analytics will allow for even more personalized, student-centered approaches.

AIやデータ分析の進歩によって、さらに個人に特化された、生徒中心のアプローチが可能になるでしょう。

flipped classroom [名]反転授業、逆転授業

 定義 an educational model in which students engage with learning materials, such as recorded lectures or readings, outside of the classroom, while class time is dedicated to hands-on activities, problem-solving, and collaboration

教育モデルの一つで、生徒は録音された講義や文章などの教材に教室外で取り組む一方、教室内では体験活動や問題解決、共同作業を行う

2030 Teachers will become more like facilitators as the education paradigm shifts.
教育のパラダイムシフトに伴って、教師はよりまとめ役に近い役割を担うでしょう。

hybrid instruction [名]ハイブリッド指導

 定義 an educational approach that combines elements of face-to-face instruction and online learning, offering a flexible and adaptable learning experience that caters to the diverse needs and preferences of students

対面授業とオンライン学習を組み合わせた教育手法で、生徒の多様なニーズや嗜好に柔軟に対応可能な学習体験を提供するもの

2030 Increased access to broadband and digital devices will make hybrid instruction more widely available and equitable.
ブロードバンドやデジタル機器へのアクセスが増えれば、ハイブリッド指導がより広く、公平に行き渡るようになるでしょう。

inquiry-based learning [名]探究型学習

 定義 a student-centered approach to education that emphasizes active exploration, questioning, and problem-solving through the investigation of complex, real-world problems and challenges

生徒主体の教育手法の一つで、複雑な現実世界の問題や課題の調査を通じた、積極的な探求、質問、問題解決を重視するもの

2030 Advances in technology will enable more sophisticated virtual labs and simulations to support inquiry-based learning experiences.
テクノロジーの進歩によって、より高度な仮想実験室やシミュレーションの実施が可能となり、探究型学習体験を後押しするでしょう。

project-based learning [名]課題解決型学習、課題に基づいた学習

 定義 an instructional method in which students actively explore real-world challenges and problems through extended projects, developing critical thinking, problem-solving, and collaboration skills

指導方法の一つで、生徒が幅広い活動を通じて現実世界の課題や問題を積極的に探求し、批判的思考、問題解決、共同作業の技能を身につけるもの

2030 AI will be used to match students with project-based learning opportunities that align with their interests and career goals.
AIを用いて、生徒の興味やキャリア目標に沿った課題解決型学習の機会が提供されるでしょう。

synthetic tissue

090

[名] 合成組織

解説

Synthetic tissues are a valuable tool for studying disease mechanisms and developing new therapies. For instance, synthetic skin constructs have been developed for wound healing and cosmetic testing, while bioengineered blood vessels offer potential solutions for cardiovascular diseases. Additionally, **synthetic tissues** have been used in organ-on-a-chip technologies, enabling researchers to simulate and study complex biological interactions in a controlled environment.

合成組織は、病気のメカニズムを研究し、新しい治療法を開発するための貴重な道具だ。例えば、創傷治癒や化粧品検査のために合成皮膚が開発されてきたが、一方で生物工学によって作られた血管が、心血管系疾患の治療策となる可能性を秘めている。さらに、合成組織は臓器チップ技術に使用され、研究者は管理された環境の下で複雑な生物学的相互作用を模擬実験したり研究したりすることができるようになっている。

定義 artificial tissue created in a laboratory setting, designed to replicate the structure and function of natural tissue
天然組織の構造や機能を再現するために実験室で作られた人工組織

 Synthetic tissue will be used widely in pharmaceutical testing, reducing the reliance on animal models.
合成組織が医薬品の実験に広く使用されるようになり、動物実験に依存する度合いが低減するでしょう。

bioscaffold [名]バイオスキャフォールド

定義 a three-dimensional structure, typically made of biodegradable materials
3次元構造の一つで、一般的に生分解性材料で作られたもの

 Biodegradable materials will be used in bioscaffolds to ensure that scaffolds degrade as new tissue forms.
生分解性材料がバイオスキャフォールドに使われるようになり、確実にスキャフォールドが分解されて新しい組織形状を作り出すようになるでしょう。

OoCs [名]臓器チップ

定義 short for "organs-on-chips," microengineered devices that contain living human cells designed to mimic the structure and function of human organs for drug testing and research purposes
「臓器チップ」を縮めた形で、生きた人間の細胞を含むマイクロ工学的な装置のこと。これらは、薬物検査や研究目的で人間の臓器の構造と機能を模倣するように設計されている

 The mass production of OoCs will make them accessible for widespread use in pharmaceutical research and personalized medicine.
臓器チップは、大量生産されることによって、医薬品の研究や個人に特化した医療に広く利用できるようになるでしょう。

biofabrication [名]バイオファブリケーション

定義 the process of using additive manufacturing techniques to construct complex biological structures or tissues using living cells, biomaterials, and bioactive factors
付加製造技術を使った工程で、目的は、生体細胞や生体材料、生理活性因子を用いて複雑な生体構造や組織を構築することにある

 Biofabrication will enable the development of entirely new biological structures designed to perform specific tasks or deliver targeted therapies.
バイオファブリケーションによって、特定の役割を果たしたり標的療法を提供したりするように設計された全く新しい生物学的構造物の開発が可能となるでしょう。

bioink [名]バイオインク

定義 a biomaterial, often composed of living cells and other components, that is used as a medium in bioprinting processes to create structures
生体材料の一つで、多くの場合、生きた細胞をはじめとする材料でできている。バイオ印刷の工程において、構造体を作るための媒体として使われる

 Bioinks with smart properties, such as self-healing and stimuli-responsiveness, will emerge.
自己修復性や刺激応答性など、高度な特性を持つバイオインクが現れるでしょう。

telehealth

091

［名］遠隔医療

Thanks to **telehealth**, patients can now receive medical consultations and treatment from the comfort and convenience of their homes. Furthermore, **telehealth** has expanded access to specialized healthcare providers who may be located in different cities or even countries. The flexibility of **telehealth** allows for timely and efficient healthcare delivery, especially for individuals in rural or underserved areas.

遠隔医療のおかげで、今や患者は自宅にいながらにして診察や治療を受けられる。さらに、遠隔医療によって、市外どころか国外にいる専門医の医療提供を受けられるまでになってきた。遠隔医療の柔軟性により、特に地方や医療施設に恵まれない地域に住む人々が、適時に効率よく医療の提供を受けられる。

定義 the use of digital technologies, such as video conferencing and remote monitoring devices, to deliver healthcare services and consultations remotely

ビデオ会議や遠隔監視装置などのデジタル技術を活用し、遠隔地から医療サービスや診察を提供すること

 Doctors will administer more medical checkups remotely.
医師が遠隔で行う検診が増えるでしょう。

e-patient [名] e患者

 定義 an individual who actively participates in their healthcare by using digital technology and online resources to gather information, make informed decisions, and manage their health

デジタル技術やオンラインリソースを利用して、情報収集や、十分な知識を持った上での意思決定、自らの健康への対処を行い、自分の健康管理に積極的に関与する人のこと

2030 E-patients will be equipped with advanced personal health monitoring devices, enabling real-time, continuous health data collection and analysis for preventative care.

e患者は、高度な個人健康監視装置を装備し、リアルタイムで継続的な健康データの収集と分析を行い、予防医療を実現するでしょう。

---

telemonitoring [名] 遠隔監視

 定義 the remote monitoring of patients' health status, vital signs, symptoms, or medical data using connected devices or sensors

接続された機器やセンサーを使用して、患者の健康状態やバイタルサイン、症状、医療データなどを遠隔で監視すること

2030 Telemonitoring will be a common approach for chronic disease management.

遠隔監視は、慢性疾患を管理するための一般的な手法となるでしょう。

---

telemedicine [名] 遠隔治療

 定義 the practice of delivering medical care remotely using digital technologies, such as video consultations, remote patient monitoring, and electronic health records

ビデオ診察や遠隔患者モニタリング、電子カルテなど、デジタル技術を駆使して遠隔地から医療を提供する行為

2030 Integration of telemedicine with AI-powered diagnostic tools will lead to more accurate and efficient diagnoses.

遠隔治療とAIを用いた診断ツールの統合で、より正確で効率的な診療が実現するでしょう。

---

telesurgery [名] 遠隔手術

 定義 a surgical procedure performed remotely using robotic technology and a telecommunications link, allowing a surgeon to control the surgical instruments from a distance

ロボット技術と電気通信回線を使って遠隔操作で行われる外科手術のことで、外科医が離れた場所から手術器具を操作できるようにするもの

2030 The reliability of next-generation telecommunications networks will enable more complex remote procedures.

次世代通信網の信頼性が高まり、より複雑な遠隔操作が実現するでしょう。

183

TradFi

092

［名］従来型金融

解説

TradFi is watching DeFi evolve with unease. New technologies like smart contracts and dApps have the potential to render many TradFi products and services irrelevant. But TradFi has an established infrastructure and regulatory framework that DeFi lacks. If TradFi institutions are to survive, they'll need to adapt and embrace the innovative aspects of DeFi while leveraging their existing strengths.

従来型金融の側から見れば、分散型金融の進化は不安材料だ。自動化契約やdAppsのような新しいテクノロジーは、多くの従来型金融の商品やサービスを無意味なものにする可能性を秘めている。しかし、従来型金融には、分散型金融にない確立されたインフラと規制の枠組みがある。従来型の金融機関が生き残るには、既存の強みを生かしながら、分散型金融の革新的な側面に適応し、それらを受け入れる必要がある。

定義 short for "traditional finance," a term used to describe the conventional financial system, including banks, stock markets, and other regulated institutions

traditional finance（従来型金融）の省略形で、銀行、株式市場、その他規制された機関を含む従来の金融システムを表す用語

 TradFi will encroach on DeFi territory, causing many DeFi companies to be acquired or shut down.

従来型金融が分散型金融の領域を侵食し、多くの分散型金融企業が買収されたり、閉鎖されたりするでしょう。

GameFi [名]ゲームファイ、ゲーミファイ

 定義 a fusion of gaming and decentralized finance, where users can earn rewards or tokens by participating in blockchain-based games

ゲームと分散型金融の融合のことで、ブロックチェーンを利用したゲームに参加することによって報酬やトークンを得られる仕組み

 2030 The e-sports market will be valued at more than $5 billion, partly due to the introduction of GameFi elements.

e スポーツの市場規模が 50 億ドルを超える見込みですが、その理由の一つがゲーミファイの要素の導入です。

ICO [名]新規仮想通貨公開

定義 short for "initial coin offering," a fundraising method used by cryptocurrency startups to raise capital, where investors purchase newly issued tokens in exchange for established cryptocurrencies or fiat currencies

「新規仮想通貨公開」の頭字語で、暗号通貨のスタートアップ企業が資金調達に用いる資金調達手法。投資家は新たに発行されたトークンを、既存の暗号通貨や不換通貨と交換して購入する

 2030 An increasing number of companies will raise funds via ICOs rather than IPOs.

新規株式公開ではなく、新規仮想通貨公開で資金調達を行う企業が増えていきます。

NFT [名]非代替性トークン

定義 short for "non-fungible token," a digital token representing ownership or proof of authenticity for a unique digital or physical asset, typically on a blockchain

「非代替性トークン」の頭字語で、通常ブロックチェーン上で、固有のデジタル資産または物理資産の所有権、あるいは真正性の証明となるデジタル・トークンのこと

 2030 NFTs will come standard with many purchases from music to clothing.

非代替性トークンが、音楽から衣料品まで、多くの買い物場面で当たり前に利用されるようになるでしょう。

rug pull [名]ラグプル

定義 a deceptive act in the cryptocurrency space where the developers or organizers of a project abruptly abandon it after attracting significant investments, causing investors to suffer substantial financial losses

暗号通貨の分野における詐欺行為の一つで、多額の投資を集めた後に開発者や主催者が突然プロジェクトを放棄し、投資家に大きな金銭的損失を与えるもの

 2030 Rug pulls will become more common as more cryptocurrencies emerge.

暗号通貨が増えるにつれて、ラグプルがより一般的になるでしょう。

093

Diversity 多様性

transgender

［形］トランスジェンダー

解説

Transgender individuals have been increasingly visible and vocal in recent years. As society becomes more accepting of diverse gender identities, **transgender** rights and recognition have gained momentum. This shift has led to increased advocacy for healthcare, legal protections, and social inclusion tailored to the unique experiences and needs of **transgender** individuals.

近年、トランスジェンダーはますます人の耳目に触れるようになってきた。社会が多様な性自認を受け入れるようになるにつれ、トランスジェンダーの権利や評価についての議論が勢いを増している。この変化は、トランスジェンダー特有の経験やニーズに合わせたヘルスケア、法的保護、社会的包摂などの支持の活発化につながっている。

定義 referring to individuals whose gender identity does not align with the sex they were assigned at birth
人の性自認が出生時に与えられた性別と一致しない

 Medical and psychological support systems will greatly improve despite conservative pushback.
医療面や精神面での支援体制が、保守派の抵抗があろうとも、大きく改善されるでしょう。

passing [名]パッシング、パス

 the ability to be perceived by others as the gender they identify with, often considered in terms of physical appearance and social presentation
自認する性として他者から認識される能力のことで、多くの場合、外見や社会的な表現の観点で判断されるもの

2030 As understanding of gender diversity increases, the pressure for individuals to pass as a specific gender will decrease.
ジェンダーの多様性への理解が深まれば、特定の性別で通すことへの圧力は低下していくでしょう。

gender-affirming [形]ジェンダーアファーメーションの、本当のジェンダーを肯定する

 referring to treatments, practices, or environments that support and validate an individual's gender identity, such as healthcare services, pronoun usage, or clothing choices
医療サービスや代名詞の使用、衣服の選択といった、人の性自認を支援・検証する治療、実践、環境の

2030 Gender-affirming surgeries will be covered under most insurance policies.
性適合手術に、ほとんどの保険が適用されるようになるでしょう。

gender dysphoria [名]性別違和感

 the distress or discomfort experienced when one's assigned gender at birth does not align with one's gender identity
生まれつきの性別が自分の性自認と一致しない場合に経験する苦痛や不快感

2030 Early detection and intervention of gender dysphoria will be standard in mental healthcare, leading to improved outcomes for transgender individuals.
性別違和感の早期発見と対策を行うことがメンタルヘルスケアの標準となり、トランスジェンダーの人たちにとってより良い結果をもたらしていくでしょう。

transition [名]性転換

 to undergo social, medical, or legal processes to align one's physical appearance and/or social recognition with their gender identity
身体的外観や社会的認知を性自認と一致させるために、社会的、医学的、または法的な措置を受けること

2030 Medical transitions will become safer and more affordable due to advances in healthcare.
医療の進歩によって、医学的な性転換措置がより安全で、より安価なものになるでしょう。

urbanization

［名］都市化

094

解説

Since the 18th century, **urbanization** rates have grown, with over half of the world's population now residing in urban areas. **Urbanization** offers benefits like improved standards of living and enhanced economic opportunities. There are downsides, however, as it often stresses infrastructures and exacerbates social inequality. Sustainable urban planning is a critical 21st-century concern.

18世紀以降、都市化率が高まり、現在では世界人口の半数以上が都市部に居住している。都市化には、生活水準の向上や経済的機会の増大といったメリットがある。しかし、インフラに負担がかかり、社会的不平等が深刻化するなどのマイナス面もある。持続可能な都市計画は、21世紀における重要な課題だ。

定義 the process by which an increasing proportion of a population lives in cities and urban areas, often due to migration from rural areas
人口のうち、都市部に住む人口の割合が増加する過程のことで、多くの場合、農村部からの移住に起因する

Sixty percent of the global population will live in urban areas.
世界人口の 60 パーセントが都市部で暮らすようになるでしょう。

gentrification [名] 高級化、中産階級化

 定義 the process of renovating and improving a neighborhood or area, often resulting in the displacement of lower-income residents due to rising property values

地域や区域を再開発・再建する工程のことで、資産価値の上昇により低所得者層が追い出されることが多い

2030 Gentrification will reduce diversity as long-term residents seek more affordable housing elsewhere.

中産階級化によって、ある場所に長く暮らしてきた人たちがより手頃な価格の住宅を他所に求めるようになり、多様性が低下するでしょう。

brick-and-mortar [形] 実店舗の、インターネット上ではない、リアルな

 定義 referring to physical business establishments, such as stores and offices, as opposed to online or virtual operations

オンラインやバーチャルな運営とは逆で、店舗や事務所などの事業所が物理的に存在する

2030 Brick-and-mortar shopping will place an increasing emphasis on the customer experience to differentiate it from online shopping.

実店舗での買い物は、オンラインショッピングとの差別化のために、顧客体験の価値がいっそう重視されるようになるでしょう。

bike lane [名] 自転車専用道路、自転車専用レーン

定義 a designated area of a roadway or path, typically marked by painted lines, intended for the exclusive use of bicycles

車道や通路の上の指定された区域の一つで、通常はペイントされた線によって示され、自転車での利用に限定する目的がある

 2030 Bikers will see the addition of thousands of miles of protected bike lanes and off-road trails.

自転車愛好家たちは、新たに何千マイルもの保護された自転車専用道路やオフロードトレイルを楽しめるようになるでしょう。

cultural displacement [名] 文化的転移、文化的置き換え

定義 a situation where a community's cultural identity is eroded or replaced as a result of migration, colonization, globalization, or the influence of a dominant culture

移民、植民地化、グローバル化、または支配的な文化の影響によって、地域の文化的アイデンティティーが損なわれたり置き換わったりする状況

 2030 Those who are culturally displaced will lose the safety and familiarity of the environment with which they're familiar.

文化的転移を経験する人たちが、なじみ深い環境の安全性や親しみやすさを失っていくでしょう。

vegetarian

095

［形］ベジタリアンの、菜食主義者の

解説

The rise in environmental and health concerns, along with increasing awareness of animal welfare, has contributed to the growing popularity of **vegetarian** diets. Many people have embraced a **vegetarian** lifestyle, and food industries have responded by offering an extensive range of **vegetarian** products. As a result, the cultural and culinary landscape has evolved to accommodate diverse dietary preferences.

環境や健康への関心の高まりと、動物愛護への意識の高まりが、菜食の人気を増大させている。 多くの人々が菜食主義者のライフスタイルを受け入れ、食品業界もそれに応えて、菜食主義者向けの製品を幅広く提供してきた。その結果、文化や料理にまつわる世界は、多様な食の嗜好に対応できるよう進化を遂げた。

---

 referring to a diet that excludes meat but may include other animal products such as dairy and eggs
食肉以外で、乳製品や鶏卵などの動物性食品は含まれる可能性のある食事についての

 Innovations in food science and technology will bring more diverse and appetizing vegetarian options.
食品科学技術の革新によって、より多彩でおいしいベジタリアン食品が現れるでしょう。

vegan [形] ビーガンの

 定義 referring to a dietary and lifestyle choice that excludes the consumption of all animal products, including meat, poultry, fish, dairy, eggs, and honey

精肉、魚介、乳製品、鶏卵、蜂蜜を含むすべての動物性食品の消費を排除した食事やライフスタイルの

2030 The development of lab-grown meat will provide ethical and sustainable protein alternatives, blurring the line between vegan and meat-eating diets.

人工肉の開発によって、倫理的で持続可能なタンパク質の代替品が供給されるようになり、ビーガンと肉食の境界線があいまいになるでしょう。

dairy-free [形] 乳製品を含まない、乳製品不使用の

 定義 referring to a diet or product that contains no dairy or dairy-derived ingredients, such as milk, cheese, or butter

牛乳、チーズ、バターなどの乳製品や乳製品に由来する成分を含まない食事や製品の

2030 New dairy analogs will lead to dairy-free alternatives that don't compromise taste or texture.

新しい乳製品類似食品が、味や食感を損なわない乳製品不使用の代替品につながるでしょう。

plant-based [形] 植物由来の

 定義 referring to a diet or food product that is primarily or entirely composed of plant-derived ingredients

植物に由来する材料で大半またはすべてを構成する食事や食品の

2030 Plant-based diets will be promoted as a sustainable solution to address global food security.

世界の食糧安全保障に対処するための持続可能な解決策として、植物由来の食生活が推進されるでしょう。

lactose-intolerant [形] 乳糖不耐症の、乳製品を受け付けない

 定義 describing a person who is unable to fully digest lactose, a sugar found in milk and dairy products, due to a deficiency of lactase enzyme

ラクターゼ酵素の欠乏により、牛乳や乳製品に含まれる糖質、乳糖を十分に消化することができない

2030 The discovery of new enzymes will lead to treatments that alleviate and possibly cure lactose intolerance.

新しい酵素の発見が、乳糖不耐症の症状緩和や治療法につながるでしょう。

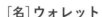

wallet

［名］ウォレット

096

解説

Cryptocurrency **wallets** allow users to store, send, and receive cryptocurrencies securely. Unlike traditional **wallets**, these digital platforms don't actually store physical currency. Instead, they track and secure the digital codes, or "keys," that represent ownership of cryptocurrencies. These **wallets** can exist in various forms, including software, hardware, or even paper.

暗号通貨のウォレットは、ユーザーが暗号通貨を安全に保管、送受信できるようにする。従来の財布とは異なり、これらはデジタルプラットフォームであって、実際に物理的な通貨を保管するものではない。その代わりに、暗号通貨の所有権を表すデジタルコード、つまり「鍵」を追跡し、保護する。こうしたウォレットは、ソフトウェア、ハードウェア、あるいは紙など、さまざまな形態を取ることができる。

定義 a digital tool or device used to store, manage, and access cryptocurrency holdings securely
暗号通貨を安全に保管・管理・利用するためのデジタルツールやデバイス

 People will leave their physical wallets at home as their smartphones function as a place to store credit card information alongside cryptocurrencies.
スマートフォンが暗号通貨とともにクレジットカード情報を保管する場として機能するので、人々は物理的な財布を家に置いたままにするでしょう。

exchange [名]取引所

 a platform or marketplace where users can buy, sell, or trade cryptocurrencies and other digital assets, often for fiat currencies or other cryptocurrencies

ユーザーが暗号通貨やその他のデジタル資産を、たいていは不換貨幣やその他の暗号通貨と交換できるプラットフォームまたは市場

Traditional foreign exchanges will become a thing of the past as people use cryptocurrencies to access digital exchanges.

人々が暗号通貨を使ってデジタル取引所にアクセスすることで、従来の外国為替取引所は過去のものとなるでしょう。

hardware wallet [名]ハードウェアウォレット

 a physical device, often resembling a USB drive, designed to store the private keys of cryptocurrency holdings securely offline

暗号通貨の秘密鍵をオフラインで安全に保管するために設計された物理的なデバイスのことで、多くの場合 USB ドライブに似ている

Hardware wallets will be baked directly into smartphones and other portable devices.

ハードウェアウォレットは、スマホなどの携帯端末に直接組み込まれることになるでしょう。

hot wallet [名]ホットウォレット

 a digital wallet connected to the Internet, providing easy access for managing and transacting cryptocurrencies but with potential security risks

インターネットに接続されたデジタルウォレットのことで、暗号通貨の管理や取引に簡単に利用できるが、潜在的なセキュリティーリスクもある

Hot wallets will become ubiquitous, although they will also become ready targets for hackers.

ホットウォレットはユビキタスな存在になるでしょうが、ハッカーの格好の標的になる可能性もあります。

cold storage [名]コールドストレージ

 a method of storing cryptocurrency holdings offline, such as on a hardware wallet or paper wallet, to minimize the risk of theft or hacking

暗号通貨をハードウェアウォレットやペーパーウォレットなどを使ってオフラインで保管し、盗難やハッキングのリスクを最小化する方法

Instead of hiding money in a mattress or burying it in the garden, people will keep the majority of their crypto holdings securely in cold storage.

お金をマットレスの中に隠したり、庭に埋めたりする代わりに、人々は保有する暗号通貨の大部分をコールドストレージに安全に保管するようになるでしょう。

097

water scarcity

［名］水不足

解説

The UN described a drought in a region of Africa in 2017 as the "worst humanitarian crisis since the Second World War." Meanwhile, two-thirds of the global population is predicted to live in water-scarce areas by 2025. As climate change makes droughts more frequent and freshwater sources dwindle, conflict will surely follow.

国連は、2017年にアフリカのある地域で起きた干ばつを「第二次世界大戦以来最悪の人道危機」と表現した。一方、2025年には世界の人口の3分の2が水不足の地域に暮らすと予測されている。気候変動によって干ばつが頻発し、淡水源が減少すれば、必ずや紛争が起こるだろう。

---

 a situation where the demand for freshwater resources exceeds the available supply, resulting from factors such as population growth, climate change, and unsustainable water use practices

淡水資源に対する需要が利用可能な供給量を上回る状況のことで、人口増加や気候変動、持続不可能な水の利用方法などが原因である

 There will be violent clashes as groups attempt to secure access to freshwater sources.

淡水資源へのアクセスを確保を巡って、集団間で暴力的な衝突が起きるでしょう。

desalination ［名］脱塩

定義 the process of removing salt and other impurities from seawater or brackish water to produce freshwater
海水や汽水から塩分などの不純物を取り除き、淡水を作る工程

2030 New technologies will lead to commercial desalination plants appearing in many coastal cities.
新しい技術によって、多くの沿岸都市に商業目的で海水を淡水化するプラントが造られるでしょう。

drought ［名］干ばつ

定義 an extended period of abnormally low rainfall, leading to a shortage of water and adverse effects on the environment, agriculture, and human activities
降雨量が異常に少ない状態が長く続くことで、水不足に加え、環境や農業などの人間の活動への悪影響につながる

2030 Droughts will grow more severe as climate change progresses.
気候変動が進むと、干ばつがより深刻化するでしょう。

aquifer ［名］帯水層

定義 an underground layer of water-bearing permeable rock, sediment, or soil from which groundwater can be extracted, often used as a source of freshwater for human consumption and agriculture
水を含む透水性の岩石、堆積物、または土壌の地下層で、そこから地下水を採取できる。多くの場合、人の生活や農業のための淡水源として使用される

2030 Governments will implement strategies to protect major aquifer systems.
各国政府が、主要な帯水層系を保護するための戦略を立てるでしょう。

hydropanel ［名］ハイドロパネル

定義 a technology that uses solar power to extract water vapor from the air and convert it into clean, drinkable water
太陽光発電による電力で空気中の水蒸気を取り出し、きれいな飲料水に変える技術

2030 Many new residential buildings will have hydropanels installed on their roofs.
多くの新築住宅で、屋根にハイドロパネルが設置されるでしょう。

wearable technology

098

［名］ウェアラブル技術

解説

Mainstream digital **wearable technology** came about in 1975 with the invention of the first calculator wristwatch. Today's wearables use sensors to interact with people and the environment, offering an array of advanced functionalities and personalized experiences. While smart fabrics and other technologies will help wearables evolve, they may be just the precursor to a cyborg revolution.

デジタルウェアラブル技術の本流は、1975年の最初の電卓付き腕時計の発明によってもたらされた。今日のウェアラブル機器は、センサーを使って人や環境と相互に作用し、数々の高度な機能と個人向けに特化された体験を提供している。スマートファブリックなどの技術がウェアラブル機器の進化を後押しするだろうが、それはサイボーグ革命の前兆に過ぎないのかもしれない。

定義 the technology for electronic devices designed to be worn on the body, typically as accessories, that collect, analyze, or display data related to the user's activities and health

体に装着するように設計された電子機器のための技術。機器は通常、アクセサリーとして用いられ、ユーザーの活動や健康に関連するデータを収集・分析・表示する

 Wearables will track blood pressure, blood glucose levels, and hydration levels.

ウェアラブル機器が、血圧や血糖値、水分補給量などを記録するようになるでしょう。

smart fabric [名]スマートファブリック

 a textile material that has been engineered with digital components or sensors to provide functionality beyond traditional fabrics
デジタル部品やセンサーを搭載し、従来の布を超える機能を実現した織物素材

2030 Smart fabrics will automatically adjust their thermal properties based on ambient temperature and body heat to provide optimal comfort in any environment.
スマートファブリックが、周囲の温度や体温に基づいて熱特性を自動的に調整し、あらゆる環境で最適な快適さを提供してくれるようになるでしょう。

biosensor [名]バイオセンサー、生体内感知装置

 a device or sensor that combines biological components, such as enzymes or antibodies, with electronic systems to detect and analyze biological substances or processes
酵素や抗体などの生体成分と電子システムを組み合わせた装置やセンサーのことで、生体物質や生体内作用を検出したり分析したりする

2030 Biosensors will be miniaturized to nanoscale dimensions, allowing for more non-intrusive health monitoring systems.
バイオセンサーはナノレベルまで小型化され、より非侵入性の高い健康監視システムを実現するでしょう。

energy harvesting [名]環境発電

 the process of capturing and storing small amounts of energy from external sources, such as solar, thermal, or kinetic energy, to power electronic devices
太陽光や地熱、運動エネルギーなどの外部の資源から少量のエネルギーを取り込んで蓄える工程のことで、これを用いて電子機器に電力を供給する

2030 Wearables will incorporate advanced energy harvesting materials so they never need to be removed to recharge.
ウェアラブル機器が、高度な環境発電素材を組み込むようになり、充電のために取り外す必要がいっさいなくなるでしょう。

conductive fibers [名]伝導性繊維

 specialized fibers that have inherent electrical conductivity, allowing the transmission of electrical signals or currents through their structure
電気伝導性を持つ特殊な繊維で、その構造を通じて電気信号や電流の伝送を実現する

2030 Conductive fibers will enable users to interact with their wearable devices by simply touching specific areas on their clothes.
伝導性繊維によって、ユーザーは衣服の特定の場所に触れるだけで、ウェアラブルデバイスとのやり取りできるようになるでしょう。

197

woke

099

[形] ウォークな、社会的不公正に対する意識の高い

解説

Woke culture has been applauded for amplifying marginalized voices and challenging systemic injustices, sparking much-needed conversations on race, gender, and social inequality. However, it has also faced criticism, with detractors citing concerns about cancel culture, suppression of free speech, and oversensitivity. The polarity of views underscores the complexity of navigating social progress in contemporary society.

ウォークな行動様式は、社会から疎外された人々の声を増幅させ、制度的な不正に挑戦し、人種やジェンダー、社会的不平等に関する必要な議論を喚起することで称賛されている。しかし、批判もあり、反対派は、キャンセル文化や言論の自由の弾圧、過敏性についての懸念を挙げている。このような両極端な意見は、現代における社会的進歩の複雑さを浮き彫りにしている。

定義 being socially and politically aware, especially regarding issues of systemic oppression, inequality, and injustice, often accompanied by a desire for social change and activism

社会的・政治的に意識が高い。特に制度的抑圧や不平等、不公正の問題について、社会変革や活動への意欲を伴って

 A younger, predominantly woke generation will exert pressure on governments to adopt more progressive policies.

若めで、とりわけ社会的不公正に対する意識の高い世代が、政府に対してより進歩的な政策を取り入れるよう圧力をかけるでしょう。

liberal [形] リベラルな、革新的な

 定義 favoring progressive or reformist ideas, policies, or principles that prioritize individual freedoms, social equality, and the protection of civil liberties

個人の自由、社会的平等、市民的自由の保護を優先する進歩的な、あるいは改革的な思想、政策、原則を支持する

2030 The term "liberal" will evolve to encompass support for radical technological progress and space exploration.

「革新的な」という言葉は、急進的な技術の進歩や宇宙開発への支持を包含するように進化するでしょう。

progressive [形] 進歩的な

 定義 advocating for or favoring social reform, innovation, and advancements in societal structures, policies, or values, often with a focus on inclusivity, equality, and positive change

社会変革や改革、社会構造や政策、価値観に関する進歩を提唱または支持するような。多くの場合、包摂性、平等、前向きな変化を重視する

2030 Progressive movements will increasingly emphasize the interconnectedness of social issues, recognizing that systems of oppression and discrimination intersect.

進歩的な運動は、抑圧と差別の仕組みが交錯していることを認識し、社会問題の相互の関連性をますます重視するようになるでしょう。

CRT [名] 批判的人種理論

 定義 short for "critical race theory," an intellectual framework that examines the ways in which race and racism are ingrained in social structures, institutions, and everyday life

「批判的人種理論」の頭字語で、人種や人種差別が社会構造や制度、日常生活にどのように根付いているかを検証する知的枠組み

2030 CRT will continue to inspire social justice movements like Black Lives Matter.

批判的人種理論は、ブラック・ライブズ・マターのような社会正義のムーブメントを鼓舞し続けるでしょう。

antifa [名] アンティファ、反ファシズム運動

 定義 short for "anti-fascist," a loosely organized movement that opposes fascism and other forms of extreme right-wing ideology

「反ファシスト」の頭字語で、ファシズムやその他の極右思想に反対する緩やかな組織的運動

2030 Antifa's online activism will facilitate broader discussions on political extremism and social justice.

反ファシズム運動のオンライン活動は、政治的過激主義や社会正義に関するより広範な議論を促進するでしょう。

199

XR

100

[名]クロスリアリティー、エクステンデッドリアリティー

解説

Mainstream adoption of **XR**, which begins in 2024, will catalyze a sea change in health, education, and a number of industries. People will become geographically untethered as **XR** technologies enable immersive and interactive experiences regardless of physical location. Teachers and students, co-workers and colleagues, doctors and patients, everyone will exist side-by-side in virtual space.

2024年に始まるクロスリアリティーの本格的な導入は、健康や教育をはじめ、多くの産業に大きな変化をもたらすだろう。XRのテクノロジーは、物理的な場所に関係なく没入的でインタラクティブな体験を可能にするので、人々は地理的に縛らずに済むようになる。教師と生徒、同僚と同僚、医者と患者など、すべての人が仮想空間の中では隣り合うことになるのだ。

定義 short for "extended reality," an umbrella term that encompasses AR, VR, and MR technologies, referring to all immersive digital experiences
「エクステンデッドリアリティー」を短くした形で、拡張現実、仮想現実、複合現実の技術を包括する言葉。すべての没入型デジタル体験を指す

 XR will become as common as tablets and laptops in schools.
クロスリアリティーは、学校でタブレットやノートパソコンと同じように普及していくでしょう。

MR ［名］複合現実

 定義 short for "mixed reality," a combination of real and virtual environments where digital and physical elements interact in real time
「複合現実」の頭字語で、デジタルと物理的な要素がリアルタイムで相互作用する、現実と仮想の環境の組み合わせ

2030 MR training will become standard in the military.
複合現実による訓練が、軍隊での標準になるでしょう。

AR ［名］拡張現実

 定義 short for "augmented reality," a technology that overlays digital content, such as images, videos, or text, onto the user's view of the real world
「拡張現実」の頭字語で、画像や動画、文字などのデジタルコンテンツをユーザーの現実世界観に重ねる技術のこと

2030 AR devices will be a common tool used in automobile repair.
拡張現実の機器が当たり前の道具となり、自動車の修理に使われるようになるでしょう。

VR ［名］仮想現実

 定義 short for "virtual reality," a computer-generated simulation of a three-dimensional environment that users can interact with using specialized equipment
「仮想現実」の頭字語で、コンピューターが作り出した3次元環境を模したもの。ユーザーは専用の機器を使用してやり取りできる

2030 Courtrooms will make use of VR for crime scene reconstruction.
法廷では、仮想現実を活用して犯罪現場が再現されるようになるでしょう。

telepresence ［名］テレプレゼンス

 定義 the state or perception of being physically present in a location while being physically elsewhere, facilitated by advanced communication and virtual reality technologies
実際には別の場所にいながら、物理的にその場所に存在している状態、あるいはそのような感覚を作り出すことで、高度な通信や仮想現実の技術によって実現する

2030 Telepresence robots will be a common sight in hospitals, allowing doctors to monitor and interact with patients remotely.
テレプレゼンス型ロボットが、病院でもよく見かけられるようになり、医師が遠隔で患者を監視したり、患者と対話したりできるようになるでしょう。

PART 2

この500タームで

多様な分野の近未来に精通する

（本文中の見出しは太字のみ表記）

absenteeism ［名］常習的欠勤、無断欠勤、ずる休み

定義 the practice of regularly being absent from work, school, or other obligations, often without a valid reason or explanation

職場、学校、その他の責務の場を、しばしば正当な理由や説明なしに定期的に欠席すること

◀ Related Words and Phrases ▶

presenteeism ［名］プレゼンティーイズム、病気などでも出勤すること

定義 the practice of being physically present at work despite illness or other circumstances that hinder productivity, often resulting in reduced effectiveness and increased health risks

病気や生産性を妨げるその他の状況にあるにもかかわらず、職場に出勤することで、しばしば効率の低下や健康リスクの増大をもたらす慣習

productivity ［名］生産性

定義 the effectiveness and efficiency with which tasks are completed, often measured in terms of output per unit of input

仕事を完了させる上での有効性と効率性のことで、多くの場合、単位入力あたりの出力量で測定される

burnout ［名］燃え尽き症候群

定義 a state of physical, emotional, or mental exhaustion, often caused by prolonged stress or overwork

肉体的、情緒的、または精神的に疲弊している状態のことで、多くの場合、長期のストレスや過労によって引き起こされる

workplace culture ［名］職場文化

定義 the shared values, attitudes, and practices that characterize an organization, influencing employee behavior and satisfaction

従業員の行動や満足度に影響を与える、組織を特徴づける共通の価値観、態度、慣行

blockchain [形] ブロックチェーン

[定義] a decentralized, digital ledger that records transactions across a network of computers, ensuring transparency and security

コンピューターのネットワーク上で取引を記録し、透明性と安全性を確保する分散型デジタル台帳

Related Words and Phrases

block [名]ブロック

[定義] a collection of data, often related to transactions, that is securely linked to other blocks in a blockchain

データの集合体のことで、多くの場合、経済活動に関連し、ブロックチェーンの他のブロックと安全につながっている

layer-1 [形]レイヤー1の

[定義] referring to the fundamental infrastructure or underlying protocol that forms the basis of a blockchain or decentralized network, providing security, consensus, and transactional capabilities at the core level

コアレベルでセキュリティー、コンセンサス、取引機能を提供するような、ブロックチェーンや分散型ネットワークの基盤となる基本インフラや基礎プロトコルに関する

layer-2 [形]レイヤー2の

[定義] referring to a secondary framework or protocol built on top of an existing blockchain to improve scalability and efficiency

拡張性や効率性を高めるために既存のブロックチェーンの上に構築される、二次的なフレームワークやプロトコルの

ledger [名]台帳

[定義] a record of financial transactions or other data, maintained in a structured and organized manner

構造化され組織化された方法で維持される、金融取引またはその他のデータの記録

gig economy [名] ギグエコノミー

定義 an economic system characterized by the prevalence of short-term contracts, freelance work, and independent contractors
短期契約やフリーランス、独立した業務委託契約者の普及を特徴とする経済の仕
組み

◀ Related Words and Phrases ▶

coworking [名]コワーキング、共同スペースで働くこと

定義 a style of work where individuals from different professions or organizations share a
common workspace, often fostering collaboration, community, and flexibility
異なる職業や組織の個人が共同のワークスペースを共有する働き方のことで、協業、共通性、柔軟
性が促進されやすい

creator economy [名]クリエーターエコノミー

定義 an economic system driven by independent content creators who generate revenue
through platforms such as social media, blogs, and podcasts
ソーシャルメディア、ブログ、ポッドキャストなどのプラットフォームを通じて収益を上げる、独
立したコンテンツクリエイターが牽引する経済の仕組み

crowdfunding [名]クラウドファンディング

定義 the practice of raising funds for a project or cause from a large number of people,
typically through online platforms
あるプロジェクトや大義のために、多くの人々から資金を集めることで、通常はオンラインプラッ
トフォームを通じて行われる

couch surfing [名]カウチサーフィン

定義 the practice of temporarily staying with friends, family, or acquaintances, often as a
cost-effective alternative to paid accommodations
友人、家族、あるいは知人の家に一時的に滞在することで、多くの場合、有料の宿泊施設での滞在
に代わる費用対効果の高い方法として用いられる

mine [動]（〜を）採掘する、マイニングする

定義 to perform complex calculations to validate transactions and secure a blockchain network, typically receiving newly created cryptocurrency as a reward

通常、報酬として新たに発行された暗号通貨を受け取る前提で、取引の検証とブロックチェーンネットワークの保護を目的として、複雑な計算を実行する

⊰ Related Words and Phrases ⊱

hashrate [名]ハッシュレート、暗号通貨採掘時の処理速度

定義 the speed at which a miner or a network of miners is able to perform the mathematical calculations required for mining a cryptocurrency

採掘者または採掘者のネットワークが、暗号通貨の採掘に必要な数学的計算を実行できる速度

proof of stake [名]プルーフ・オブ・ステーク、出資額の証明

定義 a consensus mechanism in which participants validate transactions and create new blocks based on their proportional ownership of a cryptocurrency

参加者が暗号通貨の所有比率に応じて取引を検証し、新しいブロックを作る上での合意形成の仕組み

proof of work [名]プルーフ・オブ・ワーク、作業量の証明

定義 a consensus mechanism requiring participants to solve complex mathematical problems to validate transactions and mine new blocks, expending computational resources and energy

参加者が複雑な数学的問題を解決して取引の検証や新しいブロックの採掘を行うよう求める、合意形成の仕組みのことで、計算資源やエネルギーを消費する

block reward [名]ブロック報酬

定義 the amount of new cryptocurrency given to miners for validating and adding a new block of transactions to the blockchain

新しい取引のブロックを検証し、ブロックチェーンに追加するために採掘者に与えられる、新しい暗号通貨の量

premiumization [名] プレミアム化、上質化、高級化

定義 the process of upgrading products or services to appeal to more affluent consumers or enhance the perception of quality and exclusivity

より豊かな消費者に訴求するため、あるいは品質や特別感の認識を高めるために、製品やサービスを格上げする段階

━━◄ Related Words and Phrases ►━━

prestige [名] 名声

定義 a high level of respect, admiration, or reputation associated with someone or something based on their achievements, social status, or perceived excellence

業績、社会的地位、または認められる卓越性に基づいた、人物または事物に関連する高水準の敬意、賞賛、あるいは評判

masstige [名] マステージ

定義 a marketing strategy that combines aspects of mass-market products with prestige elements to appeal to a broader consumer base

マスプロダクトの側面とプレステージの要素を組み合わせて、より広い消費者層にアピールするマーケティング戦略

affluence [名] 豊かさ、富

定義 the state of having a lot of money and material possessions, often associated with a high standard of living

多くの金銭や物品を所有している状態のことで、多くの場合、高い生活水準と関連付けられる

upmarket [形] 高級市場向けの、高所得者層向けの

定義 high in quality and often high in price, typically aimed at affluent consumers

高品質で、たいてい高額で、一般的に富裕な消費者向けの

sat [名] サトシ（ビットコインの最小単位）

定義 short for "Satoshi," the smallest unit of the Bitcoin cryptocurrency, equal to one hundred millionth of a single Bitcoin (0.00000001 BTC)

「サトシ」の略で、暗号通貨ビットコインの最小単位。1 ビットコインの 1 億分の 1（0.00000001 BTC）に相当する

≫ Related Words and Phrases ≫

moon [名]ムーン、仮想通貨の急騰（チャート）

定義 a significant and rapid increase in the value of a digital asset

デジタル資産の価値の著しい急騰

diamond hands [名]ダイヤモンドハンド、高いリスク許容度

定義 a phrase used by investors, particularly in the cryptocurrency community, to describe holding onto an asset despite market volatility or declining prices

特に暗号通貨コミュニティーの投資家の間で使用されるフレーズで、市場の不安定さや価格の下落にもかかわらず、資産を持ち続けること

whale [名]大口投資家

定義 an individual or organization that holds a large amount of a cryptocurrency, often having the potential to influence market trends

暗号通貨を大量に保有する個人または組織のことで、多くの場合、市場動向に影響を与える可能性を持つ

HODL [動]買い持ちする

定義 an intentional misspelling of "hold," originating from an online forum post to encourage holding onto cryptocurrency assets during price fluctuations

オンラインフォーラムの投稿に由来する hold の意図的なスペルミス。価格変動中に暗号通貨資産を保持することを奨励する

diplomacy [名] 外交

定義 the art and practice of conducting negotiations between countries, especially in politics and international relations
特に政治や国際関係において、国家間で交渉を行う上での技術や慣行

◄ Related Words and Phrases ►

bilateral [形] 2国間の

定義 involving two parties, usually countries, in a formal agreement, contract, or negotiation
公式な合意、契約、または交渉において、2者――通常は国家――が関与して

partisan [形] 支持した、盲従した、党派的な

定義 strongly supporting a particular party, cause, or person, often without considering other perspectives
特定の政党、大義、または人物を強く支持し、しばしば他の観点が考慮されないような

unilateral [形] 一方的な

定義 involving or performed by only one party or individual without the participation or agreement of others
他者の参加または合意を得ずに、一当事者または一個人のみが関与して、または実行して

coalition [名] 連立政権、連立政府、連合

定義 a temporary alliance of several groups or parties, especially in politics or international affairs
特に政治や国際問題において、いくつかのグループや政党が結ぶ一時的な同盟関係

elite [名] エリート

定義 a select group of people with a high social status or superior skills and abilities, often with considerable power or influence

社会的地位が高いか、または優れた技術や能力を持ち合わせ、多くの場合、かなりの権力や影響力を持つ選ばれた人々の集団

Related Words and Phrases

class warfare [名] 階級闘争

定義 conflict or tension between different social or economic classes, often involving disputes over wealth, resources, or power

異なる社会的または経済的階層間の対立や緊張のことで、しばしば富や資源、権力をめぐる争いが含まれる

dark money [名] 黒い金、ダークマネー

定義 money that is used to fund political campaigns or advocacy efforts but whose source is not easily traceable due to loopholes or lack of transparency in campaign finance laws

政治運動や支援活動の資金として使用されるが、政治資金法の抜け穴や透明性の欠如により、その出所を容易にたどれない金

hegemony [名] 覇権、支配

定義 dominance or control of one group, state, or country over others, especially in political, economic, or cultural aspects

特に政治的、経済的、文化的側面において、ある集団、国家、国が他者に対して優位に立つこと、または支配すること

oligarch [名] オリガルヒ、(ロシアの) 新興財閥、大富裕層

定義 a wealthy individual who has significant political influence or control, often through their ownership of major companies or media outlets

政治的に大きな影響力や支配力を持つ富裕層のことで、多くの場合、大手企業やメディアを所有することで力を行使する

211

polarization ［名］二極化、二極分化

定義 the division of a group or society into opposing factions, often along political, social, or ideological lines
集団や社会が、しばしば政治的、社会的、あるいは思想的な路線を巡って、対立する勢力に分割されること

◄ Related Words and Phrases ►

popular vote ［名］一般投票、一般有権者票
定義 the collective total of individual votes cast by eligible citizens to determine the outcome of an election or referendum
選挙や国民投票の結果を決定するために投じられた、有権者の個々の票の総計

ranked-choice voting ［名］順位付け選択投票
定義 an electoral system in which voters rank candidates by preference, and votes are redistributed until a candidate receives a majority
有権者が候補者を好みで順位付けし、候補者が過半数を獲得するまで票が再配分される選挙制度

voter turnout ［名］投票率
定義 the percentage of eligible voters who cast a ballot in an election
選挙で投票権を持つ有権者のうち、投票した人の割合

gerrymander ［動］党利党略のために〜（選挙区）を改定する
定義 to manipulate the boundaries of an electoral district in a way that gives an unfair advantage to one political party
選挙区の境界を操作して、特定の政党が不当に有利になるようにする

autism spectrum [名] 自閉スペクトラム症、自閉症スペクトラム障害

定義 a range of neurodevelopmental conditions characterized by differences in social communication, interaction, and restricted or repetitive behaviors, varying in severity and presentation

社会的コミュニケーションや人付き合いの仕方が人と違う、行動に限界があったり同じ振る舞いを繰り返したりするなどの特徴を持った、一連の神経発達障害の症状のことで、重篤度や発症の仕方に幅がある

◤ Related Words and Phrases ◢

stimming [名] 自己刺激的行動

定義 self-stimulating behaviors, often repetitive and soothing, that individuals with autism or other sensory-processing disorders use to regulate their emotions or sensory input

自己を刺激する行動のことで、多くの場合、反復的で鎮静効果を持つもの。自閉症やその他の感覚処理障害を持つ人が、感情や感覚的な刺激を調節するために行う

coping mechanism [名] 対処メカニズム

定義 strategies or behaviors that individuals use to manage stress, anxiety, or difficult emotions, often as a response to challenging situations

人がストレス、不安、あるいは苦しい感情を制御するために取る対処策または行動のことで、たいていは困難な状況への反応として現れる

perseverate [動] 保続する、執拗に繰り返す

定義 to repeatedly engage in a thought, action, or behavior, often associated with developmental or cognitive disorders, but also seen in typical development

ある思考、行動、行為を繰り返す。多くの場合、発達障害や認知障害と関連付けられるが、通常の発達過程でも見られるもの

developmental disability [名] 発達障害

定義 a group of conditions affecting an individual's physical, learning, language, or behavior development, often present from birth or early childhood

人の体や学習、言語、行動などの発達に影響を与える複数の条件・状態をひとまとめに捉えたもので、出生時または幼児期から現れることが多い

corporate social responsibility [名]企業の社会的責任

定義 the strategic approach by which organizations aim to balance profit-making activities with social and environmental considerations, recognizing their role as responsible corporate citizens

企業が、責任ある社会の一員としての役割を認識し、利潤追求活動と、社会と環境への配慮のバランスを取ることを目指した戦略的なアプローチ

◄ Related Words and Phrases ►

emotional tax [名]精神的な負担

定義 the psychological burden experienced by individuals who feel pressured to suppress their emotions or cultural identity in a workplace or social environment

職場などの社会的な環境において、感情や文化的アイデンティティーを抑え込まなければならないと感じる人が経験する心理的負担

ERG [名]従業員リソースグループ

定義 short for "employee resource group," a voluntary, employee-led group within an organization that focuses on fostering a diverse and inclusive workplace by supporting specific demographics or interests

「従業員リソースグループ」の頭字語で、組織内の従業員主導の自主的な集団のこと。特定の層や派閥に属する人たちを支援することによって、多様かつ包括的な職場の育成に重点を置く

work-life effectiveness [名]ワークライフバランス、仕事と生活のバランスを取ることの有効性

定義 the successful management and balance of professional responsibilities and personal life tasks, leading to both career satisfaction and personal well-being

職務上の責任と私生活での課題を上手に管理し、バランスを取ること。仕事での満足と個人的な幸福の両立につながる

crisis management [名]危機管理

定義 the process of preparing for, responding to, and recovering from an unexpected event or emergency, with the goal of minimizing negative impacts on an organization or community

予期せぬ出来事や緊急事態に備え、対応し、そこから回復する工程のことで、組織やコミュニティーへの悪影響を最小限に抑えることを目的としている

digital citizenship ［名］デジタル市民権

定義 the responsible, ethical, and productive use of technology and participation in digital communities
責任ある、倫理的で生産的なテクノロジーの使用とデジタルコミュニティーへの参加

⬤⬤⬤⬤⬤◀ Related Words and Phrases ▶⬤⬤⬤

digital literacy ［名］デジタルリテラシー

定義 the ability to find, evaluate, use, and create digital content effectively and responsibly, including understanding the basics of technology and online navigation
デジタルコンテンツを効果的かつ責任を持って見いだし、評価し、利用し、作成する能力のこと。これにはテクノロジーやインターネットの閲覧に関する基本的な理解が含まれる

cyberethics ［名］サイバー倫理

定義 the study and application of ethical principles and values in the context of digital technologies, particularly regarding issues such as privacy, intellectual property, and online behavior
デジタル技術の文脈における倫理原則と価値観の研究や応用のことで、特にプライバシー、知的財産、オンラインでの振る舞い方などの問題に関するもの

critical thinking ［名］批判的思考

定義 the ability to analyze, evaluate, and synthesize information objectively and logically, often used to solve problems, make decisions, and form well-founded opinions
客観的かつ論理的に情報を分析・評価・統合する能力。問題解決や意思決定、根拠のある意見の形成に用いられることが多い

media literacy ［名］メディアリテラシー

定義 the ability to access, analyze, evaluate, and create media content in various formats, understanding the role of media in society and its impact on individuals and culture
社会におけるメディアの役割と個人および文化への影響を理解しながら、さまざまな形式のメディアコンテンツを利用・分析・評価・創造する能力

dystopian [形] ディストピアの、暗黒郷の

定義 describing an imagined society characterized by extreme suffering, oppression, or societal dysfunction, often used as a warning or critique of current societal trends

多くの場合、現在の社会的傾向に対する警告や批評として用いられながら、極度の苦痛、抑圧、社会的機能不全を特徴とする想像上の社会を描写した

◄ Related Words and Phrases ►

megacity [名]メガシティー、巨大都市

定義 a very large urban area with a population of more than ten million people
人口 1,000 万を超える超大型都市圏

black swan [名]想定外の事態

定義 an unpredictable, highly improbable event with significant and widespread consequences, often used in the context of finance, economics, and risk management to describe unforeseen crises or disasters

重大かつ広範な結果を伴う予測不可能で非常に起こりにくい事象のことで、予期せぬ危機や災害を表すために、金融、経済、リスクマネジメントなどの文脈でよく使われる

disaster relief [名]災害救助、災害救援活動

定義 the provision of aid, resources, and support to individuals and communities affected by disasters, including emergency response, recovery assistance, and long-term reconstruction efforts

被災した個人やコミュニティーに対する援助、資源、および支援の提供のことで、緊急対応や復旧支援、長期的な復興事業を含む

housing crisis [名]住宅危機、住宅難

定義 a situation in which the supply of affordable, quality housing is insufficient to meet demand, often resulting in increased homelessness, overcrowded living conditions, and financial hardship for many individuals and families

手頃な価格で質の高い住宅の供給が不十分で需要を満たせない状況のことで、多くの場合、ホームレスの増加や、過密な生活環境、多くの個人や家庭の経済的苦境につながる

FIRE ［名］経済的自立と早期退職、ファイヤー

定義 short for "financial independence, retire early," a financial and lifestyle movement focused on achieving financial independence and early retirement through frugality, savings, and investment

「経済的自立と早期退職」の頭字語で、倹約や貯蓄、投資を通じて経済的自立と早期退職を達成することに焦点を当てた財務とライフスタイルに関する動きのこと

◄ Related Words and Phrases ►

LeanFIRE ［名］リーンファイヤー

定義 a variation of the FIRE movement that emphasizes extreme frugality and minimalism, with the goal of achieving financial independence and early retirement on a lower level of savings and investment

FIRE 運動の一種で、極端な倹約とミニマリズムを重視し、より小規模の貯蓄と投資で経済的自立と早期退職を達成することを目指すもの

DINK ［名］ディンクス

定義 short for "dual income, no kids," couples who both work and do not have children, often associated with greater financial flexibility and discretionary spending

「共稼ぎで子どもなし」の頭字語で、共働きで子どもを持たない夫婦のこと。通常、経済的な柔軟性が高く、裁量的な支出が大きいことが連想される

DINKY ［名］ディンキー

定義 short for "dual income, no kids yet," couples who both work and do not have children but plan to have them in the future, often enjoying greater financial flexibility before starting a family

「共稼ぎでまだ子どもがいない」の頭字語で、共働きで子どもはいないが、将来的に子どもを持つつもりでいる夫婦のこと。たいてい、子どもが生まれる前に、より大きな経済的な柔軟性を享受している

yuppie ［名］ヤッピー

定義 short for "young urban professional" or "young upwardly-mobile professional," a young person with a well-paid job and a fashionable lifestyle

「若い都会派職業人」または「若く将来有望な職業人」のことで、給料の高い仕事とファッショナブルなライフスタイルを持った若者

gatekeeping [名] ゲートキーピング

定義 the act of setting standards or norms that determine what is considered acceptable or valid, often leading to the exclusion or marginalization of certain individuals or perspectives

何が許容され、何が有効と見なされるかを決める基準や規範を設定する行為のことで、しばしば特定の個人や見方の排除や除外につながる

◄ Related Words and Phrases ►

tone policing [名] トーンポリシング

定義 a rhetorical tactic used to silence or discredit someone's argument or opinion by criticizing their emotional tone or perceived aggressiveness rather than addressing the substance of their argument

相手の主張や意見を封じたり、信用を失墜させたりするために用いられる修辞的な戦術で、主張の本質に触れるのではなく、相手の感情に基づく口調や攻撃性を批判することによるもの

white fragility [名] 白人の脆弱性

定義 the defensive reactions and avoidance behaviors exhibited by some white people when confronted with issues of racial inequality, discrimination, or privilege

人種的不平等、差別、特権の問題に直面したときに一部の白人が見せる防衛反応や回避行動

virtue signal [動] 美徳シグナリング、徳が高いというアピール

定義 to publicly express opinions or take actions that demonstrate one's moral values or social consciousness, often with the primary intention of gaining praise, approval, or social status rather than genuinely supporting a cause

自分の道徳的価値観や社会的意識を示すために、公に意見を述べたり行動を起こしたりすることで、多くの場合、純粋に大義を支持するというよりも、賞賛や承認、社会的地位を獲得することを主な目的としている

cancel culture [名] キャンセルカルチャー

定義 a social practice where individuals or groups are publicly shamed or boycotted due to perceived offensive actions, statements, or ideologies, often occurring on social media

攻撃的な行動、発言、またはイデオロギーが見られるという理由から、個人や集団が人前で恥をかかされたり、ボイコットされたりする社会的慣行のことで、多くの場合 SNS 上で起こる

Generation Alpha [名] アルファ世代

定義 the demographic cohort immediately following Generation Z
ジェネレーション Z の直後に当たる人口統計学的集団

◄ Related Words and Phrases ►

Generation Z [名] Z 世代

定義 the demographic cohort born between 1997 and 2012, often characterized by their digital nativity and fluency with social media, technology, and other forms of digital communication
1997 年から 2012 年に生まれた人口統計学的集団。基本的にデジタルネイティブで、SNS やテクノロジー、その他のデジタル通信手段に精通していることを特徴とする

Millennials [名] ミレニアル世代

定義 the demographic cohort born between 1981 and 1996, often characterized by their technological savviness, adaptability, and a focus on work-life balance
1981 年から 1996 年に生まれた人口統計学的集団で、基本的にテクノロジーに精通し、適応力があり、ワークライフバランスを重視することを特徴とする

Generation X [名] X 世代

定義 the demographic cohort born between 1965 and 1980, often characterized by its adaptability, independence, and skepticism toward traditional institutions
1965 年から 1980 年に生まれた人口統計学的集団で、基本的に適応性、独立性、伝統的な制度に対する懐疑心を特徴としている

boomer [名] ベビーブーマー

定義 a member of the baby boomer generation, the demographic cohort born between 1946 and 1964, characterized as being out of touch with contemporary culture, values, and technology
ベビーブーマー世代、すなわち 1946 年から 1964 年に生まれた人口統計学的集団の一員のことで、現代の文化や価値観、技術に疎いとされる

panopticontent ［名］パンオプティコンテンツ

定義 user-generated content, particularly on social media, that contributes to a sense of constant surveillance and self-policing, as individuals are aware that their actions and expressions are visible to others and subject to scrutiny

特にソーシャルメディア上の、ユーザーが生成したコンテンツのことで、常に監視・管理されているという感覚を醸成する。これは、人が自分の行動や表情が他者に見えており、監視の対象になっていると認識するからだ

◄ **Related Words and Phrases** ►

self-document ［動］〜を自分で記録する

定義 to create and share content, often through photos, videos, or text, that documents one's own life, experiences, and thoughts

自分の人生、経験、考えを記録したコンテンツを、写真、動画、文書などで作成し、共有する

clout ［名］影響力、権威

定義 the influence, impact, or perceived authority an individual or brand wields within social media platforms

個人や企業がソーシャルメディアプラットフォーム内で行使する影響力や効果、認識される権威

NPC ［名］非プレーヤーキャラクター

定義 short for "non-player character," someone who appears to follow a predetermined script or lacks independent thought, much like a character in a video game

「非プレーヤーキャラクター」の頭字語で、ビデオゲームのキャラクターのように、あらかじめ決められた脚本に従っているように見えるか、独自の考えを持たない人物のこと

viral ［形］（口コミで）素早く広がるような

定義 pertaining to a piece of information, a video, or an image that has been rapidly and widely circulated on the Internet within a short period of time

情報、動画、画像などがインターネット上で短期間で急速に広まって

phobia [名] 恐怖症

定義 an intense, irrational, and persistent fear or aversion toward a specific object, situation, or activity, often leading to significant distress or avoidance behavior

強烈で非合理的、かつ持続的な恐怖または嫌悪感のことで、特定の物体、状況、活動に対して抱かれる。たいてい大きな苦痛や回避行動につながる

═══ ◄ Related Words and Phrases ► ═══

homophobia [名] 同性愛嫌悪、同性愛恐怖症

定義 aversion, prejudice, or negative attitudes toward homosexuality or individuals who identify as LGBTQIA+, often resulting in discrimination, stigmatization, or marginalization

同性愛やLGBTQIA+として認識される個人に対する嫌悪、偏見、否定的な態度のことで、多くの場合、差別行動や他者の非難、疎外化につながる

xenophobia [名] 外国人嫌悪、外国恐怖症

定義 fear, dislike, or prejudice against people from other countries or cultures

他の国や文化の人に対する恐怖心や嫌悪感、偏見

nomophobia [名] 携帯電話依存症

定義 the fear or anxiety of being without access to a mobile phone or being unable to use it

携帯電話が手元にないこと、あるいは携帯電話を使えないことへの不安や恐怖

technophobia [名] 科学技術恐怖症、テクノロジー恐怖症

定義 the fear or aversion to technology, often stemming from a lack of understanding or negative experiences with technological devices

テクノロジーに対する恐怖心や嫌悪感のことで、多くの場合、ハイテク機器に対する理解不足や否定的な体験から生じる

poverty [名] 貧困

定義 the state of being extremely poor, with a lack of financial resources and access to basic necessities
極端に貧しく、財力がなく、基本的な生活必需品が手に入らない状態

━━━━━◤ Related Words and Phrases ◥━━━━━

public housing [名] 公営住宅
定義 government-owned or subsidized residential buildings or units provided to low-income individuals or families, aiming to offer affordable and decent housing options within the public sector
低所得の個人や世帯に提供される、政府が所有または補助する住宅や住居のことで、公共部門内で手頃でそこそこの居住物件を提供することが目的

slum [名] スラム街
定義 a densely populated urban area characterized by substandard housing, poor sanitation, and a lack of basic necessities
標準以下の住居や劣悪な衛生環境、基本的な生活必需品の欠如などを特徴とする、人口密度の高い都市地域

wage disparity [名] 賃金格差
定義 the unequal distribution of income between different groups, such as between men and women, or different racial and ethnic groups
男女や人種、民族といった異なる集団の間で所得が不平等に分配されること

wealth gap [名] 貧富の格差
定義 the unequal distribution of assets, resources, and opportunities between different socioeconomic segments of society
社会の異なる社会経済的領域の間での、資産、資源、機会の不平等な分配

troll [名] 荒らし、ネタ

定義 a person who intentionally posts provocative or offensive messages online to upset others or cause discord

挑発的なメッセージや攻撃的なメッセージを意図的にインターネット上に投稿し、他人を動揺させたり不和を引き起こす人

◀ Related Words and Phrases ▶

sealion [動] ～にシーライオニングする、～にしつこく嫌がらせする

定義 to engage in a disingenuous and persistent form of online questioning or debate, often with the intent to annoy or undermine the targeted person

ネット上で不誠実かつ執拗な質問や討論を行う。多くの場合、対象となる人物を困らせたり、疲弊させたりする意図がある

shitpost [名] クソみたいな書き込み

定義 a low-quality or irrelevant online post, often intended to be humorous, disruptive, or provocative

低俗な、あるいは不適切なオンラインの投稿のことで、多くの場合、悪ふざけや破壊、挑発を意図している

gaslight [動] ～をだます

定義 to manipulate someone psychologically by making them doubt their own perceptions, memories, or sanity, often as a means of control or deception

誰かを心理的に操作することで、本人の知覚や記憶、正気を疑わせることによって行われ、たいてい支配や欺瞞の手段として用いられる

flame [動] ～を罵倒する、～を非難する、～にかみつく

定義 to engage in hostile or aggressive online communication, often involving insults, criticism, or personal attacks

敵対的、あるいは攻撃的なオンラインコミュニケーションを行うことで、たいてい侮辱、批判、個人攻撃が含まれる

refugee [名] 難民

定義 a person who has been forced to leave their country in order to escape war, persecution, or natural disaster
戦争、迫害、自然災害から逃れるために自国を離れることを余儀なくされた人

◄ Related Words and Phrases ►

asylum [名] 亡命、庇護

定義 the protection granted by a country to an individual who has left their home country as a political refugee
政治的難民として母国を離れた個人に対して、国家が与える保護

migrant [名] 移住者

定義 a person who moves from one place to another, typically in search of better opportunities, such as work or education
ある場所から別の場所へ移動する人のことで、多くは仕事や教育などで、より良い機会を求めている

undocumented [形] 不法滞在の、密入国の

定義 describing an individual who resides in a country without the necessary legal authorization or documents
必要な法的認可や書類手続きを経ずに、ある国に居住する個人についての

refugee camp [形] 難民キャンプ

定義 a temporary settlement built to provide shelter, basic necessities, and support to large groups of displaced people
大規模な避難民の集団に、避難所や基本的な生活必需品、支援を提供するために建設された一時的な居住場所

Diversity 多様性

awareness ［名］気づき、自覚、認識

定義 conscious understanding of social inequities, discrimination, and exclusion, promoting empathy and commitment to equity and inclusion

社会的不平等、差別、排除を意識的に理解することで、共感や公平性、包摂への関与を促すもの

◄ Related Words and Phrases ►

ally ［名］同調者、支持者、協力者

定義 a person who actively supports and advocates for the rights and well-being of a marginalized group, even though they are not a member of that group themselves

社会的に疎外された集団の権利や福祉を、その集団の一員ではないにもかかわらず、積極的に支援し、擁護する人

advocacy ［名］擁護、支援活動

定義 the act of publicly supporting, promoting, or recommending a particular cause or policy, often to bring about change or address social issues

特定の運動や方針を公に支持、宣伝、推奨する行為で、多くの場合、変化をもたらすため、または社会問題に対処するためのもの

inclusion ［名］包含、包摂、受け入れ

定義 the practice of ensuring that individuals or groups, particularly those who have been historically marginalized, are welcomed and fairly represented within a community or organization

個人または集団、特に歴史的に疎外されてきた人々が、コミュニティーや組織に歓迎され、公平に一員と認められること

safe space ［名］安全な空間、安全な場所

定義 an environment in which individuals, particularly those from marginalized backgrounds, can feel secure and supported, free from discrimination or harassment

個人、特に社会から疎外された環境にある人々が、差別やハラスメントから解放され、安心して支援を受けられる環境

ethnicity [名] 民族性、民族意識

定義 the categorization of people based on shared cultural characteristics, such as language, religion, traditions, or ancestry
言語、宗教、伝統、祖先など、共有する文化的特徴に基づいて人々を分類すること

Related Words and Phrases

Latinx [形] ラテンアメリカ系住民の

定義 refering to people of Latin American origin or descent, often as an alternative to the gender-specific terms "Latino" or "Latina"
ラテンアメリカの出身者、またはその子孫の。たいてい性別を特定した語 Latino（ラテンアメリカ系男性の）または Latina（ラテンアメリカ系女性の）に代わって使われる

AAPI [名] アジア・太平洋諸島系アメリカ人

定義 short for "Asian American and Pacific Islander," encompassing a diverse range of people from Asia, the Pacific Islands, and the United States with Asian or Pacific Islander heritage
「アジア・太平洋諸島系アメリカ人」の頭字語で、アジアや太平洋諸島の出身者、および米国のアジアや太平洋諸島人の血を引く多様な人々を幅広く指す

MENA [名] 中東と北アフリカ

定義 short for the "Middle East and North Africa," a geopolitical region that encompasses countries from the Middle East and North Africa, often characterized by shared historical, cultural, and linguistic ties
「中東と北アフリカ」の頭字語で、中東と北アフリカの国々を含む地政学的な地域のこと。そこでは多くの場合、歴史的、文化的、言語的なつながりが共有されている

BiPoC [名] 黒人、先住民と有色人種

定義 short for "Black, Indigenous, and people of color," a term used to collectively describe individuals from non-White racial or ethnic backgrounds while acknowledging the unique experiences of Black and Indigenous communities
「黒人、先住民と有色人種」の頭字語で、黒人や先住民のコミュニティーのユニークな経験を認めつつ、非白人の人種的、民族的背景を持つ個人を総称するために使われる言葉

ism [名] 主義、イズム

定義 a set of beliefs or ideologies that promote prejudice, bias, and unfair treatment based on certain characteristics such as race, gender, or religion

偏見や先入観、不当な扱いを助長するような一連の信念やイデオロギーのことで、人種や性別、宗教といった特質に基づいたもの

═══ ◄ Related Words and Phrases ► ═══

ageism [名] 年齢差別

定義 discrimination or prejudice based on a person's age, often manifesting in stereotypes, marginalization, or exclusion of older or younger individuals

人の年齢に基づく差別や偏見。多くの場合、年上または年下の人に対する固定観念や、排斥、排除という形で現れる

classism [名] 階級差別、階級主義

定義 discrimination or prejudice based on a person's social class, often resulting in the marginalization or exclusion of individuals from lower-income or working-class backgrounds

社会階級に基づく差別や偏見のことで、低所得者や労働者階級の出身者が疎外されたり排除されたりすることが多い

tokenism [名] 形だけの平等主義、名ばかりの差別撤廃

定義 the practice of making a superficial effort to include or represent minority groups, often to create an appearance of diversity or inclusivity without addressing underlying systemic issues

少数派を取り込んだり表に出したりするために表面的な努力をすること。たいては、根本的な構造上の問題に取り組むことなく、多様性や包摂性の外観を作り上げる

adultism [名] アダルティズム、子どもは大人の支配下にあるという考え

定義 discrimination or prejudice against young people, often manifesting in the dismissal, marginalization, or exclusion of youth from decision-making processes or opportunities

若者に対する差別や偏見のこと。多くの場合、意思決定の過程や機会から若者を排除したり、疎外したり、排除したりすることで顕在化する

misogyny ［名］女性憎悪、女性蔑視

定義 hatred, contempt, or prejudice against women or girls, manifesting in various forms such as discrimination, objectification, or violence

女性や少女に対する憎しみや蔑み、偏見のことで、差別や偽物化、暴力といったさまざまな形で現れる

━━━━━ ◄ Related Words and Phrases ► ━━━━━

manspreading ［名］大股座り

定義 the act of a man sitting with his legs wide apart, often taking up more than one seat on public transportation or in other shared spaces

公共交通機関やその他の共有スペースで、男性が脚を大きく広げて座る行為のこと。たいてい、複数の座席を占有する

mansplain ［動］（〜を）男性が女性に偉そうに説明する

定義 as a man, to explain something to a woman in a condescending or patronizing manner, often assuming she has little knowledge of the subject

男性が女性に対して、慇懃無礼または恩着せがましい態度で何かを説明する。多くの場合、女性がそのテーマについてほとんど知識がないという思い込みがある

slut-shaming ［名］スラットシェーミング

定義 the act of criticizing or stigmatizing a person, typically a woman or girl, for perceived promiscuity

人、主に女性や少女に対して、規範に反しているように見えると言って批判したり汚名を着せたりする行為のこと

incel ［名］インセル、不本意な禁欲主義者

定義 short for "involuntary celibate," a person, typically a man, who is unable to find a romantic or sexual partner despite desiring one, often expressing resentment or hostility toward women or society

「非自発的独身者」を縮めた形で、恋愛や性的なパートナーを欲しているにもかかわらず見つけられない人、主に男性を指す。たいてい、女性や社会に対する憤りや敵意を表現している

intrinsic motivation [名] 内因性動機づけ

定義 the internal drive to engage in an activity because it is personally rewarding, enjoyable, or meaningful rather than for external rewards or recognition

ある行動に関わろうとする内的な衝動のことで、外から与えられる報酬や評価のためではなく、個人的にやりがいを感じ、楽しい、または有意義だと思うことが理由となる

━━━━ ◄ Related Words and Phrases ► ━━━━

extrinsic motivation [名] 外的動機づけ

定義 the drive to engage in an activity or task due to external factors, such as rewards, recognition, or the avoidance of negative consequences, rather than for the inherent enjoyment or satisfaction

ある行動や課題に従事しようとする衝動のうち、報酬や承認、否定的な結果の回避などの外的要因によるもののこと。本来の楽しさや満足感に基づくものではない

grit [名] 気概、根性

定義 a personality trait characterized by perseverance, passion, and resilience in the pursuit of long-term goals, often associated with overcoming obstacles, maintaining effort, and achieving success despite challenges

忍耐力、情熱、長期的な目標を追求する上での立ち直りの早さなどを特徴とする性格特性のことで、障害を克服し、努力を続け、困難があっても成功を収めやすい

growth mindset [名] グロースマインドセット

定義 the belief that one's abilities, intelligence, and talents can be developed and improved through effort, learning, and perseverance

努力や学習、忍耐によって、自分の能力、知性、才能を開発し、向上させることができるという信念

extracurricular [形] カリキュラム外の、課外の

定義 referring to activities or pursuits that are not part of a school's formal academic curriculum, such as clubs, sports, volunteer work, or hobbies

クラブ活動、スポーツ、ボランティア、趣味など、学校の正規のカリキュラムに含まれない活動や追求課題の

STEM [名] 科学・技術・工学・数学、理系

定義 short for "science, technology, engineering, and mathematics," which represents an interdisciplinary approach to education focused on these fields
「科学・技術・工学・数学」の頭字語で、これらの分野に特化した学際的な教育へのアプローチのこと

Related Words and Phrases

STEAM [名] 科学・技術・工学・芸術・数学

定義 an acronym that expands upon STEM (science, technology, engineering, and mathematics) by incorporating the arts, highlighting the importance of creativity, design, and critical thinking alongside the traditional STEM subjects
STEM に芸術を加えた頭字語で、従来の STEM 科目に加えて、創造性やデザイン、批判的思考の重要性を強調するもの

humanities [名] 人文科学

定義 a group of academic disciplines that study human culture, history, language, literature, philosophy, and the arts, emphasizing critical thinking, analysis, and communication skills
人間の文化、歴史、言語、文学、哲学、芸術を研究し、批判的思考や分析、コミュニケーション能力を重視する学問分野群

ELA [名] ELA、イングリッシュ・ランゲージ・アーツ

定義 short for "English language arts," an academic subject that encompasses reading, writing, speaking, and listening skills, as well as the study of literature, grammar, and composition
「イングリッシュ・ランゲージ・アーツ」の頭字語で、読む・書く・話す・聞く技能、文学や文法、作文の学習を含む学術科目

SEL [名] 情操学習、情操教育

定義 short for "social and emotional learning," a holistic approach to education that focuses on the development of social skills, emotional intelligence, and personal well-being to enhance academic achievement and lifelong success
「情操学習」の頭字語で、社会的技能や情操、個人の幸福感などの育成に焦点を当て、学問的目標達成と生涯にわたる成功を後押しするための総合的な教育アプローチ

universal design [名] ユニバーサルデザイン

定義 an approach to designing products, environments, and experiences to be accessible and usable by as many people as possible, regardless of age, ability, or background

年齢や能力、経歴などに関係なく、できるだけ多くの人が手を伸ばしやすく、使いやすい製品、環境、体験をデザインするアプローチ

◀ Related Words and Phrases ▶

LMS [名] 学習管理システム

定義 short for "learning management system," a software application or platform that facilitates the delivery, management, and tracking of educational courses, resources, and activities in online or blended learning environments

「学習管理システム」の頭字語で、オンラインまたはブレンディッドラーニングの環境における教育課程や教材、活動の提供や管理、追跡を容易にするソフトウェアアプリケーション、あるいはプラットフォームのこと

MOOC [名] ムーク、大規模公開オンライン講座

定義 short for "massive open online course," an online course that is freely accessible to a large number of participants, offering education on various subjects from renowned institutions or experts

「大規模公開オンライン講座」の頭字語で、多数の参加者が自由にアクセスでき、著名な教育機関や専門家からさまざまなテーマの教育を受けられるオンライン講座のこと

smartboard [名] スマートボード、電子黒板

定義 a large touchscreen display used in educational settings to facilitate interactive learning, collaboration, and multimedia presentations

教育現場で、インタラクティブな学習、協働、マルチメディアによる発表などを促進するために使用される大型のタッチスクリーンディスプレーのこと

gamification [名] ゲーミフィケーション

定義 the application of game design elements, such as point systems, competition, and rewards, to non-game contexts, like education or training, to increase motivation, engagement, and learning outcomes

ポイントシステムや競争、報酬といったゲームの設計要素を、教育や研修などのゲームではない活動に適用し、動機づけや関与の度合い、学習成果を高めること

106

aesthetic ［名］美学、美感

定義 a distinctive style, appearance, or visual theme that characterizes a person's taste or preferences in art, fashion, or design

個性的なスタイル、外観、視覚的なテーマで、芸術、ファッション、デザインにおける人の趣味や嗜好を特徴づけるもの

≺ Related Words and Phrases ≻

beat ［名］ビート

定義 a well-applied, flawless makeup look

しっかりした非の打ちどころのない化粧姿

drip ［名］ドリップ

定義 an individual's fashionable or stylish appearance, particularly in relation to clothing, accessories, or overall aesthetic

ファッショナブル、あるいはスタイリッシュな人の外観のことで、特に衣服やアクセサリー、または全体的な美感に関わるもの

lewk ［名］ルック

定義 a distinctive, well-coordinated, and fashionable outfit or appearance that makes a statement or showcases a person's unique style

個性的で、うまくコーディネートされた、ファッショナブルな服装や外見のことで、人のユニークなスタイルを主張したり、アピールしたりするもの

glow-up ［名］グローアップ

定義 a significant and positive transformation in a person's appearance, style, or overall well-being, often occurring over time or through personal effort

人の外見やスタイル、あるいは全体的な幸福感における、重要かつ肯定的な変化。多くの場合、長い時間や個人の努力によってもたらされるもの

athleisure [名] アスリージャー

定義 a style of clothing that combines athletic wear and leisurewear, often worn in casual and social settings beyond the gym or sports activities
スポーツウェアと普段着を組み合わせたスタイルのことで、ジムやスポーツ活動以外のカジュアルな場面や社交の場面で着用されることが多い

Related Words and Phrases

e-sports [名] e スポーツ

定義 organized, competitive video gaming events, often involving professional players, teams, and leagues, and watched by spectators both online and in-person
組織的な対戦型ビデオゲーム競技のことで、プロ選手やチーム、リーグで参加することが多く、オンラインや対面での観戦も可能なもの

magnet fishing [名] マグネットフィッシング

定義 a hobby where participants use a strong magnet attached to a rope to search for metal objects in bodies of water, such as rivers or lakes
ロープに取り付けた強力な磁石を使って、川や湖などの水辺にある金属を探す趣味

pickleball [名] ピックルボール

定義 a paddle sport that combines elements of tennis, badminton, and table tennis, played with a perforated plastic ball and paddle on a smaller court
テニスとバドミントン、卓球の要素を併せ持ったパドルスポーツで、穴の空いたプラスチック製のボールとパドルを使い、小さめのコートでプレーするもの

crossfit [名] クロスフィット

定義 a high-intensity fitness training program that combines elements of weightlifting, cardio exercises, and functional movements, aiming to improve overall physical fitness and performance
ウェートリフティング、有酸素運動、昨日運動の要素を組み合わせた、総合的な体力と動きの向上を目的とした高強度のフィットネストレーニングプログラム

bae [名] ベイ

定義 referring to something or someone that is beloved or cherished, often expressing deep affection or preference

愛されているものや人の。多くの場合、深い愛情や好みを表現する

====== Related Words and Phrases ======

stan [名] 熱狂的なファン

定義 an extremely dedicated and passionate fan of a celebrity, musician, or other public figure, often to the point of obsession

有名人やミュージシャンなどの公人の極めて熱心で情熱的なファンのこと。たいてい、その人物に取りつかれてしまっている

throuple [名] スラプル

定義 a committed romantic relationship that involves three individuals rather than the traditional two-person couple

従来の2人ではなく、3人が関わる献身的な恋愛関係のこと

ship [動] 〜をくっつける、〜をカップルにする

定義 from "relationship," to support or endorse a romantic relationship, real or imagined, between two characters or individuals

relationship から生まれた語。2人の登場人物や個人の間にある、現実あるいは想像上の恋愛関係を支持したり、推奨したりする

OTP [名] 理想のカップル

定義 short for "one true pairing," a term used by fans to describe their favorite romantic pairing of characters or individuals in a fictional work or real life

「理想のカップル」の頭字語で、フィクションの登場人物や実生活の中の個人を支持する人が、自分のお気に入りのカップルを指して用いる言葉

epicurean [形] 美食家の、食通をうならせる

定義 referring to the pursuit of pleasure, especially in food and drink
特に飲食物について喜びを追求する

════◄ Related Words and Phrases ►════

terroir [名]テロワール、土壌
定義 the unique combination of natural factors that influence the characteristics of an agricultural product, such as wine
ワインなどの農産物の特徴に影響を与える、自然要因の独特な組み合わせ

ghost kitchen [名]ゴーストキッチン
定義 a commercial kitchen that operates solely to fulfill delivery orders and has no physical dining space for customers
デリバリーの注文に応じるためだけに運営され、客のための物理的な食事スペースを持たない商用厨房

gastronomic [形]食の、美食の、調理法の
定義 relating to the art, science, and appreciation of food
食べ物に関する技術や科学、鑑賞の

single-source [形]単一産地の、単一供給源の
定義 originating from one specific location, producer, or supplier
唯一特定の場所、生産者、供給者を元とする

Culture

festivus ［名］フェスティバス

定義 a secular holiday celebrated on December 23, popularized by the TV show *Seinfeld*
12 月 23 日に祝われる非宗教的な祝日で、テレビ番組『となりのサインフェルド』によって広まったもの

Related Words and Phrases

Galentine's Day ［名］ギャレンタインデー

定義 a celebration on February 13th for women to show appreciation and support for their female friends, popularized by the TV show *Parks and Recreation*
女性が女友だちに感謝と応援の気持ちを伝えるために 2 月 13 日に行われる祝賀で、テレビ番組『パークス・アンド・レクリエーション』で広まったもの

friendsgiving ［名］フレンズギビング

定義 a celebration of Thanksgiving among friends, often held before or after the traditional family Thanksgiving gathering
感謝祭を友人同士で祝うもので、伝統的な家族の感謝祭の集まりの前か後に行われることが多い

Treat Yo' Self Day ［名］トリート・ユアセルフ・デー

定義 a day dedicated to self-care and indulgence, inspired by the popular TV show *Parks and Recreation*
セルフケアと道楽に捧げる日のことで、人気テレビ番組『パークス・アンド・レクリエーション』にちなんだもの

democracy sausage ［名］デモクラシーソーセージ

定義 a barbecue held at polling stations on election day, typically in Australia, symbolizing a celebration of democracy
選挙日に投票所で行われるバーベキュー大会のことで、通常オーストラリアで民主主義の賛美を象徴するもの

gezellig ［形］ヘゼリヒ、居心地の良い、温かい

定義 (Dutch) describing a warm, cozy, and convivial atmosphere or experience, often associated with spending time with loved ones or enjoying a pleasant environment

（オランダ語）温かい、居心地の良い、和やかな雰囲気や経験についての。多くの場合、愛する人と過ごすことや心地良い環境を楽しむことに関連する

Related Words and Phrases

koselig ［形］コーシェリ、居心地の良い、快適な

定義 (Norwegian) describing a sense of warmth, coziness, and contentment, typically associated with social interactions or relaxing environments

（ノルウェー語）温かさや居心地の良さ、満足感についての。通常、社会的な交流やくつろげる環境と関連する

hygge ［形］ヒュッゲ、居心地の良い、快適な

定義 (Danish) referring to coziness, comfort, and well-being achieved through enjoying simple pleasures and creating a warm atmosphere

（デンマーク語）シンプルな喜びを楽しみ、温かい雰囲気を作ることで得られる居心地の良さや快適さ、幸福感の

lördagsgodis ［名］ルーダスゴディス、土曜日のお菓子

定義 (Swedish) the tradition of enjoying candy or sweets specifically on Saturdays

（スウェーデン語）土曜日に特別にお菓子やスイーツを楽しむ習慣のこと

niksen ［名］ニクセン、あえて何もしないこと

定義 (Dutch) doing nothing or engaging in purposeless activity as a form of relaxation and stress relief

（オランダ語）くつろぎやストレス解消のために何もしないこと、あるいは無目的な活動をすること

107

Healthcare 医療・健康管理

allergy ［名］アレルギー

定義 an immune system reaction to a substance, such as pollen or food, that is harmless to the average person
花粉や食べ物など、平均的な人にとっては無害な物質に対する免疫系の反応

◄ Related Words and Phrases ►

asthma ［名］ぜんそく

定義 a chronic respiratory condition characterized by difficulty breathing due to inflamed and narrowed airways
気道の炎症と狭くによって呼吸困難となる慢性呼吸器疾患

---

bacteria ［名］細菌、バクテリア

定義 single-celled microorganisms that can be found in various environments, with the potential to be beneficial, harmful, or have no significant effect on humans
さまざまな環境に存在する単細胞の微生物で、人に対して有益な、あるいは有害な、あるいはとりたてて影響を与えない可能性を持っている

---

inflammation ［名］炎症

定義 the body's natural response to injury, infection, or irritation, characterized by redness, swelling, heat, and sometimes pain
けがや感染、刺激に対する身体の自然な反応のことで、赤みや腫れ、発熱、時には痛みなどの特徴を持つ

---

rhinitis ［名］鼻炎

定義 an inflammation of the mucous membrane inside the nose, often caused by an allergy or infection, resulting in sneezing, itching, and a runny nose
アレルギーや感染症によって起こる鼻の粘膜の炎症で、くしゃみ、かゆみ、鼻水などの症状が出る

epidemiology [名] 疫学、伝染病学

定義 the study of the distribution and determinants of health-related events in populations, and the application of this knowledge to control health problems
集団の中での健康にかかわる事象の分布や決定要因の研究、および健康の問題を管理するための上記知識の応用

Related Words and Phrases

clinical trial [名] 臨床試験

定義 a research study that tests the safety, effectiveness, and potential side effects of medical interventions, such as drugs, devices, or procedures
医薬品や医療機器、医療処置などの医学療法の安全性、有効性、潜在的な副作用などを検証する研究調査

mRNA [名] メッセンジャー RNA

定義 short for "messenger RNA," a molecule that carries genetic information from DNA to ribosomes, where it is used to build proteins
「メッセンジャー RNA」の省略形で、遺伝情報を DNA からリボソームへ運び、そこでタンパク質を作るために使われる分子のこと

superspreader [名] スーパースプレッダー、超感染拡大者

定義 an individual or event that results in the transmission of a contagious disease to a disproportionately large number of people
ありえないほど大勢の人に感染症を伝染させてしまう個人や出来事

symptom [名] 症状

定義 a physical or mental indication of an illness, injury, or condition
身体的または精神面での病気やけが、健康状態の兆候

euthanasia ［名］安楽死

定義 the act of intentionally ending a person's life to relieve their suffering, often in cases of terminal illness or unbearable pain

苦しみを和らげるために意図的に人の命を終わらせる行為のことで、通常、末期的な病気や耐え難い痛みを抱える患者に対するもの

═══ ◄ Related Words and Phrases ► ═══

assisted suicide ［名］自殺ほう助

定義 the act of providing a person with the means to end their own life, often due to terminal illness or unbearable suffering

人に自分の人生を終わらせる手段を提供する行為のことで、しばしば末期的な病気や耐え難い苦痛が原因となる

right to die ［名］死ぬ権利

定義 the belief that individuals have the right to decide when and how to end their own lives

人には自分の人生をいつ、どのように終えるかを決定する権利がある、という信念のこと

end-of-life care ［名］終末期ケア、終末期医療

定義 the support and medical care provided to patients with a terminal illness or advanced age, focused on relieving pain and maintaining quality of life

終末期や高齢の患者に対して、痛みの緩和や生活の質の維持に重点を置いた支援や医療を提供すること

living will ［名］生前遺言

定義 a legal document that outlines a person's preferences for medical treatment and care if they become unable to communicate or make decisions

人が、意思疎通や意思決定ができなくなった場合の医療や治療に関する自分の要望を記した法的文書のこと

gene [名] 遺伝子

定義 a segment of DNA that contains the information required for the synthesis of a specific protein or RNA molecule, influencing an organism's traits

DNA の一部で、特定のタンパク質や RNA 分子の合成に必要な情報が含まれており、生物の形質を左右するもの

≫ Related Words and Phrases ≫

epigenetics [名] 後成的遺伝学、後成学

定義 the study of changes in gene function that do not involve alterations to the underlying DNA sequence, often influenced by environmental factors

DNA 配列の変化を伴わない遺伝子機能の変化の研究のこと。この変化は通常、環境要因の影響によって起きる

gene bank [名] 遺伝子バンク

定義 a facility or database for preserving and storing genetic material, such as seeds or DNA samples, to maintain biodiversity and protect endangered species

種子や DNA サンプルなどの遺伝物質を保存・保管するための施設やデータベースのことで、生物多様性を維持し、絶滅危惧種を保護することが目的

gene therapy [名] 遺伝子治療

定義 a medical treatment that involves altering or replacing faulty genes with healthy ones to treat or prevent genetic disorders and diseases

遺伝性疾患や疾病の治療・予防のために、欠陥のある遺伝子を改変したり、健康な遺伝子と置き換えたりする医療行為

genomics [名] ゲノミクス

定義 the study of the structure, function, and evolution of genomes, which are the complete set of genetic material present in an organism

生物に存在する遺伝物質の総体であるゲノムの構造や機能、進化を研究すること

immunology [名] 免疫学

定義 the study of the immune system and its role in protecting the body from diseases and foreign substances
病気や異物から体を守る免疫の仕組みと、その役割についての研究

◆━ Related Words and Phrases ━◆

immunochemistry [名] 免疫化学

定義 the branch of chemistry concerned with studying the chemical processes and interactions involved in the immune system's response to foreign substances
化学の一分野で、異物に対する免疫系の反応に関わる化学的過程や相互作用を研究するもの

immunohistochemistry [名] 免疫組織化学

定義 a laboratory technique used in pathology and research to detect specific proteins or antigens in tissues, utilizing the binding of antibodies to target molecules, followed by visualization through the use of chemical or fluorescent markers
病理学の研究で、組織中の特定のタンパク質や抗原を検出するために使用される実験技術の一つ。抗体が標的分子に結合した後、化学マーカーまたは蛍光マーカーを使用して可視化する

immunotherapy [名] 免疫療法

定義 a medical treatment that uses the body's immune system to fight diseases by stimulating or enhancing immune responses
体の免疫システムを利用した医学的治療法の一つで、免疫反応を刺激または増強することで疾病と闘う

neutralizing antibody [名] 中和抗体

定義 an antibody produced by the immune system that specifically binds to and neutralizes the biological activity of a pathogen, toxin, or foreign substance, preventing its harmful effects
免疫系によって作られる抗体で、病原体や毒素、異物の生物学的活性に特異的に結合して中和し、その有害な影響を防ぐもの

nutrition [名] 栄養摂取、栄養素

定義 the process of obtaining and utilizing the necessary nutrients from food for the body's growth, maintenance, and repair
身体の成長、維持、修復のために必要な栄養素を食物から得て利用する過程

Related Words and Phrases

intermittent fasting [名]断続的断食

定義 an eating pattern that cycles between periods of eating and fasting, with various approaches that restrict food intake during certain hours or days
食べる期間と断食の期間を繰り返す食事のパターンのこと。さまざまなやり方があるが、いずれも特定の日時に食事の摂取を制限する

supplement [名]栄養補助食品、サプリメント

定義 a product, often in the form of a pill, powder, or liquid, intended to provide additional nutrients, such as vitamins, minerals, or amino acids, to one's diet
多くは錠剤、粉末、あるいは液状の製品で、ビタミン、ミネラル、アミノ酸などの栄養素を食事に加えることを目的としている

obesity [名]肥満

定義 a medical condition characterized by the excessive accumulation of body fat, often resulting in significant health risks and an increased likelihood of various chronic diseases
体脂肪の過剰な蓄積を特徴とする医学的な状態のことで、多くの場合、重大な健康リスクやさまざまな慢性疾患の可能性を高める

ultra-processed [形]超加工の

定義 referring to food products that have undergone extensive industrial processing and contain a high proportion of artificial additives
大幅な工業的加工が施され、人工添加物の割合が高い食品の

pathogen ［名］病原体、病原菌

定義 a microorganism, such as a bacterium, virus, or fungus, that can cause disease in a host organism
宿主に病気を引き起こす細菌、ウイルス、真菌などの微生物

◄ **Related Words and Phrases** ►

epidemic ［名］まん延、伝染病、疫病

定義 a widespread occurrence of an infectious disease in a community or region at a particular time, typically spreading quickly and affecting a large number of people
特定の時期に集団や地域の中で感染症が広く発生することで、通常、急速に広がり、多くの人々に影響を及ぼす

mutation ［名］突然変異

定義 in virology, a genetic alteration or change that occurs in the DNA or RNA of a virus, resulting in the introduction of new variations or characteristics into the viral population
ウイルス学における、ウイルスの DNA または RNA に起こる遺伝的な変化または変更のことで、ウイルスの集団に新たな変異や特性が導入される

variant ［名］変異株、変異体

定義 a version of a microorganism, such as a virus or bacterium, that is genetically distinct from the original strain and may exhibit different characteristics, such as increased transmissibility or resistance to treatments
ウイルスや細菌などの微生物の型の一つで、元の株とは遺伝的に異なり、感染力の増大や治療に対する耐性といった別の特性を示す可能性のあるもの

jab ［名］予防接種

定義 a vaccination or vaccine injection, often used in the context of immunization campaigns and public health discussions
ワクチン接種やワクチン注射のことで、予防接種キャンペーンや公衆衛生の議論の場などでよく使われる

personalized medicine ［名］オーダーメイド医療

定義 a medical approach that involves tailoring healthcare treatments, practices, and products to individual patients based on their genetic, environmental, and lifestyle factors

個々の患者に合った治療、診療、製品を提供する医療手法のことで、遺伝や環境、ライフスタイルなどの要因に基づく

◆ Related Words and Phrases ◆

pharmacogenomics ［名］薬理ゲノム学、薬理ゲノミクス

定義 the study of how an individual's genetic makeup influences their response to medications, combining pharmacology and genomics to personalize drug selection, dosage, and treatment strategies

人の遺伝子構成が薬物に対する反応にどのように影響を与えるかに関する研究で、薬理学とゲノミクスを組み合わせたもの。薬剤の選択、投与量、治療方法を患者一人ひとりに合わせることが目的

liquid biopsy ［名］液体生検

定義 a non-invasive diagnostic method that involves the analysis of circulating biomarkers, such as cell-free DNA or proteins, in body fluids to detect and monitor diseases

非侵襲的診断法の一つで、体液中の無細胞 DNA やタンパク質といった循環生体指標を分析し、疾病の検出や監視を行う

digital therapeutics ［名］デジタル治療法

定義 software-based interventions or treatments that utilize digital platforms, such as mobile apps or online programs, to deliver evidence-based therapeutic interventions

モバイルアプリやオンラインプログラムなどのデジタルプラットフォームを活用した、ソフトウェアベースの診療または治療のことで、根拠に基づく治療介入を提供する

immunogenomics ［名］免疫ゲノミクス

定義 the study of how an individual's genetic variations influence their immune system, including the identification of genetic factors associated with immune responses, disease susceptibility, and immunotherapy efficacy

人の遺伝的変異が免疫系にどのように影響するかに関する研究のことで、これには免疫応答、疾患感受性、免疫療法効果に関連する遺伝的要因の特定などが含まれる

molecular diagnostics [名] 分子診断学

定義 the analysis of genetic materials, biomarkers, or gene expression patterns to aid in disease detection, diagnosis, and treatment decisions

遺伝物質や生体指標、遺伝子発現パターンなどを解析するもので、疾病の発見や診断、治療方針の決定に役立つ

◄ Related Words and Phrases ►

transcriptomics [名] 転写学

定義 the study of an organism's complete set of RNA transcripts, providing insights into gene expression patterns, regulation, and functional analysis of the transcriptome

生物の RNA 転写物の完全な組み合わせを研究するもので、遺伝子の発現パターンや規則、トランスクリプトームの機能解析などに関する理解につながる

ctDNA [名] ctDNA、循環腫瘍 DNA

定義 short for "circulating tumor DNA," genetic material released by tumor cells into the bloodstream, which can be isolated and analyzed to detect cancer-related mutations, monitor treatment response, and assess disease progression

「循環腫瘍 DNA」を縮めた形で、腫瘍細胞から血流に放出される遺伝物質のこと。これを分離・分析することで、がんに関連する変異の検出や治療反応の監視、病気の進行の判定などを行える

biomarker [名] 生体指標、バイオマーカー

定義 a biological molecule or characteristic that can be objectively measured and evaluated, serving as an indicator of normal biological processes, disease states, or responses to therapy

客観的に測定・評価することができる、生物学的分子または特性。正常な生物学的作用や疾病の状態、治療に対する反応などの指標としての役割を果たす

genome sequencing [名] ゲノム解読

定義 the process of determining the complete sequence of an organism's DNA, including all its genes, providing information on genetic variations and potential disease risk

ある生物の、あらゆる遺伝子を含んだ DNA の全塩基配列を決定する工程のことで、遺伝的変異や潜在的な疾病リスクに関する情報を提供する

computer-aided medicine

[名] コンピューターを使った医療、コンピューター支援医療

定義 the integration of computer technology and software applications in medical practice to assist healthcare professionals in tasks such as diagnosis, treatment planning, and patient management

医療現場におけるコンピューター技術およびソフトウェアアプリケーションの統合のことで、診断や治療計画、患者の管理といった業務において医療従事者を支援するためのもの

▶ Related Words and Phrases ◀

in-silico trials [名]コンピューターによる臨床試験

定義 computer-simulated clinical trials that use computational models and algorithms to predict the safety and efficacy of medical interventions, reducing the need for human trials

コンピューターでシミュレーションを行う臨床試験のことで、計算モデルやアルゴリズムを使用して医療介入の安全性や有効性を予測し、人体による臨床試験の必要性を低減する

digital pathology [名]デジタル病理学

定義 the practice of digitizing and analyzing pathological images, such as tissue slides or microscopy samples, using digital imaging technology and computer-based platforms

組織のスライドや顕微鏡を通した標本などの病理学的画像を、デジタル化して分析すること。デジタル画像化技術やコンピューターベースのプラットフォームを使用する

surgical simulation [名]手術シミュレーション

定義 computer-based training that replicates surgical procedures, enabling surgeons to practice and refine their skills in a realistic virtual environment

外科手術を再現するコンピューターベースのトレーニングのことで、外科医がリアルな仮想環境で技能を訓練、洗練させることができる

robotic surgery [名]ロボット外科手術

定義 surgical procedures performed using robotic systems that provide enhanced precision, dexterity, and visualization to assist surgeons during minimally invasive surgeries

ロボットシステムを使用して行われる外科的処置のことで、外科医が低侵襲手術を行う際に、精度や巧みさ、可視化性能などを高めてくれる

reproductive health

［名］リプロダクティブヘルス、性と生殖に関する健康

定義 the state of complete physical, mental, and social well-being in all matters relating to the reproductive system, including fertility, contraception, and sexually transmitted infections

生殖に関するあらゆる面において、身体的、精神的、社会的に完全に良好である状態のこと。生殖能力や避妊、性感染症などの問題が含まれる

◄ Related Words and Phrases ►

fertility treatment ［名］不妊治療

定義 a medical procedure or intervention designed to assist individuals or couples in achieving pregnancy, particularly when facing infertility issues

特に不妊症の問題に直面している個人やカップルを支援し、妊娠を実現するために考案された医療処置や介入のこと

male contraceptive ［名］男性用避妊法

定義 a method or device used by men to prevent pregnancy, either by blocking sperm from reaching the egg or inhibiting sperm production

妊娠を防ぐために男性が使用する方法または用具のことで、精子が卵子に到達するのを阻止するか、精子の生成を阻害するもの

family planning ［名］家族計画、産児制限

定義 the conscious decision and practice of controlling the number and timing of pregnancies through the use of contraception, fertility awareness, and other reproductive health interventions

妊娠の回数や時期の制限を意識的に決定し、実践すること。避妊や生殖に関する啓発、その他のリプロダクティブヘルスの介入を通じて行われる

infertility ［名］不妊、不妊症

定義 the condition or state of being unable to conceive a child or achieve pregnancy

受胎や妊娠ができない体調、状態

superbug [名] スーパー耐性菌、非常に強力な細菌

定義 a strain of bacteria that has developed resistance to multiple antibiotics, making it difficult to treat infections caused by the bacteria
複数の抗生物質に対する耐性を獲得した細菌株のことで、細菌による感染症の治療を困難にするもの

═══ Related Words and Phrases ═══

antibiotics [名] 抗生剤、抗生物質

定義 drugs used to treat bacterial infections by either killing bacteria or inhibiting their growth and reproduction
細菌感染症の治療に使用される薬剤のことで、細菌を死滅させるか、細菌の成長・繁殖を阻害する

biofilm [名] 生物膜、バイオフィルム

定義 a complex community of microorganisms, such as bacteria, that adhere to a surface and produce a slimy film to protect themselves from environmental threats
細菌などの微生物が複雑に絡み合ったもので、何かの表面に付着してぬめりのある膜を作り、それが環境の脅威から自分の身を守る

macrophage [名] 大食細胞、マクロファージ

定義 a type of white blood cell that plays a crucial role in the immune system, responsible for engulfing and destroying harmful bacteria, viruses, and other foreign substances
白血球の一種で、免疫系で重要な役割を担っており、有害な細菌やウイルスなどの異物を飲み込んで破壊する

antibiotic resistance [名] 抗生物質への耐性

定義 the ability of bacteria to evolve and develop resistance to the drugs designed to kill them, rendering those antibiotics less effective in treating infections
細菌が進化して、それを殺すために作られた薬剤に対抗できるよう身につけた能力のこと。そのせいで、こうした抗生物質が感染症の治療における効果を失う

universal health coverage [名] 国民皆保険制度

定義 a healthcare system where all individuals can access necessary health services without facing financial hardship
すべての人々が財政上の問題を抱えずに、必要な医療サービスを受けられる医療制度

▶ Related Words and Phrases ◀

affordable care [名] 費用が適正な医療

定義 healthcare that is reasonably priced and accessible, allowing individuals to obtain the medical services they need without causing financial strain
費用が適正で利用しやすい医療のこと。個人が経済的な負担を背負わずに、必要な医療サービスを受けられる

health insurance [名] 健康保険

定義 a policy provided by an insurance company or government program that covers the cost of healthcare services, usually in exchange for a monthly premium
保険会社、あるいは政府の制度によって提供される保険の一種で、通常、毎月の保険料と引き換えに、医療サービスの費用をまかなうもの

out-of-pocket [形] 自己負担の

定義 referring to expenses that are paid directly by an individual rather than being covered by insurance or another third-party source
保険などの第三者の財源でまかなわれるのではなく、個人によって直接支払われる費用の

deductible [名] （保険の）控除免責額

定義 a specified amount of money an individual must pay for healthcare expenses before their insurance begins to cover the costs
保険が適用され始める前に、個人が医療費として支払わなければならない一定の金額

aerodynamic ［形］空気力学の

定義 designed to minimize air resistance and drag for more efficient movement through the air
空気抵抗や風圧を最小限に抑え、より効率的に空中を移動できるよう設計された

◄ Related Words and Phrases ►

hypersonic ［形］極超音速の

定義 relating to speeds of at least five times the speed of sound, or approximately 6,125 kilometers per hour
音速の 5 倍以上、つまり時速約 6,125 キロメートルの速度に関する

VTOL ［形］垂直離着陸の

定義 short for "vertical take-off and landing," referring to aircraft that can take off, hover, and land vertically without the need for a runway
「垂直離着陸」を短くした形。滑走路を必要とせず、垂直に離陸、ホバリング、着陸できる航空機の

jetpack ［名］ジェットパック

定義 a wearable device equipped with jet propulsion that enables a person to fly through the air
ジェット推進力を備えたウェアラブルデバイスで、人が空を飛ぶことを可能にするもの

smart road ［名］スマート道路

定義 a road equipped with advanced technology, such as sensors and communication systems, designed to improve traffic flow, safety, and efficiency
センサーや通信システムなどの先進技術を備え、交通の流れや安全性、効率を向上させることを目的とした道路

biotechnology ［名］バイオテクノロジー

定義 the use of living organisms, cells, or biological processes to develop or modify products or processes for specific purposes

生物、細胞、または生物学的作用を利用することで、特定の目的のために製品や工程を開発または変更するもの

≪ **Related Words and Phrases** ≫

GMO ［名］遺伝子組み換え生物

定義 short for "genetically modified organism," an organism modified by introducing specific changes to its DNA through genetic engineering methods

「遺伝子組み換え生物」の頭字語で、遺伝子工学的手法により DNA に特定の変化を導入して改変された生物のこと

microfluidics ［名］マイクロ流体工学

定義 the scientific field and technology that deals with the behavior, control, and manipulation of small amounts of fluids at the microscale

マイクロスケールでの少量の流体の挙動、制御、操作を扱う科学分野およびテクノロジー

bioamplifier ［名］バイオアンプ

定義 a device used to amplify biological signals, such as electrical activity from muscles, nerves, or the heart, for measurement and analysis

生体信号を増幅するために用いられる装置のことで、筋肉、神経、心臓からの電気的活動などの測定と分析が目的である

pill camera ［名］カプセル内視鏡

定義 a small, ingestible capsule containing a camera that captures images of the digestive tract as it passes through, typically used for medical diagnostic purposes

消化管を通過する際の画像を撮影するカメラを内蔵した小型の飲み込めるカプセルで、一般に医療診断の目的で使用される

room-scale VR [名] ルームスケール VR

定義 a type of virtual reality system that allows users to physically move within a designated space, with their movements tracked and translated into the virtual environment

仮想現実システムの一種で、ユーザーが指定された空間内を物理的に移動し、その動きを追跡して仮想環境に変換することができる

◄ Related Words and Phrases ►

haptics [名]触覚学

定義 the science and technology of creating touch sensations in human-computer interactions, often used to simulate the feel of objects or surfaces in virtual environments

人間とコンピューターの相互のやり取りの中で、触れる感覚を作り出す科学技術のことで、多くの場合、仮想環境における物体や表面の感触を模倣するために用いられる

base station [名]ベースステーション

定義 a stationary device that serves as a central hub or anchor point in a virtual reality setup, providing positional tracking and synchronization of VR headsets within a defined tracking area

仮想現実の設定で、中心的なハブまたは基準点として機能する据え置き型装置で、定義されたトラッキングエリア内で VR ヘッドセットの位置の追跡と同期を行う

head mounted display [名]ヘッドマウントディスプレー

定義 a wearable display device, typically in the form of a helmet or goggles, that projects images or video directly in front of the wearer's eyes, often used in virtual reality systems

通常ヘルメットやゴーグルの形を取ったウェアラブルの表示装置のことで、着用者の目の前に直接画像や映像を投影する。仮想現実システムでよく使われる

headset [名]ヘッドセット、ヘッドフォン

定義 a pair of headphones, often with an attached microphone, that is worn on the head and used for communication, listening to audio, or engaging with virtual reality systems

一対のヘッドフォンで、たいていマイクが付いている。頭部に装着し、通信や音声の聴取、仮想現実システムを利用するするために使われる

jailbreak ［動］〜を改造する、〜を改変する

定義 to remove the limitations and restrictions imposed by the manufacturer on a device, allowing for customization and access to features otherwise unavailable

メーカーが機器に課している制限や制約を取り除き、カスタマイジングや通常利用できない機能へのアクセスを可能にする

≪ Related Words and Phrases ≫

DRM ［名］デジタル著作権管理

定義 short for "digital rights management," a set of technologies and methods used to protect and control the distribution, use, and access of copyrighted digital content

「デジタル著作権管理」の頭字語で、著作権で保護されたデジタルコンテンツの配布、使用、アクセスを管理するために使われる技術や手法のこと

fair use ［名］公正利用、公正使用

定義 a legal doctrine allowing limited use of copyrighted material without obtaining permission from the rights holder, typically for purposes such as education, research, or commentary

権利者の許可を得ずに著作物を限定的に使用することを認める法原理で、通常、教育や研究、論評などの目的が想定される

firmware ［名］ファームウェア

定義 software embedded in a device's hardware that controls its functionality, often responsible for the basic operations and communication with other components

機器の本体に組み込まれたソフトウェアのことで、その機能を制御するもの。多くの場合、基本動作や他の部品類との通信をつかさどる

copyright infringement ［名］著作権侵害

定義 the unauthorized use, reproduction, or distribution of copyrighted material, such as music, movies, or software, without the permission of the rights holder

音楽、映画、ソフトウェアなどの著作物を、権利者の許可なく無断で使用、複製、配布すること

maglev ［名］磁気浮揚

定義 a transportation system that uses magnetic levitation to lift, guide, and propel vehicles, reducing friction and allowing for high speeds and energy efficiency

磁力による浮揚作用を利用した交通システムで、車両を持ち上げ、誘導し、推進することによって摩擦を減らし、高速走行やエネルギーの効率化を可能にする

≼ **Related Words and Phrases** ≽

guideway ［名］軌道、ガイドウェー

定義 a structure or path, such as rails or tracks, designed to guide and support the movement of vehicles like trains or monorails

レールや線路などの構造物や経路のことで、電車やモノレールのような乗り物の動きを誘導し支えるために設計されたもの

electromagnetic propulsion ［名］電磁推進

定義 a method of propulsion that uses magnetic fields to generate force and move objects, such as vehicles or spacecraft, without the need for traditional fuels or engines

磁界を利用した推進方法の一つで、力を発生させて、車両や宇宙船などの物体を移動させる。従来の燃料やエンジンなどを必要としない

levitation ［名］浮上、浮揚

定義 the act of lifting or suspending an object in the air without any physical support, often through the use of magnetic forces

物理的な支えなしに、物体を空中に持ち上げたり浮かべたりすることで、多くの場合、磁力を利用する

friction ［名］摩擦、摩擦力

定義 the resistance that one surface encounters when moving against another, resulting in the generation of heat, wear, and energy loss

1つの表面が別の表面上を動くときに出合う抵抗のことで、発熱や摩耗、エネルギーの損失につながる

nanotechnology [名] ナノテクノロジー

定義 the science, engineering, and technology of manipulating matter at the nanometer scale, usually ranging between 1 and 100 nanometers, to create new materials, devices, and structures

ナノメートルのスケールで物質を操る科学、工学、および技術のことで、通常、1から100ナノメートルの範囲内で新しい材料や装置、構造物を作り出す

⟫⟫⟫⟫ Related Words and Phrases ⟫⟫⟫

nanoassembly [名]ナノアッセンブリー

定義 the process of arranging and assembling molecules, nanoparticles, or other nanoscale elements into a specific order or structure to form larger, functional materials or devices

分子やナノ粒子などのナノスケールの物質を特定の順序や構造で配列し、組み立てる工程のことで、より大きな機能的な物質や装置を形成する

nanobot [名]ナノボット、ナノロボット

定義 a microscopic machine or robot capable of manipulating matter at the nanometer scale

ナノメートルのスケールで物質を操作できる微細な機械やロボット

nanolithography [名]ナノリソグラフィー

定義 a process used to create nanoscale patterns or structures on a substrate, typically employed in the fabrication of electronic components, such as semiconductor devices

基板上にナノスケールのパターンや構造を作るための工程で、一般的には半導体デバイスなどの電子部品の製造に使用される

nanomanipulation [名]ナノマニピュレーション

定義 the process of manipulating, controlling, or modifying nanoscale objects, typically using specialized tools like scanning probe microscopes or atomic force microscopes

ナノスケールの物体を操作、制御、または修正する工程のことで、走査型プローブ顕微鏡や原子間力顕微鏡のような特殊な道具が使われる

OSINT [名] オシント、オープンソースインテリジェンス

[定義] short for "open-source intelligence," a method of information gathering that involves collecting, analyzing, and disseminating data from publicly available sources, such as websites, social media, and news outlets

「オープンソースインテリジェンス」を短くした形で、ウェブサイトや SNS、報道機関など、一般に公開されている情報源からデータを収集、分析、発信する情報収集手法のこと

◀ Related Words and Phrases ▶

dox [動]他人の個人情報をインターネット上にさらす、ドキシングする

[定義] to publicly reveal someone's personal information, such as their real name, address, or phone number, without their consent, often as a form of online harassment or to incite others to harass them

本名、住所、電話番号といった、誰かの個人情報を本人の同意なしに公にする。多くの場合、オンラインハラスメントの一形態として、あるいは他人をあおって嫌がらせをするための行為

web scraping [名]ウェブスクレーピング

[定義] the process of extracting and gathering data from websites through the use of automated tools or scripts

自動化されたツールやスクリプトを使い、ウェブサイトからデータを抽出・収集する工程

data fusion [名]データ融合

[定義] the process of integrating data from multiple sources, such as sensors, databases, or other information systems, to create a more accurate, comprehensive, and useful representation of the data

複数のソースからのデータを統合する工程のことで、ソースにはセンサーやデータベース、その他の情報システムなどがある。より正確で包括的、かつ有用なデータの開示を行うことが目的

geofencing [名]ジオフェンシング

[定義] the use of GPS or other location-based technology to create virtual boundaries around a specific geographical area, allowing for the triggering of actions or notifications when a device enters or exits the defined area

GPS などの位置情報技術を使って、特定の地理的領域の周りに仮想的な境界を作ること。それによって、ある装置が定義された領域に持ち込まれたり、そこから持ち出されたりしたときに、何らかの動作や通知が発せられる

pose tracking [名] 姿勢追跡

定義 the process of monitoring and recording the position and movement of a person's body, usually through the use of cameras, sensors, or other tracking devices

人体の位置や動きを監視・記録する工程のことで、通常、カメラやセンサーなどの追跡装置が使われる

![Related Words and Phrases]

eye tracking [名] 視線追跡、視標追跡

定義 the measurement of eye movement and the direction of a person's gaze, often using specialized cameras or sensors to determine where they are looking

人の目の動きや視線の方向を測定することで、多くの場合、専用のカメラやセンサーを使って、その人がどこを見ているのかが判断される

hand tracking [名] 手部追跡、手部検出

定義 the monitoring and recording of hand movements and gestures, often using cameras, sensors, or other tracking devices

手の動きやジェスチャーを監視・記録することで、一般的にカメラやセンサー、その他の追跡装置が使われる

head tracking [名] 頭部追跡

定義 the process of detecting and measuring the position and orientation of a person's head, usually with cameras, sensors, or other tracking devices, often used in virtual reality or gaming applications

人の頭の位置や向きを検出・測定する工程のことで、通常はカメラやセンサーなどの追跡装置が用いられる。仮想現実やゲームアプリでよく使われる

positional tracking [名] 位置追跡

定義 the process of determining the location and orientation of an object or person in a physical or virtual space, often using sensors, cameras, or other tracking devices

物理的または仮想的な空間内の物体や人の位置と向きを特定する工程のことで、多くの場合、センサーやカメラなどの追跡装置が使われる

quantum mechanics ［名］量子力学

［定義］ a branch of physics that describes the behavior and interactions of matter and energy at the atomic and subatomic scales, involving principles such as wave-particle duality and quantum superposition

物理学の一分野で、原子や素粒子のスケールにおける物質やエネルギーの挙動や相互作用を説明するもの。波動・粒子の二重性や量子重ね合わせなどの原理が含まれる

◀ Related Words and Phrases ▶

quantum computing ［名］量子コンピューティング

［定義］ a type of computing that utilizes quantum bits or qubits, which can exist in multiple states simultaneously, enabling the performance of complex calculations and problem-solving tasks that are infeasible for classical computers

量子ビットを利用した演算の一種で、複数の状態を同時に存在させることができる。古典的なコンピューターでは実現不可能な複雑な計算や問題解決作業を行える

quantum dot ［名］量子ドット

［定義］ a nanoscale semiconductor particle with unique optical and electronic properties due to its small size and quantum confinement, often used in applications like display technology, solar cells, and medical imaging

小さなサイズと量子閉じ込めに起因する特有の光学的・電子的性質を持ったナノスケールの半導体粒子のことで、表示技術や太陽電池、医療画像などの用途でよく使われる

quantum entanglement ［名］量子絡み合い

［定義］ a phenomenon in quantum mechanics where the properties of two or more particles become correlated in such a way that the state of one particle cannot be described independently of the state of the other particles, even when separated by large distances

量子力学における現象の一つで、2つ以上の粒子の性質が、1つの粒子の状態が他の粒子の状態と別個に説明できないような形で相互に関連するもの。たとえ粒子同士が遠く離れていても起こる

quantum compass ［名］量子コンパス

［定義］ a navigation device that uses the principles of quantum mechanics to determine position and orientation without relying on external signals such as GPS

量子力学の原理を利用したナビゲーション装置で、GPS などの外部信号に頼らず、位置や向きを特定するもの

resolution ［名］解像度

定義 a measure of the detail and clarity of a digital image or display, typically expressed as the number of pixels in the width and height of the image or screen

デジタル画像やディスプレーの詳細性や鮮明さを表す指標のことで、通常、画像や画面の幅と高さのピクセル数で表現される

➤◄ **Related Words and Phrases** ►◄

pixel ［名］ピクセル、画素

定義 the smallest discrete unit of a digital image, usually represented as a single point in a grid and assigned a specific color

デジタル画像の最小の分離単位で、通常はグリッドの1点として表現され、特定の色が割り当てられている

polygon count ［名］ポリゴン数

定義 the number of polygons, typically triangles or quadrilaterals, used to represent the surface of a 3D model in computer graphics

コンピューターグラフィックスにおいて、3D モデルの表面を表現するために使われるポリゴン——通常は三角形または四角形——の数

field of view ［名］視野角

定義 the extent of the observable world that can be seen at any given moment through a camera, viewing device, or the human eye, typically expressed as an angle

カメラや視覚装置、あるいは人間の目を通して任意の瞬間に認識できる観察可能な世界の範囲のことで、通常は角度で表される

voxel ［名］ボクセル

定義 a volumetric pixel, or value in a regular grid in three-dimensional space, often used to represent 3D objects and data in computer graphics, medical imaging, and scientific simulations

3次元空間の規則的なグリッド内の容積画素または容積値のことで、コンピューターグラフィックスや医療画像、科学的シミュレーションなどで3次元の物体やデータを表現するためによく使われる

RFID ［名］無線自動識別

定義 short for "radio-frequency identification," a technology that uses radio waves to wirelessly identify and track objects equipped with special tags or transponders

「無線自動識別」を短くした形で、電波を利用して特殊なタグや応答装置を装着した物体を無線で識別・追跡する技術のこと

Related Words and Phrases

NFC ［名］近距離無線通信

定義 short for "near field communication," a short-range wireless communication technology that enables devices to exchange data

「近距離無線通信」の頭字語で、機器間でデータをやり取りできる近距離での無線通信技術のこと

---

smart label ［名］スマートラベル

定義 a label embedded with RFID, NFC, or other electronic components that can store, transmit, or receive information for various applications, such as tracking, authentication, or temperature monitoring

RFID や NFC などの電子部品が埋め込まれたラベルのことで、追跡や認証、温度監視といったさまざまな用途の情報を保存したり送受信したりできる

---

smart packaging ［名］スマートパッケージング

定義 a type of packaging that incorporates advanced technologies, such as sensors or RFID tags, to provide additional functionality, enhancing product safety, convenience, and user experience

センサーや RFID タグなどの先端技術を組み込んだ梱包の一種で、負荷的な機能を担い、製品の安全性や利便性、利用者の使い勝手を向上させるもの

---

tag ［名］タグ、電子タグ

定義 a small electronic device, often using RFID or NFC technology, that can store, transmit, or receive data and be attached to an object for identification, tracking, or other purposes

小型の電子装置の一つで、多くの場合 RFID や NFC 技術が使われている。データの保存や送受信が可能で、識別や追跡などの目的で物に取り付けられる

3D printing　［名］3D プリント

定義 a manufacturing process that creates three-dimensional objects by successively depositing layers of material, typically plastic or metal, based on a digital model
3 次元の物体を生み出す製造工程の一つで、素材を順次積層していくことで実現する。通常、デジタルモデルに基づいて、プラスチックや金属などの素材が用いられる

◄ Related Words and Phrases ►

additive manufacturing　［名］積層造形

定義 the process of creating objects by adding material layer by layer, as opposed to subtractive manufacturing, which removes material to create a shape
材料を層状に追加していくことで物を作る工程。材料を削って形を作る除去加工の逆に当たる

digital fabrication　［名］デジタルファブリケーション

定義 a manufacturing process that uses computer-controlled machines and tools to create objects based on digital models
コンピューター制御された機械や工具を使い、デジタルモデルに基づいて物を生み出す製造工程

rapid prototyping　［名］高速試作

定義 the process of quickly creating a physical model or prototype of a product using computer-aided design (CAD) and manufacturing technologies, such as 3D printing
ある製品の物理的な模型や試作品を迅速に作成する工程のことで、コンピューター支援設計（CAD）や 3D プリントなどの製造技術が用いられる

stereolithography　［名］光造形法

定義 a type of 3D printing technology that uses a laser to solidify a liquid photopolymer resin layer by layer, creating a three-dimensional object
3D プリント技術の一種で、液状のフォトポリマー樹脂をレーザーで層状に固め、立体物を作り出す

109

Computing コンピューティング

AGI ［名］汎用人工知能

［定義］ short for "artificial general intelligence," a form of artificial intelligence that exhibits intelligence and cognitive abilities at a level equal to or surpassing human capabilities across a wide range of tasks

「汎用人工知能」の頭字語で、さまざまな課題に対して人間の能力と同等かそれを上回るレベルの知能や認知能力を発揮する人工知能のこと

═══◄ Related Words and Phrases ►═══

intelligence explosion ［名］知性爆発

［定義］ a hypothetical scenario in which an AI system becomes capable of autonomously improving its own intelligence, leading to rapid advancements beyond human comprehension

AI システムが自律的に自らの知能を向上させることができるようになるという仮定のシナリオで、人知を超えた急速な進化を遂げるという仮説

ASI ［名］人工超知能

［定義］ short for "artificial superintelligence," the hypothetical stage of artificial intelligence where machines possess intelligence that greatly surpasses human cognitive abilities

「人工超知能」の頭字語で、人間の認知能力を大きく上回る知能を機械が持つという、人工知能に関する仮説の段階

singularity ［名］シンギュラリティー、特異点

［定義］ a hypothetical point in the future when artificial intelligence advances to a level where it triggers rapid technological growth, resulting in unforeseeable changes to human civilization

未来における仮説上の時点の一つで、人工知能の発達が急速な技術発展を引き起こし、人類の文明に予期せぬ変化をもたらすタイミングのこと

transhumanism ［名］超人間主義、トランスヒューマニズム

［定義］ a movement that advocates for the use of technology to enhance human physical, mental, and emotional capacities, potentially leading to a post-human future

人間の肉体的、精神的、感情的な能力を高めるためにテクノロジーを利用することを提唱する動向で、潜在的にポストヒューマン（仮説上の人類を超えた未来の種）の未来につながるもの

P2P [形] ピアツーピアの

定義 short for "peer-to-peer," referring to a decentralized communication model where individual devices, or peers, directly share data without the need for a central server

「ピアツーピア」を短くした形。中央のサーバーを介さずに個々の端末機、つまりピアが直接データを共有する分散型の通信モデルの

◄ Related Words and Phrases ►

MIMO [形] 多重入出力の

定義 short for "multiple input multiple output," referring to a wireless technology that uses multiple antennas to transmit and receive data simultaneously, increasing the capacity and speed of communication

「多重入出力」の頭字語。複数のアンテナを使って同時にデータを送受信し、通信量と速度を向上させる無線技術の

broadband [名] ブロードバンド

定義 high-speed Internet access that provides fast, continuous data transmission over a wide range of frequencies

高速インターネット接続サービスで、幅広い周波数帯域を使って高速かつ連続的なデータ伝送を実現するもの

mesh network [名] メッシュネットワーク

定義 a decentralized network topology in which multiple devices are interconnected to form a self-healing and self-configuring network, enabling data transmission and communication between devices without relying on a central infrastructure

分散型ネットワークの接続形態の一つで、複数の機器が相互に接続されて自己修復・自己設定可能なネットワークを作り、中央のインフラに依存せずに機器間のデータ伝送や通信を可能とするもの

cloud [名] クラウド

定義 a system of remote servers that store, manage, and process data, allowing users to access their information and applications through the Internet

データを保存、管理、処理するリモートサーバーのシステムで、ユーザーはインターネットを通じて情報やアプリケーションにアクセスすることができる

dark web [名] ダークウェブ

[定義] a concealed portion of the Internet, accessible only through specialized software, where users can maintain anonymity and engage in various activities, often illegal

インターネット上の隠された部分の一つで、専用のソフトウェアを通してのみアクセスでき、ユーザーは匿名性を保ちながらさまざまな活動ができる。ただし、多くは違法行為

≼ Related Words and Phrases ≽

VPN [名] VPN、仮想私設ネットワーク

[定義] short for "virtual private network," a technology that establishes a secure and encrypted connection over a public network allowing users to access and transmit data privately and securely

「仮想私設ネットワーク」の頭字語で、公のネットワーク上に安全で暗号化された接続を確立し、ユーザーが個人的に安全にデータにアクセスしたり、データを送信したりできるようにする技術

revenge porn [名] リベンジポルノ

[定義] the nonconsensual sharing of intimate or sexually explicit images or videos of a person, often by an ex-partner, to cause distress or harm

私的な、あるいは性的に露骨な画像や動画を本人の同意を得ずに公開することで、多くの場合、別れたパートナーによって苦痛や危害を与える目的で行われるもの

deepfake [名] ディープフェイク

[定義] a manipulated video or audio file that uses artificial intelligence to convincingly replace a person's likeness or voice with another's

人工知能を使用して改ざんされた動画や音声ファイルで、人の姿や声をもっともらしく別のものに作り替えたもの

darknet [名] ダークネット

[定義] a private network that requires specific authorization or software to access, often used for illegal activities, communication, or file sharing

特定の承認やソフトウェアがないとアクセスできない私設ネットワークで、多くの場合、違法な活動や通信、ファイル共有に使用される

encryption [名] 暗号化

定義 the method of converting data into a secret code to prevent unauthorized access or tampering
不正アクセスや改ざんを防止するために、データを秘密のコードに変換する方法

◄ Related Words and Phrases ►

end-to-end encryption [名]終端間暗号化

定義 a secure communication method where only the intended recipients can decrypt and read the transmitted data
安全性の高い通信方法の一つで、企図した受信者だけが送信されたデータを解読して読める

passwordless authentication [名]パスワードレス認証

定義 a method of verifying a user's identity without requiring a traditional password, often using biometrics, tokens, or devices
従来のパスワードを必要とせずにユーザーの身元を確認する方法のことで、多くの場合、生体認証やトークン、機器を使用する

private key [名]秘密鍵、プライベートキー

定義 a secret cryptographic key used in asymmetric encryption systems, which only the owner should know to decrypt data or sign messages
非対称暗号化システムで使用される秘密の暗号鍵で、鍵の所有者だけが把握し、データの復号化やメッセージへの署名のために用いる

public key [名]公開鍵、パブリックキー

定義 a secret cryptographic key used in asymmetric encryption systems intended to be openly shared with others
非対称暗号システムで使用される秘密の暗号鍵で、他者と広く共有することが企図されている

hactivism [名] ハクティビズム

定義 the act of using hacking techniques and computer knowledge for political or social activism
ハッキング技術やコンピューターの知識を政治活動や社会活動に利用する行為

⊰ Related Words and Phrases ⊱

cyber disobedience [名]サイバー抗議

定義 the intentional use of hacking or other digital methods as a form of nonviolent protest
ハッキングやその他のデジタルな手法を非暴力的な抗議活動の一形態として意図的に使うこと

online sit-in [名]オンライン座り込み(活動)

定義 a form of digital protest where a large number of Internet users simultaneously access a specific website or online service
デジタル抗議活動の一形態で、多数のインターネットユーザーが同時に特定のウェブサイトやオンラインサービスにアクセスするもの

DDoS attack [名]分散型サービス拒否攻撃、DDoS攻撃

定義 short for "distributed denial of service attack," a cyberattack in which multiple systems flood a targeted server or network with an overwhelming amount of traffic, causing it to crash or become unresponsive
「分散型サービス拒否攻撃」を短くした形で、複数のシステムを標的としてサーバーやネットワークに圧倒的な量のトラフィックを発生させ、クラッシュや応答不能の状態に陥らせるサイバー攻撃

botnet [名]ボットネット

定義 a network of compromised computers, often controlled without the owners' knowledge, that can be used to perform malicious activities such as spamming or launching cyberattacks
欠陥を抱えたコンピューターのネットワークの一つで、多くの場合、所有者が知らないうちにコントロールされている。迷惑メールの送信やサイバー攻撃といった悪意のある活動に使われる可能性がある

open-world [形] オープンワールドの

定義 referring to a video game or virtual environment that offers a vast, expansive, and non-linear gameplay experience, allowing players to freely explore and interact with a virtual world without strict boundaries or linear progression

大きな広がりのある、直線的ではないゲーム体験を提供するビデオゲームや仮想環境の。プレーヤーが厳格な境界線や直線的な進行のない仮想世界を自由に探索し、交流できるような

◄ Related Words and Phrases ►

world-building [名] ワールドビルディング

定義 the process of creating a detailed, immersive, and coherent fictional universe, often used in storytelling and game design

詳細で没入感があり、首尾一貫した架空の世界を作り出す過程のことで、たいてい、物語やゲームのデザインに用いられる

MMORPG [名] 多人数参加型オンライン・ロールプレーイング・ゲーム、ネットゲーム

定義 short for "massively multiplayer online role-playing game," a genre of online video games where many players interact within a virtual world

「多人数参加型オンライン・ロールプレーイング・ゲーム」の頭字語で、オンラインゲームの一種。仮想世界の中で多くのプレーヤーがやり取りするもの

real-time rendering [名] リアルタイムレンダリング

定義 the process of generating computer graphics instantly based on user input or changes, commonly used in video games and interactive media

ユーザーの入力や変更に基づいてコンピューター画像を瞬時に生成する工程のことで、ビデオゲームやインタラクティブメディアでよく使われる

user engagement [名] ユーザーエンゲージメント

定義 the level of interaction and involvement users have with a product, service, or application, often measured by metrics like time spent and actions taken

ユーザーの、製品やサービス、アプリなどとのやり取りや関与の水準のことで、多くの場合、費やした時間や取った行動などを基準にして測定される

programming [名] プログラミング

定義 the process of creating, testing, and maintaining computer software by writing and organizing code using programming languages
コンピューターのソフトウェアを作成し、テストし、保守管理する工程のことで、プログラミング言語を用いてコードを記述し、まとめ上げる

◄ Related Words and Phrases ►

framework [名]フレームワーク
定義 a set of tools, libraries, and conventions that developers use as a foundation to build and structure software applications
開発者がソフトウェアアプリケーションを構築・構成するための基盤として使用する、ツールとライブラリーと約束事をまとめたもの

protocol [名]プロトコル、通信接続手順
定義 a set of rules and guidelines that govern how data is transmitted and communicated between computers and devices over a network
ネットワークを介してコンピューターや機器の間でデータがどのように伝わり、通信されるかを規定する一連のルールとガイドライン

library [名]ライブラリー
定義 a collection of pre-written code, functions, and resources that software developers can use to simplify and streamline the software development process
ソフトウェア開発者がソフトウェア開発プロセスの簡素化と合理化のために使用できる、あらかじめ書かれたコード、関数、およびリソースの集合

architecture [名]アーキテクチャー、基本設計概念
定義 the design, structure, and organization of a computer system or software application, including its components and their relationships and interactions
コンピューターシステムやソフトウェアアプリケーションの設計、構造、組成のことで、構成要素とそれらの関係、および相互作用などが含まれる

telecommunications ［名］遠隔通信、電気通信

定義 the transmission of information over long distances using electronic and digital technologies, such as phone lines, satellites, and the Internet
長距離の及ぶ情報伝達を行うことで、電話回線や人工衛星、インターネットといった電子技術やデジタル技術を駆使したもの

≼ Related Words and Phrases ≽

fiber optics ［名］ファイバー光学

定義 a technology that uses thin strands of glass or plastic to transmit data as light signals, allowing for high-speed communication
ガラスやプラスチックの細い繊維を使い、データを光信号として伝送する技術で、高速通信を可能にするもの

dark fiber ［名］未使用光ファイバー回線

定義 unused or unlit optical fiber cables deployed for telecommunications purposes
電気通信用に配備されたまま未使用、あるいは未点灯の光ファイバーケーブル

quantum communication ［名］量子通信

定義 a branch of science and technology that harnesses the principles of quantum mechanics to securely transmit information through quantum systems, offering enhanced privacy and protection against eavesdropping
量子力学の原理を利用した科学技術の一分野で、量子システムを通じて情報を安全に伝送することで、プライバシーを強化し、盗聴から保護する

bandwidth ［名］帯域幅

定義 the capacity of a network or communication channel to transmit data, often measured in bits per second (bps)
ネットワークや通信チャネルのデータ伝送能力のことで、多くの場合、1秒あたりのビット数（bps）で測定される

touchscreen　［名］タッチスクリーン

定義 a display that allows users to interact with a device by touching the screen with their fingers or a stylus
指やスタイラスペンで画面に触れることで、機器との情報のやり取りを実現する画面

═◄ Related Words and Phrases ►═

stylus　［名］スタイラスペン

定義 a pen-like tool used to interact with touchscreens, providing precision and control for drawing, writing, or selecting items on the screen
タッチスクリーンの操作に使われるペン様の道具で、画面上に絵を描いたり文字を書いたり、アイテムを選択したりするための正確性と操作性を提供するもの

voice recognition　［名］音声認識

定義 a technology that enables devices to understand and respond to spoken commands or questions by converting speech into text or actions
音声をテキストや動作に変換することで、機器に音声による命令や質問を理解させ、それらに応答できるようにする技術

biometric authentication　［名］生体認証

定義 a security mechanism that utilizes unique physical or behavioral characteristics, such as fingerprints, iris patterns, or voice recognition, to verify and authenticate an individual's identity
指紋や虹彩パターン、声の出し方といった、人の身体的な、あるいは動作の特徴を利用したセキュリティーの仕組みのことで、個人の身元を確認したり認証したりするためのもの

gesture control　［名］ジェスチャーコントロール、動作制御

定義 a technology that allows users to interact with a device using physical movements, such as hand gestures or body motion, without touching the device
ユーザーが、手のジェスチャーや体の動きなどの物理的な動作を使って、機器と接触せずに情報をやり取りできるようにする技術

biofuel ［名］バイオ燃料

定義 a type of fuel derived from organic materials, such as plants or animal waste, which can be a more sustainable and environmentally friendly alternative to fossil fuels

植物や、動物の排泄物などの有機物から得られる燃料の一種で、化石燃料に代わる、より持続可能で環境に優しい燃料となり得るもの

◄ Related Words and Phrases ►

biodiesel ［名］バイオディーゼル

定義 a renewable fuel made from vegetable oils, animal fats, or used cooking grease, which can be used in diesel engines

植物油脂や動物油脂、使用済み調理用油脂から作られる再生可能な燃料で、ディーゼルエンジンに使用できる

biogas ［名］バイオガス

定義 a mixture of gases produced by the breakdown of organic matter, often used for heating or electricity generation

有機物の分解によって発生するガスの混合物で、多くの場合、暖房や発電に使われる

biomass ［名］バイオマス

定義 organic material, such as plants, wood, and agricultural residues, that can be used as a renewable source of energy

植物、木材、農業残渣など、再生可能なエネルギー源として利用可能な有機物

bioreactor ［名］バイオリアクター、生物反応器

定義 a device or system that supports the growth and maintenance of living organisms, such as bacteria or algae, for various purposes, including waste treatment and biofuel production

廃棄物処理やバイオ燃料生産といったさまざまな目的で、細菌や藻類などの生物の増殖や維持をサポートする装置やシステム

circular economy [名] 循環（型）経済

定義 an economic system that aims to minimize waste and resource consumption by designing products and processes for reuse, repair, and recycling, promoting sustainability and reducing environmental impacts

廃棄物や資源の消費を最小限に抑えることを目的とした経済システムで、再利用、修理、リサイクルのための製品や工程を設計したり、持続可能性を促進したり、環境への影響を低減したりすることによって実現するもの

◄ Related Words and Phrases ►

green manufacturing [名]グリーンマニュファクチャリング

定義 a sustainable approach to industrial production that aims to minimize environmental impact by implementing eco-friendly practices, such as resource conservation, waste reduction, and the use of renewable energy sources

工業生産に対する持続可能なアプローチで、目的は環境への影響を最小限に抑えることにある。環境に配慮した取り組みを行うことで実現するもので、それには省資源、廃棄物の削減、再生可能エネルギーの利用などが挙げられる

upcycle [動]〜をアップサイクルする

定義 to transform waste materials or discarded products into new, higher-quality items

廃材や廃棄された製品を、より質の高い新しいものに生まれ変わらせる

downcycle [動]〜をダウンサイクルする

定義 to convert waste materials into new products of lower quality and functionality, potentially extending their useful life

耐用年数が延びる可能性を含ませつつ、廃棄物を品質や機能の面で劣る新しい製品に作り変える

cradle-to-cradle [形]ゆりかごからゆりかごまでの

定義 refering to a design approach that emphasizes the creation of products and systems where materials are continuously recycled or reused in a closed-loop cycle, eliminating waste and minimizing environmental impact

材料が継続的にリサイクルまたは再利用される閉じた循環の中で製品やシステムを作り出すことに重きを置いた設計手法。廃棄物をなくし、環境への影響を最小限に抑えるもの

contamination [名] 汚染、汚濁

定義 the presence of pollutants or harmful substances in an environment that can cause negative impacts on ecosystems and human health
環境の中に汚染物質や有害物質が存在し、それが生態系や人間の健康に悪影響を与えること

≈ **Related Words and Phrases** ≈

eutrophication [名]富栄養化

定義 a process in which an excessive amount of nutrients, such as nitrogen and phosphorus, enter a body of water, leading to algal blooms, oxygen depletion, and harm to aquatic life
窒素やリンなどの栄養塩が水域に過剰に入り込み、藻類の発生や酸素の欠乏、水生生物への害をもたらす過程

PFAS [名]有機フッ素化合物

定義 a group of synthetic chemicals, including perfluorooctanoic acid (PFOA) and perfluorooctane sulfonate (PFOS), used in various industrial and consumer products and linked to environmental and health risks
合成化学物質の一群で、パーフルオロオクタン酸やパーフルオロオクタンスルホン酸などが含まれる。さまざまな工業製品や消費財に使用され、環境や健康のリスクと結び付いている

pharmacoenvironmentology [名]ファーマコエンバイロンメントロジー

定義 the study of the environmental impacts of pharmaceuticals, including their potential risks to ecosystems and human health through exposure in water or food sources
医薬品が環境に与える影響についての研究のことで、水や食物への曝露による生態系や人間の健康への潜在的なリスクなどを対象とする

sewage [名]下水、汚水

定義 wastewater and waste material, often containing human excrement, that is discharged from homes, businesses, and industries
家庭や事業所、産業界から排出される廃水や、多くは人糞を含む廃棄物のこと

ecotourism　［名］エコツーリズム

定義　a form of sustainable tourism that focuses on responsible travel to natural areas, aiming to minimize environmental impact, support conservation efforts, and benefit local communities

持続可能な観光の一形態で、責任を持って自然に分け入ることに焦点を当て、環境への影響を最小限に抑え、保護活動を支援し、地域社会に利益をもたらすことを目指す

Related Words and Phrases

disposable income　［名］可処分所得

定義　the amount of money an individual or household has available to spend or save after taxes and other necessary expenses, such as housing and food, have been paid

個人や世帯が、税金や住居費、食費などの必要経費を支払った後に、使ったり貯蓄したりできる金額

biodiversity　［名］生物の多様性、種の多様性

定義　the variety of life forms, including plants, animals, microorganisms, and ecosystems, within a given region or on Earth as a whole

生命体の多様性のことで、植物や動物、微生物、はては生態系を含めた、特定の地域内、あるいは地球全体での状況

overtourism　［名］オーバーツーリズム、観光公害

定義　a situation characterized by an excessive number of tourists visiting a destination, resulting in overcrowding, congestion, and negative impacts on the local community, environment, or cultural heritage

観光地を訪れる旅行客の数が過剰になり、過密状態や混雑が生まれ、地域社会や環境、文化遺産への悪影響が生じる状況のこと

geoconservation　［名］ジオコンサーベーション

定義　the protection and management of geological and geomorphological features, such as rock formations, caves, and landscapes, to preserve their scientific, educational, and cultural value

岩層や洞窟、景観全体の地質学的・地形学的特性を保護・管理することで、その科学的、教育的、文化的価値の保全が目的

SDGs ［名］SDGs、持続可能な開発目標

定義 short for “Sustainable Development Goals,” a set of 17 global goals established by the United Nations in 2015 to address economic, social, and environmental challenges and promote sustainable development by 2030

「持続可能な開発目標」を短くした形で、2015 年に国連が定めた 17 の世界的目標のこと。2030 年までに経済・社会・環境に関する課題に取り組み、持続可能な開発を推進するもの

Related Words and Phrases

collaborative consumption ［名］協調的消費

定義 the sharing, borrowing, or renting of goods and services among individuals or communities, often facilitated by digital platforms, to reduce waste, optimize resources, and promote sustainability

個人や地域社会の間で物やサービスを共有、借用、または貸与することで、通常、デジタルプラットフォームによって促進される。廃棄物の削減や資源の最適化、持続可能性の促進が目的

environmental degradation ［名］環境劣化、環境の悪化

定義 the deterioration of the environment due to human activities, such as pollution, deforestation, and overexploitation of resources

汚染や森林破壊、資源の乱開発といった人間の活動によって環境が悪化すること

fairtrade ［名］フェアトレード

定義 a certification system and social movement aimed at promoting equitable trading conditions, fair prices, and sustainable practices for producers and workers in developing countries

公平な取引条件、公正な価格、持続可能な活動などの促進を目的とした認証制度と社会運動で、開発途上国の生産者と労働者へ向けられたもの

sustainability ［名］サステナビリティー、持続可能性

定義 the practice of meeting current societal needs without compromising the ability of future generations to meet their own needs, ensuring the balance between environmental, social, and economic considerations

将来の世代が自らのニーズを満たす能力を損なうことなく、現在の社会的ニーズを満たすことで、必ず環境・社会・経済のバランスが考慮される

thermodynamics ［名］熱力学

定義 the branch of physics that deals with the study of energy transformation and the relationships between heat, work, and other forms of energy in systems
物理学の一分野で、エネルギー変換の研究や、物事の体系の中での熱・作用・その他のエネルギー形態の間の関係を対象とする

◄ Related Words and Phrases ►

isothermal ［形］等温の

定義 occurring at constant temperature or involving processes in which temperature remains constant despite changes in other variables, such as pressure or volume
一定の温度で発生する、または、圧力や体積といった他の変数が変化しても温度が一定な工程を含んだ

evaporative cooling ［名］気化冷却

定義 a cooling process that relies on the evaporation of a liquid to remove heat from a surrounding environment or object
液体の蒸発に依存する冷却工程で、周囲の環境や物体から熱を取り除く

ionocaloric cooling ［名］イオン熱量効果冷却

定義 a cooling technology that utilizes the reversible thermal effects of ions in response to an applied electric field, enabling efficient and environmentally friendly cooling without the need for traditional refrigerants
電界印加によるイオンの可逆的な熱作用を利用した冷却技術で、従来のような冷媒を必要としない効率的で環境に優しい冷却を可能にする

adiabatic ［形］断熱の

定義 referring to a process in which no heat is exchanged with the surroundings, such as the expansion or compression of a gas, leading to changes in temperature and pressure
気体の膨張や圧縮などが起こる状況下で熱交換が行われない工程の。温度や圧力の変化につながる

toxic [形] 有毒な

定義 relating to or caused by a substance or agent that is harmful or poisonous to living organisms, often with detrimental effects on health or the environment

生物にとって有害か有毒な物質、または薬剤に関連する、またはそれらによる。通常、健康や環境に有害な影響を与える

◄ Related Words and Phrases ►

carcinogen [名]発がん物質

定義 a substance or agent that can cause cancer by damaging genetic material or disrupting cellular processes

がんを引き起こす可能性のある物質または薬剤のことで、遺伝物質を損傷したり細胞の作用を破壊するもの

effluvia [名]悪臭、放出物

定義 unpleasant or harmful odors, vapors, or emissions that emanate from a substance or source

物質や水源から発せられる不快な、あるいは有害な臭気や蒸気などの排出物

biohazard [名]バイオハザード、生物学的有害物質

定義 a biological substance, agent, or condition that poses a risk to the health of humans, animals, or the environment, often requiring specific precautions for handling and disposal

人、動物、または環境の健康にリスクをもたらす生物学的な物質や薬剤、または状態のこと。多くの場合、取り扱いや廃棄に特定の予防措置を必要とする

pesticide [名]殺虫剤

定義 a chemical substance or biological agent used to control, repel, or eliminate pests, such as insects, weeds, or fungi, that can harm crops, structures, or human health

害虫を管理、忌避、または除去するために使用される化学物質または生物学的薬剤のこと。この害虫には、作物や建物、人の健康・健全性に害を与える昆虫、雑草、菌類などが含まれる

extinction ［名］絶滅

定義 the permanent loss of all members of a species, often as a result of environmental changes, human activities, or other factors that impact their ability to survive and reproduce

ある種の全構成員が永久に失われることで、多くの場合、環境の変化や人間の活動、あるいはそれ以外の生存と繁殖の能力に影響を与える要因によってもたらされる

Related Words and Phrases

endangered species ［名］絶滅危惧種

定義 a species that is at risk of extinction due to factors such as habitat loss, overexploitation, or environmental changes, and often requiring conservation efforts to ensure its survival

生息地の喪失や乱獲、環境の変化などの要因で絶滅の危機に瀕している種のこと。多くの場合、その生存を確保するための保全活動を必要とする

Holocene extinction ［名］完新世絶滅

定義 also known as the Sixth Extinction, an ongoing mass extinction event characterized by the accelerated loss of species and ecosystems, primarily due to human activities such as habitat destruction and climate change

第6次絶滅とも呼ばれる、現在進行中の大量絶滅現象のこと。主に生息地の破壊や気候変動などの人間の活動が原因で、種や生態系が加速度的に失われることを特徴とする

Red List ［名］レッドリスト

定義 a comprehensive inventory of the conservation status of species worldwide, maintained by the International Union for Conservation of Nature (IUCN), which categorizes species based on their risk of extinction

世界中の種の保全状況を示す包括的な目録で、国際自然保護連合（IUCN）によって管理されるもの。絶滅の危険性に基づいて種が分類されている

vulnerable ［形］絶滅危惧II類の、脆弱な

定義 referring to a species that is facing a high risk of extinction or decline in population due to various factors such as habitat loss, overexploitation, or environmental changes

生息地の消失や乱獲、環境の変化などさまざまな要因により、絶滅や個体数減少の危険性が高い種の

ozone layer [名] オゾン層

定義 a region of Earth's stratosphere containing a high concentration of ozone molecules, which acts as a protective shield by absorbing harmful ultraviolet radiation from the Sun

地球の成層圏にあるオゾン分子が多く存在する領域で、太陽からの有害な紫外線を吸収し、保護用の盾として機能する

◀ Related Words and Phrases ▶

infrared radiation [名] 赤外線放射

定義 a type of electromagnetic radiation with wavelengths longer than visible light, emitted by all objects with a temperature above absolute zero, and involved in processes like heat transfer and thermal imaging

可視光よりも波長の長い電磁波の一種で、絶対零度以上の物体から放出され、熱伝導や赤外線画像などの処理に関係がある

methane [名] メタン

定義 a potent greenhouse gas with the chemical formula CH_4, produced naturally through processes like the decomposition of organic matter, and also emitted by human activities, such as fossil fuel extraction and agriculture

化学式 CH_4 で表される強力な温室効果ガスで、有機物の分解などの過程で自然に発生する。化石燃料の採取や農業などの人間の活動によって排出される

space debris [名] 宇宙ごみ、スペースデブリ

定義 human-made objects in space that are no longer functional

宇宙空間に漂う、役に立たなくなった人工物

ultraviolet radiation [名] 紫外線放射

定義 a type of electromagnetic radiation with wavelengths shorter than visible light and longer than X-rays, emitted by the Sun and other sources

電磁波の一種で、可視光線より短くエックス線より長い波長を持つ。太陽などの源から放射される

bug　［名］バグ

定義　an error or flaw in a computer program that causes it to produce an incorrect or unexpected result
コンピュータープログラムのエラーや欠陥のことで、それが原因で不正確な、あるいは予期しない結果が出る

◄ Related Words and Phrases ►

glitch　［名］異常、故障、誤作動

定義　an unexpected or temporary malfunction, error, or flaw in a system, software, or technology that produces unintended or irregular behavior
システムやソフトウェア、技術上の予期せぬ、または一時的な誤動作、エラー、欠陥のことで、意図しないような、不規則な動作が生じる

fat finger　［動］タイプミスを犯す

定義　to make an error in typing or pressing a button, especially on a computer keyboard or touchscreen, due to fingers being too large
指が太すぎて、特にコンピューターのキーボードやタッチスクリーンで、入力やボタンを押す際にミスを犯す

recall　［動］～をリコールする、～（不良品）を回収する

定義　to request the return of a product from buyers, usually due to the discovery of safety issues or product defects
通常、安全上の問題や製品の欠陥が見つかったために、購入者に製品の返品を依頼する

human error　［名］人的ミス、ヒューマンエラー

定義　a mistake made by a person rather than being caused by a poorly designed process or the malfunctioning of a machine
設計された工程の不備や機械の誤動作が原因ではなく、人が犯した誤り

byte　［名］バイト

定義 a unit of digital information in computing that consists of eight bits
コンピューターにおけるデジタル情報の単位で、8 ビットで構成される

◀ **Related Words and Phrases** ▶

tera-　［接頭辞］テラ

定義 a unit prefix in the metric system denoting one trillion, or 10 to the power of 12
メートル法の単位接頭辞で、1 兆、つまり 10 の 12 乗を表す

---

peta-　［接頭辞］ペタ

定義 a unit prefix in the metric system denoting one quadrillion, or 10 to the power of 15
メートル法の単位接頭辞で、1,000 兆、つまり 10 の 15 乗を表す

---

exa-　［接頭辞］エクサ

定義 a unit prefix in the metric system denoting 10 to the power of 18
メートル法における単位接頭辞で、10 の 18 乗を表す

---

zetta-　［接頭辞］ゼタ

定義 a unit prefix in the metric system denoting 10 to the power of 21
メートル法における単位接頭辞で、10 の 21 乗を表す

neo-Luddite [名] 現代技術懐疑派

定義 a person opposing new technologies and industrialization
新しい技術や工業化に反対する人

► Related Words and Phrases ◄

analog [形]アナログな

定義 not digital
デジタルではない

---

audio jack [名]オーディオジャック

定義 an electrical connector used in audio systems for transmitting analog sound signals
オーディオシステムで使われる電気コネクターで、アナログ音声信号の伝送が目的

---

dumbphone [名]低機能電話

定義 a mobile phone that is limited in capabilities, typically only providing voice calling and text messaging features
機能が限定された携帯電話で、一般的には音声通話とテキストメッセージ機能だけを提供する

---

landline [名]固定電話

定義 a phone that uses a metal wire or optical fiber for transmission
伝送に金属線または光ファイバーを使用する電話機

solar flare [名] 太陽フレア

定義 a sudden and intense release of energy in the form of electromagnetic radiation from the Sun's surface, often accompanied by the ejection of high-energy particles and intense bursts of light
電磁波の形を取った太陽表面からの突然で激しいエネルギーの放出のことで、多くの場合、高エネルギー粒子の放出や強烈な光の爆発を伴う

Related Words and Phrases

magnetic storm [名] 磁気嵐

定義 a temporary disturbance of the Earth's magnetosphere caused by charged particles emitted from the Sun
地球磁気圏の一時的な乱れのことで、太陽から放出される荷電粒子が原因

blackout [名] 磁気嵐停電

定義 a failure of electrical power supply, causing a total loss of power in a particular area
電力供給の停止のことで、特定の地域の電力が完全に失われることにつながる

smart grid [名] 次世代送電網、スマートグリッド

定義 an advanced electrical power distribution network that utilizes modern technologies, including digital communication and automation, to enhance the efficiency, reliability, and sustainability of electricity generation, transmission, and consumption
デジタル通信や自動化などの最新技術を活用した高度な配電網で、発電や送電、電力消費の効率と信頼性、持続可能性を高めるもの

coronal mass ejection [名] コロナガスの噴出

定義 a massive release of plasma and accompanying magnetic field from the Sun's corona
太陽のコロナからの大量のプラズマ放出と、それに伴う磁場のこと

slow travel [名] スロートラベル

定義 a philosophy of travel that promotes a more relaxed, unhurried, and sustainable journey, allowing travelers to delve deeper into destinations, connect with local communities, and gain more of an appreciation of the places they visit

よりくつろいだ、急がない、持続可能な旅を促進する旅行哲学のことで、旅行者が目的地をより深く知り、地域社会とつながり、訪問した場所をより深く理解することが可能となる

◄ Related Words and Phrases ►

glamp [動] グランピングをする

定義 from "glamor" and "camp," to camp in a style that combines the simplicity and natural setting of traditional camping with the added comforts, conveniences, and lavishness associated with high-end travel and accommodation

glamor（魅惑）と camp（キャンプをする）を併せたように、従来のキャンプの単純さと自然環境に、高級な旅行や宿泊に伴う快適さや便利さ、贅沢さを加えたスタイルでキャンプをする

wellness retreat [名] ウェルネスリトリート

定義 a type of vacation or getaway focused on promoting individuals' health and well-being through physical, psychological, or spiritual activities

長期休暇または短期休暇の一種で、身体的、心理的、あるいは精神的な活動を通じて個人の健康と幸福を促進することに焦点を当てたもの

microadventure [名] マイクロアドベンチャー

定義 a short, accessible, and typically low-cost outdoor adventure or exploration undertaken close to home, allowing individuals to experience the thrill of outdoor activities within a limited time frame

短期間に身近な場所で、たいてい低料金で実施される野外での冒険や探検のことで、限られた時間の中で野外活動のスリルを味わえる

staycation [名] ステイケーション

定義 a vacation spent at home or within one's local area, typically involving relaxation, entertainment, or exploration of nearby attractions

自宅や地元地域で過ごす休暇のことで、一般的にはくつろいだり娯楽を楽しんだり、身近な観光スポットを見て回ったりする

goblin mode ［名］ゴブリンモード

定義 a lifestyle or mood that involves disregarding societal expectations in favor of comfort, solitude, and doing whatever one wants

社会的な期待を無視して、快適さや孤独、好きなことを優先するライフスタイルや気分

◄ **Related Words and Phrases** ►

binge-watch ［動］〜（テレビ番組のシリーズなど）を一気にすべて見る

定義 to watch multiple episodes or an entire season of a television series or streaming content in a continuous and indulgent manner, often for an extended period of time

テレビ番組のシリーズやストリーミングコンテンツの複数のエピソードやシーズン全体を、継続的かつはまり込んで、たいてい長時間にわたって視聴する

social norms ［名］社会規範

定義 the unwritten, culturally established rules and expectations that guide acceptable behavior and interactions within a given society or social group

文化的に確立された不文律や期待のことで、特定の社会や社交集団の中で受け入れられる行動や人付き合いの仕方につながる

self-indulgent ［形］好き勝手な、やりたい放題の

定義 characterized by excessive or gratifying indulgence in one's own desires, whims, or pleasures, often without consideration for others

欲求やその場の思いつき、快楽などに過剰に、満足するまでおぼれ、たいていは他人を顧みないような

meh ［間投詞］別に、まあね

定義 a term that expresses a lack of interest or enthusiasm

興味や熱意がないことが表れる言葉

absolute unit
［名］巨漢、大物、特別に大きい人や物

af
［副］めっちゃ、とんでもなく、as fuckの頭字語

all-in
［形］すべて込みの、込み込みの、完全な

amirite
だよね、ですよね、…, am I right?（私は正しい？）の発音表記

bench
［動］〜を関与させない、〜を寄せ付けない

bet
いいよ、オッケー

bruh
相棒、友人への呼びかけの言葉

canceled
［形］オワッテル、ないわー

cap
［動］うそをつく

catfish
［動］〜になりすます、オンラインで偽の身分を装い、誰かをだましたり誤解させたりする

CEO
［名］シャチョウ、大家、何かを極めて得意とする人

chef's kiss
カンペキ、素晴らしい

close of play
［名］今日中（に）、退社時刻（までに）

creeper
［名］怪しいやつ、キモいやつ

dad bod
［名］オヤジ体形、中年太り

dead
［形］［副］最高すぎる、めっちゃ、死ぬほど

dish
［動］うわさ話に興じる

dodgy
［形］怪しい、信用できない

dronie
［名］ドローン自撮り、ドローンで撮影した自撮り写真

dumpster fire
［名］大惨事、大混乱

ecoanxiety
[名] 環境問題心配性

edgelord
[名] 重度厨二病患者、わざと攻撃的な行動を取って注目を集めようとする人

entitlement
[名] 根拠なく自分を特別だと見なす感覚

F
哀悼、不幸なニュースや誰かのネガティブな経験に対する哀悼や同情の簡潔な表現

facepalm
[動] あきれてみせる、手のひらで顔を覆う

fail
[名] 赤っ恥、恥ずかしい失敗

fam
[名] 家族同様の連中

fika
[名] コーヒータイム、休憩、スウェーデンの習慣を表す語

FOMO
[名] 乗り遅れ嫌い、fear of missing out（逃すことへの恐怖）の頭字語

FTW
（〜は）最高、これで決まり、for the win（絶対に、たしかに）の頭字語

full send
[副詞] パワー全開で

ghost
[動] 幽霊化する、突然連絡を断つ

go hard
[動] 頑張る、全力を尽くす

GOAT
[名] 史上最高の人、greatest of all time の頭字語

headdesk
[動] ガックリする、頭を机に打ち付ける

healthie
[名] 健康アピール自撮り、自分の健康に関連する事物をアピールするための自撮り写真

heard
了解、聞いたよ

hinky
[形] アヤシイ、疑わしい

I can't (even)
たまらん、ムリ、不信感や圧倒的な面白さや興奮などを伝える言葉

IDEK
全然知らない、I don't even know. の頭字語

jelly
［形］嫉妬深い、やきもちを焼いた

Karen
［名］カレン、自分には特権があり何でも自分
の思いどおりにできると思い込んでいる無礼
な白人女性に対する蔑称

keep it one hundred
［動］とことんやる、本気で行動する

killing it
最高だ、すごい

left on read
［形］既読スルー、メッセージが読まれたまま
返信がない状態

legend
［名］レジェンド、偉業を達成した人物

lowdown
［名］内情、秘密情報

lowkey
［副］少し、感情の度合いが低く控えめな

main character syndrome
［名］主人公症候群、ある状況下で自分が主役
で他人は脇役だと認識する傾向

mental health day
［名］ストレス解消や心の健康増進を目的とし
た休日

mood
分かるよ、その気持ち分かる

peep this
これ見て

peeps
［名］やつら、人々

phubbing
［名］一緒にいる人を無視して、自分の携帯電
話に集中すること

pod
［名］小群、部外者を寄せ付けない少人数の集
団

potato
［名］イモ、品質や解像度の低い画像や動画

preach
それな

receipt
［名］証拠、証拠品

salty
［形］ムカつく、イラッときて

savage
［形］半端ない、ヤバい

seen

見た、分かった、メッセージを確認したり理解や同意を示したりする言葉

self-own

［名］ジコチュー、自己認識に欠けているせいで自らをおとしめる行為

selfie

［名］自撮り写真

shredded

［形］体を絞った、体脂肪を削った

simp

［名］一途すぎるやつ、女性に尽くしすぎる男

skinny

［名］特ダネ、内部情報

slay

［動］うまくいく、キメる

SMH

ダメだこりゃ、shaking my head（頭を横に振っている）の頭字語で不信感や失望感、憤りを表す

snowflake

［名］弱っちいやつ、過敏に反応したり、気分を害しやすい人を指す蔑称

spit take

［名］意外な出来事や面白い発言に対して、飲み物を吐き出す反応

squad

［名］ダチ、ツレ、しょっちゅう一緒に遊び歩く仲の良い集団

stealthie

［名］周りに気づかれないように撮った自撮り写真

stress

［名］イラッとすること

sus

［形］アヤシイ、suspicious（疑わしい）を縮めた形

swole

［形］筋肉モリモリの、マッチョな

tea

［名］ゴシップ、ネタ、事の真相

TFW

〜のときのあの気持、that feeling when の頭字語

thicc

［形］（主に女性の体形が）曲線美の

TL;DR

（メッセージなどが）長すぎて読まなかった、too long; didn't read の頭字語

tope

［形］イケてる、tight（格好いい）と dope（いかした）の合成語

trigger

［動］～をいらつかせる、～を怒らせる

turnt

［形］興奮した、熱狂した

velfie

［名］自撮り動画、video selfie の合成語

verklempt

［形］あぜんとした、感極まった

vibe

［動］～に共鳴する、～とつながる

vibe check

意味不明、どういうつもり？　SNS の不愉快
な投稿に対する嫌味

weak

［形］オモシロすぎな、めちゃおもろい

work-life balance

［名］ワークライフバランス

workation

［名］ワーケーション、休暇先で仕事をこなす
こと

WTF

何てこった、What the fuck! の頭字語

yas

よっしゃ、興奮したときに使う yes の変形

yeet

［動］～を激しく投げ捨てる

YOLO

人生は一度きりさ、You only live once. の頭
字語

zombie

［名］幽霊化してしばらくたってから突然連絡
を再開してくる者

カテゴリー別索引

Society 社会

Diversity, Equity, and Inclusion
多様性、公平性、包括性

Education　教育

Culture, Fashion, Art and Sports
文化、ファッション、アート、スポーツ

Healthcare　医療・健康管理

Computing　コンピューティング

Environment and Sustainability
環境、持続可能性

Slang and Casual Conversation
俗語、日常の会話

アルファベット順索引

303

305

313

English Conversational Ability Test
国際英語会話能力検定

● **E-CATとは…**
英語が話せるようになるための
テストです。インターネット
ベースで、30分であなたの発
話力をチェックします。

www.ecatexam.com

● **iTEP®とは…**
世界各国の企業、政府機関、アメリカの大学
300校以上が、英語能力判定テストとして採用。
オンラインによる90分のテストで文法、リー
ディング、リスニング、ライティング、スピー
キングの5技能をスコア化。iTEP®は、留学、就
職、海外赴任などに必要な、世界に通用する英
語力を総合的に評価する画期的なテストです。

www.itepexamjapan.com

2030年までに知っておきたい
最重要ボキャブラリー1000

2023年8月4日　第1刷発行

著　　者　アンドリュー・ロビンス

編者・訳者　岡本茂紀

発 行 者　浦　　晋亮

発 行 所　IBCパブリッシング株式会社
　　　　　〒162-0804 東京都新宿区中里町29番3号 菱秀神楽坂ビル
　　　　　Tel. 03-3513-4511　Fax. 03-3513-4512
　　　　　www.ibcpub.co.jp

印刷所　　株式会社シナノパブリッシングプレス

© Andrew Robbins 2023
© Office LEPS, Inc. 2023

Printed in Japan

ISBN978-4-7946-0770-6

ISBN978-4-7946-0770-6
C0082 ¥2400E

定価（本体2,400円+税）
IBCパブリッシング

9784794607706

1920082024000

2030年までに知っておきたい1000のボキャブラリーを

経済、政治、社会、多様性、公平性、包括性、教育、文化、

ファッション、アート、スポーツ、健康管理、

テクノロジー、コンピューティング、

環境、持続可能性、気候変動、俗語、日常の会話など

さまざまなカテゴリーに分けて、

日英対訳で徹底解説！